TABLE AND TRADITION

D0643041

Books by Alasdair I. C. Heron
Published by The Westminster Press

Table and Tradition
The Holy Spirit
A Century of Protestant Theology

TABLE AND TRADITION

by

ALASDAIR I. C. HERON

CONCORDIA UNIVERSITY LIBRARY
PORTLAND, OR 97211

The Westminster Press
Philadelphia

Copyright © 1983 A. I. C. Heron

Published by The Westminster Press®
Philadelphia, Pennsylvania

PRINTED IN THE UNITED STATES OF AMERICA
9 8 7 6 5 4 3 2 1

Library of Congress Cataloging in Publication Data

Heron, Alasdair.
  Table and tradition.

  Bibliography: p.
  1. Lord's Supper—History. I. Title.
BV823.H47 1983   264'.36   83-14762
ISBN 0-664-24516-1 (pbk.)

CONTENTS

FOREWORD

The lectures on which this book is based were first given in the spring of 1978 on the invitation of the Trustees of the Kerr Lectureship in the University of Glasgow. Their appearance in print as required by the terms of the Trust is now long overdue, and I must couple my thanks to the Trustees for the honour done me with some explanation of the delay.

The explanation will come as no surprise to those who have undertaken similar projects. First, in spite of all noble intentions of having a finished manuscript before giving the lectures, I found myself regularly burning the well-after-midnight oil before driving from Edinburgh to Glasgow the next morning to inflict on a remarkably patient and generously appreciative audience my last-minute discoveries and hunches. Second, I then found the material gathered very useful for teaching courses in New College, Edinburgh, and took my time, year by year, in slowly improving (as I hoped) the form of presentation, and at the same time considerably increasing the length of the manuscript, which it would now certainly take more than twice the original span of eight hours to deliver. By the summer of 1981, however, when on the point of moving from Edinburgh to Erlangen, I did manage to get a sort of final manuscript together. Third came the familiar but sometimes (as on this occasion) depressing experience of reading a publisher's reader's report, which in this case was particularly critical of the chapter on Calvin and the Reformation. To make matters worse, I had to agree that the reader was right: the extent to which that chapter concentrated almost exclusively on quoting Calvin, the *Scots Confession* and the *Westminster Confession* suited well enough the original setting in which the lectures were given, but could not do for a book intended to circulate more widely. My agreement with the reader's judgment was reinforced by the fresh concentration on the history of the sixteenth century forced upon me by the move to Erlangen. So I agreed to re-write the offending part of the manuscript, and at the same time to develop the last chapter, and hoped – nay, I fear, promised – to have this done by the autumn of 1982. Fourth, I did not get it done by then, for which I am sure I could think up many cogent reasons, but they would probably by now be of little interest. The tragi-comic nature of the situation should be clear enough without further elaboration. At any rate it is now done; and if 'twere well that 'twere done quickly, perhaps it is better than nothing that it has been done at all, albeit at snail's pace.

More seriously, one aim that has if anything made the task harder rather than easier was my concern so far as possible to retain the original character of the lectures *as lectures* – that is, to present a reasonably simple narrative which would contain the important material in the text, resist the temptation to explore all manner of fascinating academic by-ways, and above all not reduce to an encyclopaedic series of notes on a vast list of secondary literature (what might be described as the card-index method of composition so much beloved in scholarly circles). Contrary to what might be imagined, there is nothing easier, with access to a decent library and mastery of the elementary techniques of note-taking, than the production of immensely impressive-looking studies running to many hundreds of pages, most of them footnotes, and concluding with a select bibliography of, say, five hundred titles. The difficulty with such artefacts is not writing them, but reading them. (Paying for them is also becoming an increasing problem.) What led me to choose this subject in the first place was not a desire to engage in recondite research for its own sake, though that is something I have also engaged in in the past and doubtless shall again, nor even any conviction that I had some blazing original insight to offer, but a desire to study the matter more fully than I had previously done, and to see if the results of that study could be presented in a form that would be helpful for the intended audience – by which I had in mind students and ministers in the Reformed Churches who might find interest and value in such an account and in its attempt to consider the biblical and historical material, and the relation in past and present between Roman Catholic and Reformed views of the theme. In all the considerable literature that I have ploughed through over the years, I have not so far come across a book that does that modest job in the way that is attempted here. But it is a modest job. This is not a book for specialists, who will rightly say that it brings nothing that everyone who knows anything would not know already, and brings what it does bring in, on the whole, a very simple, not to say over-simplified form. But there is a place for such studies – I suspect a larger one than the specialists often realise.

So much for explanation and apologia; something must also be said about the scope. In the final chapters I concentrate very much on Roman Catholic and Reformed positions, with some consideration of the Lutheran-Reformed relations. The heritage of Eastern Orthodoxy appears only in the chapter on the early church, and Anglican thinking is virtually ignored. A more ambitious study could have drawn them both in, and fruitfully – but only at the cost either of compressing the material in a way I have tried here to avoid (hence the extensive quotations in the text) or of increasing the length yet further. But with an eye on my own tradition, on the context in which the lectures were first conceived, and on the continuing dialogue between the World Alliance of Reformed Churches and the Vatican, I felt and feel that what is covered here is enough to be going on with. That it is enough will be witnessed by my wife, who read the proofs, by my Assistant, Alan Torrance, who prepared the Indexes, and by my children, who at least intermittently allowed me spaces of peace to get on with writing. To all, my grateful thanks!

A further reminiscence and wish. It was in 1973-1974, during my all-too-brief time at the Irish School of Ecumenics, that I first attempted to teach a course on the Eucharist. The School's motto is *floreat ut pereat* – may it flourish in order to perish – meaning that the aim of ecumenical institutions and ecumenical theology must be to work themselves out of business by overcoming the divisions that provisionally make them necessary. It may be (and some of the thoughts in the last chapter suggest it) that that time may yet lie some way in the future. Certainly the *pereat* would be premature. All the more reason, then, to urge the *floreat*. Ten years on from my first joining it in April 1973 it gladdens me to know that the Irish School of Ecumenics is still flourishing. May it continue to do so as long as the task is unfinished.

The book was already in proof when news came of the sudden death of the friend who was particularly responsible for my being invited to give the Kerr Lectures. He had hoped to see them in print; now, sadly, they must appear as a posthumous tribute. He was a preacher, a teacher and a Christian man whose learning was combined with kindness and humour. May the Lord of the church continue to call and send such servants as

Ian Adair Muirhead

(1913-1983)

who is remembered with gratitude and affection.

ALASDAIR HERON

Erlangen, July 1983

PROLOGUE

If an explorer from another planet were to land in, say, Glasgow and begin studying the beliefs and opinions of the population, he would soon discover that fairly large groups identify themselves as 'Catholic' and 'Protestant'. It might take him rather longer to make out what these names mean, or what the main differences are. If he persisted, he might come across a whole series of debatable issues, including the meaning of a rite performed with bread and wine. Depending on where he got his further information, he might send home a report of this kind:

> In some ways these groups have a great deal in common. Both belong to a religious cult whose history runs back for many centuries. Apparently, however, they represent divergent branches, and on both sides their disagreements seem to be more important than their shared heritage. One of these disagreements has to do with a special ceremony, which each carries out and understands rather differently.
>
> Essentially this ceremony is a kind of symbolic meal in which bread or wafers are eaten and wine or fruit juice drunk. The rite is very ancient: both groups agree that it was introduced by one Jesus Christ, whose story is told in a holy book they both still read, though it is now two thousand years old, in parts even older. He is the central figure in their belief, and is held by them to have been divine. He was in fact executed by the authorities in his own country. Both Catholics and Protestants teach that he was brought back to life, and that his death was a special sacrifice to God his Father. Because of that sacrifice his followers are forgiven for their evil actions. The symbolic meal is seen as a way of sharing in the benefits of that sacrifice, and the bread and wine are sometimes called 'the body and blood of Christ'.
>
> In other details, however, the opinions of the two groups are quite different. The religion of the Catholics is organised by a special class called 'priests'. The celebration of this rite is one of their main and most jealously guarded functions. 'Priest' means 'one who offers sacrifice to God', and the ceremony, which they call 'the Mass', is understood to be the sacrifice of the priest. Only he can make it. He does this by using a special power, given him by a superior priest called a 'bishop'. This enables him to change the bread and wine into the body and blood of Christ by repeating Christ's own formula: 'This is my body; this is my

blood.' In this way, the sacrifice of Christ is made present again for the priest and those who are worshipping with him. The carrying out of the ceremony also releases a further beneficial power which can be directed to assist others who are not present, whether or not they are still alive.

The Protestants too have a priestly caste; but they generally call these people 'ministers' rather than 'priests'. As a rule, these ministers alone are authorised to perform the rite, which the Protestants normally call 'Holy Communion'. But they are not believed to possess any power to transform the bread and wine into the body and blood of Christ, nor do they 'repeat' his sacrifice or 'make it present'. Rather, the entire ceremony is an act of remembering what was done by Christ himself. Protestants thus do not 'offer his sacrifice to God', nor do they secure benefit from it for anyone else. It has been explained to me that they do not regard Christ as entirely absent in the rite, but as being 'really present' in some different fashion from that maintained by the Catholics.

One other contrast is also possibly significant. The Catholics perform the ceremony very frequently – daily for priests, and weekly for regular attenders at church. Protestants do so much less frequently – often only once or twice a year. Further, while it seems obvious enough to me that the ritual is essentially similar in each case, it is widely believed by members of each group that only its own form is valid, and that the other is so dreadfully distorted or inadequate as to make it positively harmful.

This hypothetical report is obviously something of an over-simplification, not to say a caricature. But it may serve to introduce some of the distinctive emphases and points of conflict between Roman Catholic and Reformed understandings of the matter.

First there is the simple – yet perhaps not so simple – matter of terminology. Roman Catholics commonly speak of 'the Mass', Protestants of 'Holy Communion' or 'the Lord's Supper'. Roman Catholics do also speak of 'Holy Communion', but with a slightly different emphasis: they usually mean by it the act of reception of the elements of bread and wine rather than the entire sacrament. This is therefore not the best name to use in speaking in general about it. Equally, both 'Mass' and 'Lord's Supper' are strongly loaded terms, at least by association. I have heard it argued that the word 'Mass' is strictly meaningless, as it is derived simply from the closing words of the Latin liturgy: *ite, missa est*; and that it is therefore a perfectly neutral word, quite well suited to ecumenical discussion. Most English speakers, however, understand it to mean 'the Roman Catholic Mass', and that severely limits its usefulness. In much the same way, 'Lord's Supper' is a characteristically Protestant label. It was introduced quite deliberately by the Reformers from I Cor. 11.20 to underline the nature of the sacrament as a shared meal, and to contrast with the ritualistic conception of the Mass which had developed in the previous centuries. So 'Lord's Supper' and 'Mass' are convenient labels for the sacrament as understood and practised in the Protestant and Roman Catholic settings, but we really need another word for it as well.

The one which most obviously offers itself is 'Eucharist'. It is unfortunately unfamiliar to many Protestants, and in some quarters is looked upon as a kind of Trojan horse, used by ecumenical fanatics to smuggle in unreformed ideas about the sacrament. In fact, the Greek word *eucharistia* means simply 'thanksgiving'. The verb *eucharistein*, 'to give thanks' is used in all four New Testament accounts of the Last Supper: all describe Jesus as giving thanks either over the bread or over the cup. Very early in the ancient church, 'Eucharist' became the established name for the sacrament, as is recorded around the middle of the second century by Justin Martyr[1] and perhaps even earlier.[2] It has remained in use ever since in both the Eastern, Greek Church and the Latin, Western Church; and appropriately so, for this is the great act of thanksgiving at the very heart of Christian worship. Calvin himself spoke of 'the kind of sacrifice which we have called eucharistic' (i.e. the sacrifice of thanksgiving), and insisted 'this kind of sacrifice is indispensable in the Lord's Supper'.[3] It is no very great jump from Calvin to restore the word itself as an alternative to 'Supper'; and by doing so we make available to ourselves the most universally used and understood name for the sacrament, one which is free from narrower denominational or confessional associations, and which has for that reason been increasingly employed in modern ecumenical dialogue. Taken along with 'Lord's Supper' and 'Mass' it gives us the vocabulary we need to speak not only of the distinctive Reformed and Roman Catholic conceptions, but also, beyond these, of the sacrament itself.

Moving beyond the question of terminology, we can recognise in our visitor's remarks at least some of the traditional points of contrast between the Supper and the Mass. On the Roman Catholic side he has emphasised priesthood, the offering of sacrifice, the changing of the elements, the presence of Christ and the benefits obtained by means of the celebration of the sacrament. Among the Protestants he has found a very different picture, which omits some of the most typical Roman Catholic features and stresses above all remembrance, and an apparently rather vaguely conceived 'presence' of Christ. While with fuller information he might well have extended his lists (and deepened his analysis), he has succeeded in picking out the issues which have tended to come to the fore through the centuries of disagreement which followed the Reformation, and certainly those which have most impressed themselves on the minds of large numbers of church members.

What kind of contrast is here coming into view? Is it simply that there are a number of distinct points on which Roman Catholics and Protestants disagree? If so, they could be taken one by one and discussed in turn. In fact, however, the real difference lies deeper. If one looks more closely at the list, it begins to seem that Roman Catholics tend to believe *more* than Protestants, and that a substantial part of the Protestant platform is constituted by the *rejection* of particular Roman Catholic convictions. This should cause no surprise if we remember the extent to which the Reformers did indeed reject elements in previous teaching which they believed to be unwarranted additions to the teaching of the Bible. But the Reformers did not simply reject arbitrarily; behind their rejections lay very positive conceptions of the truth which was to be maintained. At bottom the contrast in eucharistic theology which finds expression in the points mentioned is between two rather different overall views of the sacrament. The centre of gravity tends in each view to lie in a different place, and to be grasped and formulated in rather different fashions. The Roman Catholic approach, at least in those aspects of it which have been pointed up, puts a special emphasis on *what is done* in the sacrament, particularly on *what is done by the priest*, and on the whole action as a *sacrificial offering to God*. By contrast the Protestant stress is on *what has been done by Christ*, on the *remembering* of that by his people, and in general on *receiving in thankfulness* rather than on *offering*. It is not merely a matter of conflict on this particular point or that, but of contrasting overall approaches to the matter.

This is not to imply that these divergent overall approaches have now been satisfactorily defined. So far all we have done is to notice some pointers to their character which can help to direct our enquiry. What is now clear is that it will not do merely to pick out such issues as transubstantiation or sacrifice and concentrate on them alone. Instead we must dig deeper and try to see inside both views of the Eucharist in order to ask why one finds it right and necessary to talk of it in one way while the other believes it right and necessary to use quite different and contradictory conceptions. Only so can we hope to come closer to the real points of agreement and disagreement between them.

The most helpful way of doing this is to look back and see how classical Roman and Reformed eucharistic theology took shape. Behind them, however, lies the theology of the early church; and behind that the New Testament itself. There is the place where we must begin, not only in order to trace the development from the start, but in order to find if there lies in it a key to the overcoming of subsequent differences.

PART ONE
THE EUCHARIST
IN THE NEW TESTAMENT

I

THE INSTITUTION NARRATIVES

The Last Supper of Jesus with his disciples is described five times in the
New Testament – in all four Gospels, and also in I Cor. 11. With the
exception of the Fourth Gospel, these passages all repeat in fairly similar
form the story of how Jesus took bread and wine and gave them a new
meaning in the light of his approaching death. The versions given by
Mark and Matthew are almost identical:

Mark 14.22-25	Matthew 26.26-29
And as they were eating,	Now as they were eating,
he took bread,	Jesus took bread,
and having blessed (God),	and having blessed (God),
he broke (it),	he broke (it),
and gave (it) to them,	and giving (it) to *the disciples*,
and said,	said,
'Take,	'Take, *eat*,
this is my body.'	this is my body.'
And taking a cup	And taking a cup,
and having given thanks,	and having given thanks,
he gave it to them,	he gave it to them,
and they all drank from it.	saying,
And he said to them,	*'Drink from it, all of you*;
'This is my blood of	for this is my blood of
the covenant	the covenant
which is poured out for many.	which is poured out for many
	for the forgiveness of sins.
Truly I tell you,	I tell you,
I shall not drink again	I shall not drink again
of the fruit of the vine	of this fruit of the vine
until that day when I drink	until that day when I drink
it new in the kingdom	it new *with you* in *my Father's*
of God.'	kingdom.'

Apart from minor verbal differences, the main contrast here lies in the
phrases in Matthew's version which we have set in italics. He seems to
lay slightly more weight than Mark on the part of the disciples and on
the explicit command to eat and drink, and also emphasises that the

covenant is for the forgiveness of sins. Overall, however, the two records are very similar indeed. Here, as in so many other places, it is likely that Matthew has copied from Mark, and that in the two versions we possess a single tradition in two forms, Matthew's being somewhat later and fuller.

More significant contrasts come to light if we compare Mark's account with the forms in which the Last Supper is described by Luke and by Paul. Paul's version in I Cor. 11.23-26, which is in all probability the oldest of the four, differs from Mark's in several respects, as the words in italics illustrate:

> For I received from the Lord what I also handed on to you, that the Lord Jesus on the night when he was delivered up took bread, and having *given thanks,* he broke (it), and said, 'This is my body *which is for you. Do this for my remembrance.*' In the same way also the cup *after supper,* saying, '*This cup is the new covenant in my blood. Do this, as often as you drink it, for my remembrance.*' For as often as you eat this bread and drink the cup, you proclaim the death of the Lord, until he comes.

Leaving aside the opening and closing phrases which supply the framework within which the account of Jesus' words and actions is set, there are four main differences from Mark in the account itself. The first is purely verbal: Paul has 'having given thanks' (*eucharistēsas*) over the bread where Mark has 'having blessed' (*eulogēsas*). Both in effect mean the same: they refer to the grace in which God was blessed over the bread at the beginning of a Jewish meal. The second is a significant detail: Paul tells us that the cup of wine came *after* the meal; Mark and Matthew do not. The other two contrasts are more substantial still. Paul reports Jesus' instruction to *repeat* what he has done 'for my remembrance', while Mark and Matthew do not. He also gives the words spoken by Jesus over the bread and the cup in rather different form:

Mark, *Take,* this is my body.
Paul: This is my body *which is for you.*
Mark: This is *my blood of the covenant which is poured out for many.*
Paul: This cup is *the new covenant in my blood.*

Finally, where Mark quotes Jesus' own resolve never again to drink wine until the coming of the kingdom, Paul tells the Corinthians in the last sentence we quoted that in celebrating the 'Supper of the Lord' (*kuriakon deipnon* – v. 20) they are themselves looking forward to Christ's return. What lies in the foreground in Paul is *the celebration of the Eucharist by the church,* and he also offers what, as we shall see, is a significantly different account of what Jesus actually said at the Last Supper. We shall return to these variations below, but first we must turn to the fourth version, in Luke 22.14-20.

Peculiar complications arise with the Lukan description, for the ancient manuscripts offer a longer and a shorter version. The shorter ends in the middle of v. 19, omitting the rest of that verse and the whole of v. 20, and runs as follows:

> And when the hour came, he sat at table, and the apostles with him. And he said to them, 'I have earnestly desired to eat this Passover with you before I suffer; for I tell you that I shall not eat it again until it is fulfilled in the kingdom of God.' And taking a cup, and having given thanks, he said, 'Take this and divide it among you; for I tell you that from now on I shall not drink of the fruit of the vine until the kingdom of God comes.' And taking bread, and having given thanks, he broke it and gave it to them, saying, 'This is my body.'

The longer version continues on from this point:

> '. . . which is given for you. Do this for my remembrance.' And the cup in the same way after supper, saying, 'This cup is the new covenant in my blood, which is poured out for you.'

The shorter version thus gives an account which is in some respects similar to Mark's, but also differs from his; for it records the giving of a cup *before* the bread, and reports Jesus as saying *twice* that he would abstain *both* from the Passover *and* from wine until the coming of the kingdom, and as mentioning his own future *suffering*. If the short version is taken on its own, it appears to be a quite distinct third account of the Last Supper, independent of those of Paul and Mark. The longer version, on the other hand, includes material very similar indeed, though not wholly identical, to that in I Cor. 11. Here it appears that Luke's material does not offer us a third account of the entire Last Supper, but only a variant description of the first part of the occasion, offering some further details. This poses the question whether the longer or the shorter version should be accepted as Luke's own. If the longer, then the Last Supper according to the tradition he received must have included more than one ceremonial cup, one before the bread, and one after the meal. If the shorter, then Luke will have handed on to us a third and rather different account of the Last Supper, to which other material was later added to bring his description into closer harmony with Paul's. In that case, the twofold mention of the cup should be taken as evidence that the longer version is a conflation of two quite different traditions, in one of which the cup came before the bread, and in the other, after.

It would be of great help to us if we could settle whether or not the longer version is such a conflation. Unfortunately the question is uncertain.[1] The manuscript evidence can be interpreted either way: it is equally possible that the additional material in the longer version fell out when a manuscript was being copied, or was added in. As we shall see later, if the Last Supper was a Passover meal, it would have included no fewer than four different cups of wine at different stages, and on that score the account given in the longer version could well be correct. On the other hand, the long version does look suspiciously like a conflation of material from two sources, one peculiar to Luke, one closely resembling Paul's. To make matters even more complicated, even if it could be shown that Luke did originally write the longer version, that would still not exclude the possibility that Luke himself had simply combined and attempted to harmonise two different reports.

This problem with the text of Luke 22.19b-20 shows how much care is needed in interpreting the 'institution narratives' as they are commonly called. None of them is likely to be an eye-witness account, though Paul (and possibly also Mark) had known eye-witnesses. The oldest, I Cor. 11, dates from around A.D. 55, more than twenty years after the event; the Gospels are later still. Each of the descriptions is very brief, highlighting only certain significant details, and casting them in a condensed, even stereotyped form, smoothed by much repetition through decades of re-telling in teaching and in worship. The form in which they report what Jesus said and did reflects the handing-down of the material in the early church and the particular situations in which it was used. This is not to say that they are unreliable evidence for the Last Supper. There are in fact very few occasions in the ancient world for which we possess as much evidence, or of such quality. But *they describe it as it was remembered and thought upon by the Christians of the first and second generations.* That is the kind of evidence they offer, and the context which must be taken into account in their interpretation.

This rules out two ways in which we might think of trying to reconstruct the original events of the Last Supper from these sources. One would be simply to run them all together, to combine all their various details, on the principle that everything they record must have taken place. This cannot, however, be done without some fairly drastic trimming of one account to fit another; and that in turn will require some principle of selection in deciding which version is to be preferred where there are obvious differences of the kind we have already noticed. The result, too, could well be a rather 'flat' picture of the Last Supper, in which the distinctive emphases and meanings in the different descriptions had been too harshly smoothed away. As an alternative to that, it might then seem better simply to pick out what all the four narratives have in common, and take it as the reliable minimum core of evidence for what really happened. That however would leave us very little indeed; for all that Mark, Paul and the shorter version of Luke have in common is that Jesus took bread, gave thanks over it, broke it and gave it to the disciples with the words, 'This is my body'; and that either before or after that he also took and gave a cup with words quite different in Luke's short account from those in either Paul or Mark. This is no doubt a reliable minimum, but it is minimal indeed and offers us a great deal less alike of information and understanding than any of the separate versions on its own.

In order to get a more adequate view of the original Last Supper itself, we need some means of discovering the distinctive bearing of each of the different accounts upon the event, and this can best be done by attempting to locate them in their setting in the early church and to trace the influences which may have shaped them. This has been attempted in a variety of ways, as three of the most important studies of the last half-century can illustrate: those of Hans Lietzmann, Joachim Jeremias and Johannes Betz. In a brilliant pioneering investigation, Lietzmann argued that there were two kinds of Eucharist in the early days of the church.[2] One is that mentioned in Acts 2.42 and other passages as 'the breaking of bread' (with no mention of wine). This he held to be a kind of fellowship-meal, which originated in Jerusalem in the earliest days after the crucifixion and resurrection of Jesus, which the disciples saw as a continuation of the meals they had shared with Jesus in his lifetime, and in which they celebrated his victory and looked forward to the meal they would share with him on his eventual return. The other kind of Eucharist was a cultic, sacramental meal, an occasion of communion with Jesus Christ, in which attention was focussed upon his death and its meaning. This rite, Lietzmann maintained, must originally have developed in Hellenistic circles in the early church, and its roots lay in Hellenistic ideas of mystical communion through sacred memorial meals. Against that background, Jesus' death came to be seen as a sacrifice of which the Christian Eucharist was a memorial and a representation. The language to be found in both Paul and Mark (and in the longer version of Luke), with its emphasis on Jesus' death, on the covenant and blood, and on sharing in these, reflected that Hellenistic Christianity, but did not stem directly from Jesus himself, from the Last Supper, or from the earlier, Jerusalem type of Eucharist. What it reflected was rather the theological and ritual interpretation of Jesus' death which came to be central in Hellenistic Christian communities. Lietzmann was followed by many others, including Rudolf Bultmann. Bultmann believed that Jesus' own words at the Last Supper had probably been simply, 'This is my body ... This is my blood.' Everything else was the product of Hellenistic Christian sacra-mentalism.[3]

While Lietzmann did open up a fascinating new angle of enquiry into the Eucharist in the early church, his broad thesis is no longer making the running (though it or similar interpretations are still to be met in quite recent literature). Impressive though his hypothesis was, it was open to at least two major objections. First, it relied very much upon an extremely sharp distinction between Jewish and Hellenistic ways of thinking, and then ascribed everything 'sacramental' to the latter. But it is now widely recognised that the distinction in this form was seriously over-drawn; that much that was treated as Hellenistic (and therefore as secondary) in the approach which both Lietzmann and Bultmann represent is in fact better explained by reference to the Jewish background to the New Testament; and that this applies in particular to some of the very elements in the New Testament accounts of the Last Supper which it treated as non-Jewish. Second, this approach leaves us with no very convincing interpretation of the Last Supper itself, or of the words which it still leaves in Jesus' mouth; nor does it offer any very detailed explanation of how the allegedly Hellenistic interpretation of the Eucharist might in fact have grown up. It is not really adequate to make a rather vaguely defined 'Hellenism' the comprehensive explanation for everything, and Lietzmann's particular theory rests in fact upon an extremely fragile and tenuous argument from a very few scraps of evidence about 'memorial meals' in the Hellenistic world. It falls very far short of a convincing explanation of the emergence of what, according to his hypothesis, was a totally new kind of Eucharist. This short way of coping with the material is altogether too drastic and sweeping.

A very different line was taken by Jeremias, whose work has more recently dominated the field in the sense that although not all his arguments have been generally accepted he has set the entire discussion on a new basis. His *Die Abendmahlsworte Jesu* first appeared in 1935, and was then much altered in the second and third editions. The third was published in 1960 and translated into English in 1966.[4] Jeremias set out to show that the Last Supper was a Passover meal, and to interpret the words ascribed to Jesus in the various narratives against that background. He found that all the leading ideas contained in them could be interpreted satisfactorily in that way; for, he argued, the Passover itself was a sacrifice, an act of remembrance which was at the same time one of hope for future deliverance, and linked closely with the theme of the covenant between God and Israel. In addition, it was part of the Passover ritual that the head of the family should recount the story of the Exodus and interpret the various elements in the meal. So the new meaning given by Jesus to the bread and the wine, his speaking of his death as a sacrifice and the basis of a new covenant, and his command, 'Do this for my remembrance,' could all be seen as reflecting and re-interpreting the Passover ceremony itself, as could also the looking forward to the coming of the kingdom of God. In effect, Jesus was identifying himself as the Passover lamb, and instituting the Eucharist as the new Passover which would be a 'remembrance' of his self-offering. Jeremias also interpreted this 'remembrance' in a new way. He held that it did not refer to *a remembering by the disciples* of Jesus and his death, but rather *a calling on God to remember him*, and to hasten the coming of the kingdom for which he had sacrificed himself. So, he maintained, once the Last Supper was seen in the light of the Passover, all the main motifs in the various accounts became readily comprehensible. There was no need to appeal to the influence of Hellenistic Christianity to explain the prominence of the themes of sacrifice, of remembrance, or of sharing in Jesus' death, nor need it be held that there had been in the early church the two quite different types of Eucharist which Lietzmann had suggested.

The impact of Jeremias' work has deservedly been very considerable, but it is open to certain criticisms. His re-interpretation of 'remembrance' in particular has been widely criticised.[5] More important, however, is the question whether he has not read too much into the Passover setting. The Passover lamb was certainly 'sacrificed', but it was not a 'sacrifice for sin'; nor does Jewish thought at that time appear to have made any very close connexion between the blood of the Passover lamb and the 'blood of the covenant'. The words ascribed to Jesus, however, imply both the removal of sin by sacrifice and the making of a covenant in his own blood. The Passover, taken on its own, does not really serve to explain these emphases.[6] Moreover, while Jeremias did briefly discuss the different narratives and the influences which may have underlain their various wordings, he did not offer any very clear or full map of their development in their various distinct forms. Instead he concentrated chiefly on arguing in a general way that most of what they say is substantially accurate and broadly traceable back to Jesus himself. A more detailed study of the way in which these accounts emerged and were transmitted in the early church might offer a more solid working basis than Jeremias has done for the reconstruction of the original events and words of the Last Supper, and cast a clearer light on the variations between the reports.

Such a study has more recently been offered by Betz in a monumental and as yet incomplete work entitled *Die Eucharistie in der Zeit der Griechischen Väter* ('The Eucharist in the Age of the Greek Fathers').[7] Betz, unlike the others we have mentioned, is Roman Catholic, and is primarily concerned to show that the Roman Catholic understanding of the presence of Christ in the Eucharist is in harmony with the teaching of the New Testament and the early church. His work is thus in part a running debate with much recent Protestant scholarship. Here, however, we are chiefly concerned with the broad outline of his critical historical reconstruction of the growth and the shaping of the institution narratives. This marks a major advance upon Jeremias, but has not so far received the recognition it deserves, at least not among English-speaking Protestant scholars. As the two volumes together run to over 550 footnote-packed pages, we can only offer the barest sketch of his interpretation; but it will give us what we need for our own survey.

Betz' starting-point is that all the institution narratives must be recognised as being *liturgical texts*: they are not merely records of the Last Supper, but records which reflect the transmission of the story of the Last Supper in the celebration of the Eucharist in the church in the decades which followed. Their *Sitz in Leben*, the living context in which they must be seen, is early Christian worship. The variations between them must therefore be investigated from that angle. Two important general principles are to be kept in mind here. First, it is likely that particular wordings and specific emphases in this or that account will reflect to some degree debates and controversies and the general development of interpetation of the Eucharist in the early church. Second, texts which are used liturgically, and thus regularly and solemnly repeated, tend naturally to be modified in certain recognisable ways. For example, familiar expressions are often abbreviated because the full meaning can be taken as read, and only needs to be expressed in a condensed fashion. Equally, new explanatory additions are sometimes made in order to clarify what has become obscure or disputed. Again, there is a common tendency to make phrases which were originally distinct and different in form more similar to each other, a tendency towards parallelism. Principles of this sort can be applied in the light of such other evidence as is available – evidence concerning the relative ages of the different sources, their geographical origins, the influencing of one by another, traces in them of semitic rather than Greek forms of thought and expression, and so on – to piece together the probable course of the development of the tradition.

The oldest of all the documents is I Cor. 11, written about the year 55. In that passage, Paul says he is repeating what he himself had 'received from the Lord', and had already previously handed on to the congregation in Corinth. As the formulation of the narrative is in various ways different from Paul's normal language, and as indeed it has the ring of a standard formula, there is every reason to believe Paul's statement that it is one which he had himself been given 'from the Lord' – most probably in the instruction which he received after his conversion. The passage dealing with Jesus' resurrection in I Cor. 15.3ff begins in strikingly similar fashion: 'For I handed on to you in the beginning what I also received, that Christ died for our sins according to the Scriptures, and that he was buried, and that he was raised ...' In both cases it would appear that Paul is reciting the teaching he had been given, either in the same form in which he had heard it, or in one closely resembling it. It is therefore reasonable to conclude that this account, in more or less this form, is somewhat older than I Corinthians itself, and that it takes us back to the description of the Last Supper as circulated in the forties of the first century among Greek-speaking Christians. The additional material in Luke's longer version, which is similar but not wholly identical to Paul's, probably stems from the same source. Detailed comparison of these two texts can therefore help to suggest the most probable early form of that Greek description of the Last Supper. When that account is further modified by including in it certain elements from Mark which seem likely to be particularly ancient, the following version of the central core of Jesus' words can be constructed:

And taking bread, and having blessed (God), he broke it and gave it to them, and said, 'This is my body which is given for many. Do this for my remembrance.' In the same way also the cup after supper, saying, 'This cup is the new covenant in my blood.'

With this, we do not necessarily have the precise words of Jesus himself, but the earliest recoverable version of them as transmitted in the Greek-speaking church within a relatively few years of the Last Supper. This is as far back as we can go in tracing the tradition; but it is not very probable that any very major transformation of what Jesus had in fact said could have taken place within such a short period. This reconstructed text thus offers a reasonably solid basis for interpreting the Last Supper itself.

It is an important part of Betz' argument that the various narratives we now possess in the New Testament can plausibly be derived from this earlier version when likely liturgical and theological influences are taken into account. Paul and Luke's long text remain fairly close to it, but the changes which can be traced in them are all readily comprehensible. Paul alters 'my body which is given for many' to 'my body which is for you.' Both the abbreviation, dropping out the 'given', and the shift from 'many' to 'you' could have come about quite naturally as the familiar story was told and retold in the celebration of the Eucharist in local communities. Paul also reveals the tendency towards parallelism which has already been mentioned: so he gives the command to repeat what Jesus did *twice*, with the cup as well as with the bread. Similar tendencies lead in Luke's long version to slightly different results. He says that the body 'is *given for you*'; and while he only once quotes the instruction, 'Do this for my remembrance', he adds a parallel explanation to the word over the cup: 'which is *poured out for you*'. So he makes the words over the bread and the cup more similar to each other.

Further shifts still can be observed when we turn to the later accounts in Mark and Matthew. The meal which both Paul and Luke mention as coming between the bread and the cup is no longer referred to. There is an obvious probable explanation for this, in the light of what seems to have happened in the eucharistic worship of the early church. It very early appears to have brought the bread and the cup together to form a distinct act of worship and celebration which *followed*, instead of *bracketing*, a common meal (the 'Agape'). Before many generations had passed, the Eucharist and Agape were entirely separated, and the Agape finally disappeared altogether. If, as is likely, this gradual dissociation of the meal from the Eucharist was already taking place in the primitive church, the reference to the place of the cup *after* the meal would naturally come to seem irrelevant or even embarrassing, and so simply fall out of the narrative. Again, both Mark and Matthew omit the command to repeat what Jesus had done – not, presumably, because the churches they knew did not celebrate the Eucharist, but because the celebration and its propriety could be taken so much for granted that no special justification by dominical command was felt to be needed.

More significant than these shifts, however, are other changes of emphasis which are apparent in Mark and Matthew. In Mark, Jesus says, '*Take*; this is my body,' and it is also underlined that when he gave the cup, 'they all drank of it.' Matthew carries the same theme even further: Jesus says, 'Take, *eat*; this is my body,' and, 'Drink of it, all of you.' A new and stronger stress appears here to be placed on the fact that the bread and wine were *eaten and drunk*. In addition, while Mark does not say of the bread that it is 'given for many' or 'given for you', he does say that the blood of the covenant 'is poured out for many' (thus partly resembling Luke's long text with its 'poured out for you'); and Matthew not only repeats this explanation, but adds as well, 'for the forgiveness of sins.' Thus alongside the new insistence on eating and drinking, there appears in Mark and Matthew to be a special interest in the cup, leading to an expansion of the words spoken over it. This brings us to the most remarkable of all the contrasts between Mark and Matthew on the one hand and the older forms of the narrative on the other.

In Paul and Luke, and also in Betz' reconstruction of the underlying earlier Greek text, the bread is identified as Jesus' body and the cup as the covenant in his blood. 'Body' and 'covenant' are the key terms. In Mark and Matthew, the equivalents are 'body' and 'blood': 'This is my body ... This is *my blood of the covenant*.' No new terms as such have been introduced, but there is a noticeable shift of focus. Attention has moved from 'the covenant (in my blood)' to 'my blood (of the covenant)'. Behind this shift of focus, Betz suggests that there lies a change in theological perspective.

The older narratives of the Last Supper, Betz argues, describe Jesus as speaking in terms which are drawn very much from the picture of the Servant of God painted in the 'Servant Songs' in Isaiah, chs. 42, 49, 50 and 52-53. The reference to 'the many' for whom Jesus says his body is given is reminiscent of Isa. 53.11-12: 'By his knowledge shall the righteous one, my servant, make many to be accounted righteous . . . he bore the sin of many.' Again, closely bound up with the Servant Songs are two passages which speak of the Servant as a 'covenant' – Isa. 42.6: 'I have given you as a covenant to the people, a light to the nations,' and Isa. 49.8: 'I have kept you and given you as a covenant to the people.' The covenant is thus personified in the person here addressed by God: he is not merely a sign of the covenant, or a means by which it will be made, but rather is himself the bond of alliance between God and the people, the pledge of God's faithfulness. Against this background, the most likely meaning of Jesus' saying, 'This is the new covenant in my blood,' is something like, 'This is the covenant which I myself am, and which I shall seal by my own death.' Jesus himself is the meaning of the cup, Jesus with his death is the covenant of God.

When in Mark and Matthew these words are turned around to read, 'This is my blood of the covenant,' attention is being more closely directed to Jesus' death, and the wine in the cup linked directly with his covenant-blood. The ideas and associations evoked here no longer have to do chiefly with the Servant in Isaiah, but with other Old Testament passages instead, especially with Exodus 24.5-8, part of the record of the covenant made by God with Israel at Sinai:

> And Moses sent young men of the people of Israel, who offered burnt offerings and sacrificed peace offerings of oxen to the Lord. And Moses took half of the blood and put it in basins, and half of the blood he threw against the altar. Then he took the book of the covenant, and read it in the hearing of the people; and they said, 'All that the Lord has spoken we will do, and we will be obedient.' And Moses took the blood and threw it upon the people, and said, '*Behold the blood of the covenant* which the Lord has made with you in accordance with all these words.'

The centre of interest has now become Jesus' pouring out of his blood. At the same time, and as part of that same shift, his death is being interpreted primarily as a sacrifice, and the Eucharist itself as a sharing in it. This understanding of the matter is not of course new in Mark: it is to be found already in Paul, for example in I Cor. 10.16: 'The cup of blessing which we bless, is it not a sharing in the blood of Christ?' But in Mark and Matthew, these emphases have come right into the heart of the institution narrative itself.

This shift in the emphasis upon the cup seems to be paralleled by a somewhat similar shift in respect of the bread in an even later strand of the New Testament, the sixth chapter of the Fourth Gospel. All four institution narratives describe the bread as Jesus' *body* (in Greek, *sōma*). We cannot be sure what word Jesus himself would have used, but it may well have been either the Hebrew *basar* or the Aramaic *bisra*. Both words mean 'body' or 'flesh', but also carry the sense of 'person' or 'self'. The semitic mind did not make the same sharp distinction as the Greek between the physical and the spiritual, the body and the soul, the outer form and the inner self. Where the Greeks (and many of us still today) inclined to think of the human person as a soul imprisoned in a body, from which it was in principle detachable, the Hebrew was more likely to think of him as a living body, whose material, physical reality was of his very essence. To speak of 'my body' was thus a way of speaking of 'my self', and it is this sense which is conveyed, though not entirely adequately, by the Greek *sōma*. Just as the 'covenant' is essentially Jesus himself, so too is his 'body'. 'This is my body' and 'This is the covenant in my blood' both point to Jesus and identify *him* with his life and death 'for many' as the meaning of the bread and wine.

Just as the shift of focus from the *covenant* to the *blood of the covenant* brought a new concentration on Jesus' death and on the sacrificial meaning of his blood, so too it could naturally link up with an new emphasis on his *physical flesh*, so that the bread could come to be understood primarily as 'flesh' rather than 'self' or 'whole person'. And precisely this shift in respect of the bread appears to have taken place in John 6.51ff, where the author clearly has the Eucharist in mind, and where indeed he appears to be quoting a different version of Jesus' word over the bread, which we print in italics:

'I am the living bread which has come down from heaven. If anyone eats of this bread, he shall live for ever. And *the bread which I shall give is my flesh for the life of the world.*' So the Jews began to dispute among themselves, saying, 'How can this man give us his flesh to eat?' So Jesus said to them, 'Truly, truly I tell you, unless you eat the flesh of the Son of Man and drink his blood, you do not have life in you. He who chews my flesh and drinks my blood has eternal life, and I will raise him up on the last day. For my flesh is true food and my blood is true drink. He who chews my flesh and drinks my blood abides in me and I in him.'

What is being stressed here is not so much the whole person of Jesus (though that is of course implied throughout) as his 'fleshliness' and the demand to eat his flesh and drink his blood. This emphasis in the Fourth Gospel accordingly fits very well with the development traced by Betz in the institution narratives proper, and supports his thesis of a gradual shift in focus from 'body' and 'covenant' to 'flesh' and 'blood', and so to a greater emphasis on Jesus' death and its sacrificial character, and on the Eucharist as a participation in it.

How is this development to be explained? In part at least through the interpretation of the Eucharist itself in the light of theological emphases which, though ancient, were not present within the older institution narrative, but eventually came to influence its later forms. But it is also very probable that the general movement of thought and the eruption of controversy concerning the Eucharist itself could have played a significant role. The Fourth Gospel, together with the Johannine Epistles, reflects the need to combat docetic tendencies which were in the air, tendencies to believe that because Jesus came from God he could not have been a real man of flesh and blood, could not have been born of woman, and certainly could not have died on a cross. Against them, this strand of the New Testament insists that in Jesus the eternal Word *became flesh* (Joh. 1.14), and that it is through his flesh, his physical human life and history, his death and resurrection, that redemption was won. John 6 further suggests that the Eucharist itself needed to be defended: presumably those who had difficulty in accepting the reality of Jesus' flesh and blood had no less difficulty in believing that material bread and wine could have any part to play in their salvation. Hence the insistence of the whole passage both on the flesh and blood of the Son of Man and on the necessity of consuming them. In these circles at least, it may well have been controversy about the Eucharist itself that led to this sharpening of expression and concentration on flesh and blood. (Betz also suggests that the Epistle to the Hebrews reflects a similar situation, and that those who have 'profaned the blood of the covenant' (Hebr. 10.29) have in fact rejected or abused the Eucharist. His argument is a plausible one, and may well be correct. The Hebrews passages are however so indirect in their allusions that it is difficult to be sure.)

The main points in Betz' analysis may therefore be summed up as follows. The four institution narratives fall into two pairs, Paul and Luke's longer version, and Mark and Matthew. The first pair are generally closer to the oldest Greek account of Jesus' original words and actions, and so enable its provisional reconstruction. In it, Jesus describes himself in terms drawn from the Servant passages in Isaiah, and attention is concentrated upon his person and the covenant in him. In the later narratives, his flesh and blood and sacrificial death come increasingly to the fore. In this way, the centre of gravity shifts under the impact both of theological reflection upon the meaning of his death and of controversy concerning the meaning of the Eucharist itself.

This reconstruction has two chief merits. First, it offers a reasonable explanation for the diversity of the various narratives, one which can do justice to their differences but yet see them as fitting into a coherent development. Second, it offers at least a tentative sketch of what may have been the earliest recoverable form of the tradition concerning the Last Supper, and with it a means of drawing closer to the meaning of the Supper itself. Thus it does supply the kind of map which we have suggested is necessary to help us to thread our way through the different accounts. This is not to say that it is necessarily correct in every detail: historical investigation of this kind rarely leads to that sort of totally conclusive result, and new evidence, or new light on old evidence, may at any time shift the questions and answers around again. In particular, the shorter version of Luke still stands out as an awkward problem, and the possibility cannot be excluded that the narratives offered by it, and by Mark and Matthew, rest on older and more authentic traditions than has here been suggested. Overall, however, Betz' account seems at present to be the most satisfactory so far presented, and by giving it as much attention as we have, we have allowed it to introduce us to the complexities of the material and to some of the issues which it raises.

One other point must be made. It is no part of Betz' argument that the shift in focus in the later accounts of the Last Supper was in any way improper or unjustified. The theology they reflect was itself older than they, and can be seen, for example, in Paul alongside the ancient form of the eucharistic words themselves. When it came to shape the narratives, it made explicit what was earlier implicit in them: that it is in and through the death of Jesus, and through sharing in that, that salvation is achieved. But behind this emphasis upon his death as a sacrifice in which we share, it is still *the whole Christ* who is the meaning of the bread and wine. In this, Betz is certainly correct; but we may also observe that such a narrowing of focus *could* involve a certain risk of isolating one central aspect of Jesus' history and losing sight of the whole. Even if the New Testament writers avoided this trap, later theology has not always been so fortunate. In the West at least, both Roman Catholic and Protestant thinking have sometimes concentrated attention so exclusively on Jesus' death as to lose sight alike of his incarnation and human life, of his resurrection and ascension to be present for us at the right hand of the Father, and of his future coming. The meaning of the Eucharist has then been located solely in the cross, with the result that a choice has come to force itself between seeing the Eucharist as a 'repetition' of his sacrifice and understanding it as a 'mere remembering' of it. To the extent that such a narrowing of vision could easily find support in the stress in the later eucharistic narratives upon Jesus' flesh and blood, and so on his death, we may well be grateful to Betz for putting these in broader perspective and reminding us that from the earliest recoverable tradition of the Last Supper it is indeed 'the whole Christ' who gives himself to us in the Eucharist as 'the new covenant' made by God.

2

THE LAST SUPPER AND THE PASSOVER

It is even today not entirely certain whether or not the Last Supper was a Passover meal. The main reason for this uncertainty is that the Gospels themselves seem to disagree on the point. Mark 14.12-16 leads up to the story of the Last Supper by describing the preparations 'for the Passover which I shall eat with my disciples' (v. 14), and Matt. 26.17-19 and Luke 22.7-13 are similar. Of the institution narratives proper, however, only Luke's refers explicitly to the Supper as a Passover, while John 18.28 states that the Passover *followed* Jesus' arrest.

This somewhat contradictory evidence has been interpreted in a variety of ways. One possibility is that the Last Supper was not a Passover, but a kind of solemn fellowship-meal which Jesus and his disciples might have been in the habit of sharing. For much of this century that has been the majority view among New Testament scholars. Another is that it was a Passover, but held a day earlier than the official one, perhaps because more than one calendar was used by different groups among the Jews. This suggestion has been quite widely canvassed in the last twenty years or so. A third possibility is that the Supper was the regular Passover, and that the Fourth Gospel has altered its timetable in order to link the Passover feast with the crucifixion itself, and so to throw into relief the meaning of Jesus as the new Passover lamb. The fact that John does not report the institution of the Eucharist as such, but appears to ground it in Jesus' death both in John 6.51-58 and in 19.34, where he mentions the *blood and water* flowing from Jesus' side on the cross, gives some support to this hypothesis. John does appear to see together the Passover, the cross, and the source of the two sacraments of baptism and the Eucharist, at which the blood and water seem to be hinting. It may therefore be that his dating of the Passover after the Last Supper reflects a theological rather than an historical concern.

In the last thirty years, the opinion that the Last Supper was indeed a Passover meal has come once more to be widely held, chiefly because of the exceedingly full and detailed study of the evidence by Jeremias.[1] While a certain uncertainty must remain, this makes it worth while to look at the Passover itself, and to see what the shape of the Last Supper as a Passover might have been. Even if, after all, it was not a Passover, it nevertheless took place under the shadow of the approaching feast, and can properly be set against that background. Either way, the Passover ritual and its meaning can cast a good deal of light upon the Supper itself.

The central Old Testament passage explaining the Passover is Exodus 12, which describes the night on which the people of Israel were led out of Egypt. In the first part of the chapter (vv. 1-20), Moses and Aaron are given instructions from God, the main part of which runs:

> This month shall be for you the beginning of months; it shall be the first month of the year for you. Tell all the congregation of Israel that on the tenth day of this month they shall take every man a lamb . . . a lamb for a household . . . and you shall keep it until the fourteenth day of this month, when the whole assembly of the congregation of Israel shall kill their lambs in the evening. Then they shall take some of the blood, and put it on the two doorposts and the lintel of the houses in which they eat them. They shall eat the flesh that night, roasted; with unleavened bread and bitter herbs they shall eat it . . . In this manner shall you eat it: your loins girded, your sandals on your feet, and your staff in your hand; and you shall eat it in haste. It is the Lord's Passover. For I will pass through the land of Egypt that night, and I will smite all the firstborn . . . and when I see the blood, I will pass over you, and no plague shall fall upon you to destroy you when I smite the land of Egypt.
>
> This day shall be for you a memorial day, and you shall keep it as a feast to the Lord; throughout your generations you shall observe it as an ordinance for ever. Seven days you shall eat unleavened bread; on the first day you shall put away leaven out of your houses . . . And you shall observe the feast of unleavened bread, for on this very day I brought your hosts out of the land of Egypt: therefore you shall observe this day, throughout your generations, as an ordinance for ever.

Another passage may also be quoted, from Deuteronomy 16.1-4:

> Observe the month of Abib, and keep the Passover to the Lord your God; for in the month of Abib the Lord your God brought you out of Egypt by night. And you shall offer the Passover sacrifice to the Lord your God, from the flock or the herd, at the place which the Lord will choose, to make his name dwell there. You shall eat no leavened bread with it; seven days you shall eat it with unleavened bread, the bread of affliction – for you came out of the land of Egypt in hurried flight – that all the days of your life you may remember the day when you came out of the land of Egypt. No leaven shall be seen with you in all your territory for seven days; nor shall any of the flesh which you sacrifice on the evening of the first day remain until morning.

Another important instruction is given later on in Exodus 12 vv. 24-27:

> You shall observe this rite as an ordinance for you and for your
> sons for ever. And when you come to the land which the Lord
> will give you, as he has promised, you shall keep this service. And
> when your children say to you, 'What do you mean by this
> service?' you shall say, 'It is the sacrifice of the Lord's Passover, for
> he passed over the houses of the people of Israel in Egypt, when
> he slew the Egyptians, but spared our houses.

Year by year, on the fourteenth day of the first month, the people of
Israel re-enacted the meal that their forefathers had shared on that last
night in Egypt. They ate the same food that had been eaten then: roasted
lamb, unleavened bread, bitter herbs. The lamb was ritually slaughtered
in the temple in Jerusalem ('the place which the Lord will choose, to
make his name dwell there': since the destruction of the temple, the
Jewish Passover has been celebrated without the sacrificial lamb). They
joined in this sacrificial meal as a celebration of the deliverance from
Egypt: the meal itself was a permanent 'memorial' (in Hebrew,
zikkaron) of what God had done for them. To that end also, the story of
the Exodus was re-told at each Passover, and the meaning of the bread,
the lamb and the bitter herbs explained. The question and answer
described in Exodus 12.24-27 became part of the Passover rite itself, and
remain so to this day. This is the form in which the question is put by a
child or by all the children present in a modern Passover liturgy:[2]

> Why is this night different from all the other nights? On all other
> nights we eat either leavened bread or *matzah* (unleavened bread);
> on this night only *matzah*.
>
> On all other nights we eat all kinds of herbs; on this night we
> especially eat bitter herbs.
>
> On all other nights we do not dip herbs at all; on this night we
> dip them twice.
>
> On all other nights we eat in an ordinary manner; tonight we
> dine with special ceremony. (p. 29)

This then leads into the *maggid*, a full narration of the events of the
Exodus and their present and future meaning. So the modern Passover
follows the same pattern as the ancient, according to the instructions we
have quoted, and taking as its guiding theme the words of Exodus 13.8:
'You shall tell your child on that day, "It is because of what the Lord did
for me when I came out of Egypt."'

The significance for Jews down through the centuries of this
celebration, this 'memorial', and this recounting of the story of the
Exodus deserves to be underlined, for otherwise we may pass it by too
easily. For the children of Israel, the Exodus was not merely an inspiring
tale from the remote past. It was the story of how God had called them

out of slavery, given them a land, and made them a chosen nation. It was
thus the story of his love and his mercy, his faithfulness not only to their
ancestors but also *to them*. The old history was the key to their own
identity as God's people; it was to be told and re-told from one
generation to another, not merely as hallowed tradition but as a
statement of their calling and destiny. An ancient rabbinic saying about
the Passover is quoted on p. 56 of *A Passover Haggadah*: 'In every
generation each person should feel as though he himself had gone forth
from Egypt . . .' A little later, it states (p. 57): 'Not only our ancestors
alone did the Holy One redeem, but *us* as well, along with them, as it is
written; "And he freed us from Egypt so as to take us and give us the land
which he swore unto our fathers." (Deut. 6.23)' The powerful sense in
the Passover of the link between past and present, and of a future hope
opening up from it, is well conveyed in two further passages from the
same modern version of the liturgy (which, it should perhaps be added,
is not a purely modern one, but rather a revision which seeks to restore as
much as possible of the most ancient recoverable Passover material as
well as supplying additional contemporary texts for use with it). The
first of these passages is the opening call to celebration: the first words of
the *kadesh*, or 'Sanctification of the Day':

> Now in the presence of loved ones and friends, before us the
> emblems of festive rejoicing, we gather for our sacred celebration.
> With the household of Israel, our elders and young ones, linking
> and bonding the past with the future, we heed once again the
> divine call to service. Living the story that is told for all peoples,
> whose shining conclusion is yet to unfold, we gather to observe
> the Passover . . . (p. 21)

The second comes rather later, before the drinking of the second cup of
wine:

> Remembering with gratitude the redemption of our fathers from
> Egypt,
> rejoicing in the fruits of our struggle for freedom,
> we look now with hope to the celebration of a future redemption,
> the building of the City of Peace in which all men will rejoice in
> the service of God,
> singing together a new song.
> We praise You, O God, Redeemer of Israel! (p. 60)

The 'remembering' involved here is not merely a matter of looking back
to a past which is remote and distant. It is rather a setting of the present in
the light of the past, a drawing of the two together in a way which
transforms the present and renews hope for the future. All this must be
kept in mind as we look back to the Passover of two thousand years ago.

Then as now, the Passover was the greatest of all Jewish celebrations.

It was a feast of liberation, and marked as such by the fact that a quite exceptional quantity of wine – four cups in all – was drunk. It was also a meal at which Jews then would commonly recline on couches rather than sit on chairs, thus symbolising their status as free people, freed by God himself. Most of the extant evidence for the pattern of the meal and the surrounding ritual dates from a little later than the time of Jesus, but it is likely that his observance was along similar lines to those which appear in the following centuries. The broad outline was probably of the following kind.

First came a preliminary course. This began with a blessing spoken over a cup of wine which was then passed round, and an hors d'oeuvre of green herbs, bitter herbs and fruit purée was served. The main course, consisting of the Passover lamb, unleavened bread, bitter herbs and fruit purée was then brought in, and a second cup of wine mixed; but before either food or wine were taken, the Passover liturgy began. The head of the family told the story of the Exodus and explained the special meaning of the various foods which were to be eaten. This was the *haggadah*, the 'interpretation', and it could last for a considerable time – half an hour or more. It would include such sayings as this ancient Aramaic one concerning the unleavened bread which is still preserved in *A Passover Haggadah* (p. 26):

This is the bread of affliction, the poor bread,
which our fathers ate in the land of Egypt.
Let all who are hungry come and eat.
Let all who are in want share the hope of the Passover.

After the *haggadah*, the first part of the Passover *hallel* (a series of psalms) was sung, and the second cup was drunk. This ended the liturgy and the meal proper could start. The head of the family took bread and spoke over it a blessing such as the common Jewish grace, 'Blessed art Thou, O Lord our God, King of the Universe, who bringest forth bread from the earth,' then shared the bread around the table. The main course was eaten, and a closing blessing spoken over a third cup of wine, the 'cup of blessing'. The ritual was then concluded by the singing of the second part of the *hallel*, followed by the blessing and sharing of yet a fourth cup of wine, the '*hallel* cup'.

The main elements in the various institution narratives can all be fitted quite neatly into this overall pattern. The first cup mentioned by Luke could be the one with which the Passover ceremony began. The bread which all the accounts describe Jesus as giving after saying the blessing could be the bread which opened the main course, after the *haggadah*. The meal recorded by both Paul and Luke's long version could be the main course of the Passover itself. Finally the cup which in both these texts and also in Mark and Matthew followed the bread could be the third cup, the 'cup of blessing' – which name Paul in fact gives it in I Cor. 10.16. On the other hand, all these points could conceivably be paralleled in a solemn religious meal other than the Passover. It is however when other features of the institution narratives are taken into account that the significance of a possible Passover setting becomes more apparent. Two points in particular, both emphasised by Jeremias, are of special importance. First is the fact that the Passover included the *haggadah*, the interpretation of the meal and its components. This supplies a very likely setting for Jesus' reinterpretation of the bread and wine with which the main course opened and closed. Such reinterpretation can hardly have been a normal or usual occurrence, but it would be much more comprehensible if it followed his giving of the *haggadah* and explaining the meaning of the Passover itself. Second, the Passover itself as an act of remembrance, a *zikkaron*, offers a context in which the command, 'Do this for my remembrance,' can be seen as a natural extension and development of the Passover ritual. It also suggests what kind of 'remembering' Jesus had in mind. It was not to be a mere looking back to his death, but a celebration of his offering of himself which would continually recall his own to their allegiance to him, and to the deliverance he had secured for them.

Now let us go on to locate in that likely context the summary of Jesus' words and actions reconstructed by Betz. It must of course be remembered that he doubtless said much more than has been recorded, and that he could presumably assume that his words then would remind his disciples of others he had previously spoken. It was not a matter of his simply uttering these few sentences on this occasion, and nothing more. But it is with the words which appear to be most reliably recorded that we must work: there if anywhere must we search for the clues to his meaning. First however we should notice a detail which is recorded in all three Gospel narratives – Jesus' *vow of renunciation*.

Mark and Matthew both end their accounts of the Last Supper with Jesus' saying that he will not drink again of the fruit of the vine until the coming of the kingdom. This gives the impression, though without saying so in as many words, that Jesus had shared the bread and the cup, but was now forswearing the use of wine. Luke by contrast begins his description in a way that may imply that Jesus neither ate the Passover himself nor drank any of the wine: 'And he said to them, "I have earnestly desired to eat this Passover with you before I suffer; for I tell you that I shall not eat of it again until it is fulfilled in the kingdom of God." And taking a cup, and having given thanks, he said, "Take this and divide it among you; for I tell you that from now on I shall not drink of the fruit of the vine until the kingdom of God comes."' It seems from this that he did not drink from the cup, and it is one possible interpretation of his earlier words that although he wanted to eat the Passover, he would not in fact do so. At any rate, it does appear that whether or not he shared in the meal and the cup(s), he did definitely renounce their future use until the coming of the kingdom for which he was giving his own life. His mind was travelling forward to the kingdom, and to the feast that he would share with his disciples then. Here there lies in the background the thought of the messianic banquet, which indeed is specifically mentioned a little later in Luke's account of the Last Supper – at 22.30: '... that you may eat and drink at my table in my kingdom'. The kingdom of God will be a great feast to which his people are invited. But the way to that feast lies only through Jesus' renunciation of feasting; it lies indeed through his death, which that vow of renunciation foreshadows. So his last meal with his followers becomes a token of his self-denial, so that they may share in his eventual victory. But it is also a pledge of the victory itself: the wine he gives them is a foretaste of the wine of the kingdom. The Last Supper itself thus looks forward to his death, but the perspective does not terminate there. It leads on beyond the cross to what the cross will bring about, when their hunger and thirst will be finally satisfied in the great banquet in the house of the Father. The Last Supper itself was an *eschatological meal*, one which already anticipates the End. This meaning was faithfully retained by the church in the early days, when the eucharistic prayers regularly included the cry, *Maranatha*, 'Come, Lord!' In later centuries, it was all too often lost to sight, and the Eucharist seen virtually exclusively as a looking back to Jesus' death. So he has been seen more as he who once died than as he who is to come. The note of gladness and anticipation has commonly been overlaid entirely by that of sombre remembrance and the antepast of the kingdom transformed into a funeral supper. But the Last Supper itself included both moments, and both are essential. As Paul put it, 'we proclaim the Lord's death *till he comes*.' (I Cor. 11.26)

This brings us to *the word over the bread*, which in Betz' reconstruction runs:

> This is my body which is given for many. Do this for my
> remembrance.

As we have already suggested, the meaning of 'body' here is best taken as *Jesus himself* rather than merely his physical body. Of himself, Jesus says that he 'is given for many'. The fact that the verb is passive, 'is given', rather than the active, 'I shall give' (which is what is to be found in John 6.51), is striking. Its probable force is that it is *God* who 'gives' Jesus for the sake of the 'many'. In I Cor. 11.23 there is a similar use of a passive verb: 'the Lord Jesus on the night on which he was delivered up (by God) took bread ...' is more likely to be correct than the common translation, 'on the night on which he was betrayed (by Judas) ...' Jewish speech commonly used passive verbs in this way to avoid naming God himself, while it is a common enough New Testament theme that it was indeed God who 'gave' Jesus (e.g. John 3.16; Acts 2.23). This 'giving' centres in his death, so the 'is given' of Luke 22.19 ought perhaps to be rendered as a future, 'will be given'. Hebrew and Aramaic do not distinguish present and future tenses in the same way as Greek or English, so that the original words translated by Luke's present could equally well have had a future reference. Behind the words 'for many' lies as has already been mentioned the description of the Servant of God in Isaiah 53.11-12: he 'will make many to be accounted righteous' and 'bore the sin of many'. 'Many' here means rather more than simply a large number: it has the effective force of 'all'. A fair paraphrase of Jesus' interpretation of the bread might therefore be, 'This is myself, whom God will give up for the sake of all' – so that the sins of all will be forgiven, and their reconciliation with the Father brought about. *How* his death will achieve this is not spelt out; *that* it will is unmistakably affirmed.

This still leaves the most difficult part of the sentence: 'This is my body' or 'This is myself.' No phrase has caused so much conflict as this through the long history of the church, and it is difficult, perhaps impossible, to approach it without having one's perception affected and perhaps also distorted by the whole range of interpretations that have been presented, and by one's own preferred understanding. But it is still worth trying, so far as may be, to ask what Jesus himself might in fact have meant – and indeed what the disciples at the time might have reasonably been expected to understand him to mean. That will not necessarily dispose of all other questions, but it may give us a new angle from which to come towards them.

The first thing to notice is that the little word 'is', which has been the very storm-centre of controversy in recent centuries, was probably not spoken at all. It is found in all the institution narratives, but the normal semitic way of speaking would simply have left it out. Jesus' own words were most probably simply, 'This my body.' The meaning – and the problems – are however still the same. Jesus identifies the bread as himself. How is this identification to be understood? The words themselves as they stand can be taken in any of a wide variety of senses, from, 'This bread is hereby miraculously transformed into my body,' to 'This bread is a picture of myself.' To attempt to fix Jesus' own likely meaning more precisely, we must look beyond the mere words to their setting in the Last Supper and to Jesus' accompanying words and actions; and beyond that, to the Passover background and to the Jewish way of thinking and speaking.

Before he spoke these words, Jesus would perform the normal

actions of a Jew saying grace before a meal. The taking of the bread in his hands, the blessing of God, the breaking and sharing of the bread were all part of that single act in which God was praised, the table-fellowship established, and the meal begun. In Christian thought the breaking of the bread has of course been generally regarded as a representation of the death of Jesus; and the symbolism does obviously suggest itself. But the main point of the whole action was the blessing of God and the receiving and eating of the bread as a gift from him. Its breaking was a necessary but incidental element in the pattern. The pattern as a whole, however, reveals a striking and rather different connexion with Jesus' words. For there is a marked parallel between the whole action of the grace and what Jesus says about the bread. In the grace it is given to be eaten as a gift from God; and Jesus identifies it as his own person, whom God will give for many. The link thus seems to be not simply between the bread and Jesus himself: it is between *bread received and shared* and *Jesus given up by God for many*.

The significance of the grace deserves to be opened up a little further. Coming as it did at the beginning of the meal, the blessing and thanks offered over the bread extended to cover the whole meal that was to follow. The bread stood for that food as well, and that food was included in the thanksgiving, whose religious and ritual purpose was to release the food (which belonged to God and came from him) for human use. What is done with the bread stretches out to include the entire meal: in this part, the whole is in a manner contained; the bread represents the whole, and the whole is as it were concentrated in the bread. Further, it was the receiving and sharing in the bread over which the grace had been said which gathered those present into a single community at the table and made the meal a shared one rather than one taken by isolated individuals who merely happened to be eating in the same place at the same time. For the Jews, as for other ancient peoples, the shared meal had a profound religious and human significance of which we in our largely secularised and functional outlook have almost wholly lost sight. Those who ate together were bound together by that simple sharing. Hence the horror of the fact that Jesus' betrayal was brought about by one who, in the phrase of Mark 14.20 and Matthew 26.23, was 'dipping into the same dish with him.' When Paul said, 'Because there is one bread, we, who are many, are one body; for we all share in the one bread,' (I Cor. 10.17) he meant it absolutely seriously. The meal itself established a bond between those who shared in it: it did not merely symbolise the bond, but actually constituted it. Thus the bread used in the grace in the ordinary way of things in Jewish practice represented the blessing of God for the meal as a whole, the receiving of the whole as his gift, and the fellowship of those taking part.

The bread used in the grace at the Passover carried all of these meanings, and with them a further significance as well. For this, as we have seen, was 'the bread of affliction which our fathers ate in the land of Egypt.' More is meant here than simply that this bread is a sign or copy of the bread eaten on the departure from Egypt. It is to be taken and eaten as *the same bread*. It is a link with the bread eaten in the past, and so with the whole history of the Exodus, which is *the history of those present now* at the Passover celebration. This unleavened bread is itself a vehicle of the 'remembrance' by which past and present are brought together, and the past is not left in distant remoteness but brought as the living past into the present. Thus the Passover bread used in the grace represented the entire meal, bound the group into a fellowship and linked the present with the past deliverance. In each of these three moments of *blessing, thanksgiving and receiving*, of *uniting* and of *remembrance*, it could not be regarded by a religious Jew as simply 'ordinary unleavened bread'. Rather it had received a special meaning, a special use, and therefore also a special identity. Not only did it symbolise all that we have outlined: all that was focussed in the bread itself. 'This is the bread of affliction which our fathers ate' is not 'mere metaphor' but solemn description.

This already points in the direction in which we must look to see the force and intention of Jesus' re-naming of the bread and also, later, of the cup. It is not merely a matter of making them 'signs' or giving them a 'purely symbolic meaning' in the common sense of these terms, according to which a 'sign' or 'symbol' has no intrinsic connexion with what it represents, and is simply arbitrarily associated with it. If these words are to be used, it must be in a much stronger fashion, one which Paul Tillich expressed by saying that a symbol 'participates in' the reality which it signifies.[3] The very nature of the bread itself as Passover bread can only be grasped in and through all these dimensions of meaning which meet in it, and which it encapsulates and conveys. Only on that level can the description of it be understood. At the same time it is equally clear that this is not a case of some miraculous or even magical alteration in the bread itself; it has not ceased to be what it previously was, nor been transmuted into something wholly different. It is still unleavened bread, and that is indeed essential to the rest of what it is; but over and above that, it is unleavened bread made for a particular reason, used in a particular setting and for a particular purpose, and therefore to be taken in all seriousness as 'the bread of affliction which our fathers ate'.

We shall see later how difficult it has proved for both Roman Catholic and Reformed theology to preserve this kind of understanding of the eucharistic bread and wine. On the one side lies the temptation to think of a material change in the bread itself; on the other, that of making so radical a distinction between the material bread and its meaning that the connexion between the two is lost or becomes more than a little tenuous. Both dangers have been heightened through the long history of Christian thought by a recurrent tendency to make an absolute, sharp division between *material things* and *spiritual or personal realities*, and so to move away from the perception of man and the world which informed ancient Jewish thinking, and which we may expect to have been familiar to Jesus and his disciples. They knew that human existence itself is physical as well as spiritual, and that the material creation is itself the handiwork of God. It is he who brings forth bread from the earth, and wine to gladden the heart of man. Even as 'ordinary food and drink', they are not 'mere things', but things given and enabled to support human life. As food and drink they are already charged with personal and even religious significance. This is not to say that there is no difference between the spiritual and the physical, between the human, the animal and the vegetable, or between living things and things inanimate. But these different levels of being, to use a modern expression, are all connected with each other: the higher depend upon the lower, and the lower find their fulfilment in the higher, and all are held together by being God's creation. This integrated vision of the coherence of things has however often been lost in the church, especially in the West, where both theology and our wider culture have been influenced by a deeply-etched dualism between mind and body, spirit and matter, person and thing, subject and object. As a result, the two tend to fall apart entirely, and the link is effectively lost between the eucharistic elements and their significance, or the attempt is made to hold them together by a crudely materialistic interpretation of that significance, which transforms their sacramental identity into something quasi-physical. Both Roman Catholic and Reformed theology have had to struggle with this problem and have done so in a variety of ways. But a way out of the dilemma can only be found if the underlying mind/body dualism is replaced by an understanding closer to that which the Jew of old took for granted. Significantly, it is not only in theology today, but also in other disciplines, such as biology and psychology, that voices are coming to be heard calling for a new discernment of the connexion between body and mind, and between living beings and 'inanimate matter'.[4]

The meaning of the unleavened bread in the Passover thus offers a horizon in which we can better understand what Jesus meant by his own new words about it. To the bread suffused with the associations of Exodus, of affliction and liberation, he gives a further intensity of significance: 'This is myself, whom God will give for the sake of all.' We have already mentioned the broad parallel between these words and what was actually done with the bread at the Passover grace. In the light of the three moments of blessing, thanksgiving and receiving, of uniting into a fellowship, and of remembrance which we have seen to be involved in that grace, this parallel may now be spelt out in more detail. The bread is received as a gift from God; and Jesus himself is God's gift. By its sharing, the group are gathered into a community; and through Jesus a new community is brought into being. As the 'bread of affliction', it is a memorial of the deliverance from Egypt, and of that deliverance as bearing upon the present and opening up the future; and Jesus now tells his disciples to repeat what he has done for his remembrance. Each of these three moments connected with the Passover bread is thus taken up and transformed in a new perspective which is defined by reference to Jesus himself. In the giving of the bread, he is given; in the sharing of the bread, he is shared; in the whole action he will be remembered in the strong sense that what he was and did will come to bear afresh upon the present time and the new future.

In what sense, however, is Jesus himself 'given' or 'shared' in the Last Supper? Is he simply 'given' in the Last Supper itself? Or is the 'giving' there merely a 'sign' of a 'giving' which will really happen somewhere else? This is another form of the dilemma concerning the identity of the bread which we have just argued is a false one; and it is equally false here. The giving of Jesus centres in his death. So he is not simply given in the Last Supper by itself; rather, the giving there has to do with his being given on the cross. At the same time, his being given up on the cross is the climax and realisation of the purpose of his whole life. Already at the Last Supper he is present as God's gift. Nor is that all. He is given *for many*: the gift reaches out to touch those for whom it is intended. In giving the bread, he is anticipating his own death and offering its fruit to his disciples. In giving the bread he is giving himself to them. The gift of Jesus centres in the cross and turns upon it, but it does not terminate there, nor is the cross an isolated moment cut off from the rest of time and history. Rather it is itself the centre on which all time and history pivot, and in which they are all gathered up. Thus the gift made there is both *once* and *for all*; and already in the Last Supper it is offered in reality, not merely in 'symbol', to the disciples. So too in the Eucharist, the same gift is offered to us again – not in the sense that the gift itself is repeated, which is neither necessary nor possible, but in the sense that it is really extended *to us*. This again is a point where Christian thinking about the Eucharist has often toppled over on the one side or the other, either seeing in it a *repetition* of Jesus' death, or interpreting it as a *mere remembering* of it as something far distant from us. But he who was given up on Calvary is still God's gift to us, and this remembrance of him is the means by which he makes us sharers in what he is and has done for us.

So too, the 'sharing' in Jesus of which the bread speaks needs to be taken seriously. Particularly among Protestants, it is often understood in a rather weak sense as either 'receiving the benefits of his saving work' or 'having a personal relationship with Jesus'. There is nothing wrong with these ways of putting the matter, so far as they go; but they do not go far enough to do justice either to the Last Supper and the Eucharist or to the range and depth of the message of the New Testament. When the attempt is made on this kind of basis to express the meaning of the Eucharist, the result is a drastic attenuation of it. Our sharing in him is not merely a reception of benefits from him (though it involves that), nor is it merely standing in a relation to him analogous to those relations of love and trust which we have with other people (though it involves that too). Above and beyond that, it means, in Paul's terms, 'I live, yet not I, but Christ within me,' (Gal. 2.20) or in John's, 'Abide in me, and I in you.' (John 15.14) What Jesus was and is, he was and is not simply in himself *apart* from us, but precisely *for us*; and it is made effective as he lives *in us*. This is not merely 'mysticism', though mystical language is one possible vehicle for expressing it. It means rather that we are included with him in all that he is and has done for us, that the centre and ground of our own existence lies in him, and that we are therefore not simply self-enclosed and self-regulating atomistic individuals, but open to him and living out of him.

This brings us on to the second part of the word over the bread: 'Do this for my remembrance.' The 'Do this' deserves a brief comment. It might at first appear that this simply means, 'Repeat this; copy what I have done.' In all probability, however, the force of the words is a stronger one, and the verb rendered in Greek as *poiein*, 'do', means more than simply 'do' – something like 'solemnly celebrate'. In Matt. 26.18 *poiein* is used of *celebrating* the Passover: *poiein to pascha*. The same use of *poiein* is to be found in the Septuagint translation of both the main Old Testament passages which we quoted in connexion with the Passover, in Exodus 12.17 ('You shall *observe* this day') and Deuteronomy 16.1 ('You shall *keep* the Passover'). When we add the fact that the Passover itself was a 'memorial', it is difficult to avoid the conclusion that when Jesus says, 'Do this for my remembrance,' he is in fact consciously giving a fresh significance *to the celebration of the Passover*, in which the meaning of the old rite will be taken up and deepened by reference to himself.

The main point of the 'remembrance' for which Jesus tells his disciples to celebrate the new feast is similarly to be seen in the light of the Passover with its bringing of the living past to bear upon the present. Now however it is Jesus who is to be remembered rather than simply the Exodus. But the same kind of powerful remembering is involved. This is not, as it has so often been treated, a rather pathetic request not to be forgotten. It is not for Jesus' benefit that he is to be remembered, but for the benefit of those who remember. The point is not so much that his disciples *should remember*, as if their remembering gave meaning to the celebration, but rather that they should through the celebration be forcefully *reminded*. Jesus gives the means by which he will call himself to their remembrance: he is and remains the centre of gravity, and they are to be the receivers. So too the Eucharist is not primarily something that *we* do, or that we have to fill with meaning generated by the intensity of our remembering and our devotion. It is something given to us to enable us to realise afresh that what Jesus was and did, he was and did for us.

In saying this, we have left aside Jeremias' interpretation of 'for my remembrance' as meaning 'that *God* may remember me'. As was mentioned earlier, this element in Jeremias' argument has been very heavily criticised since he advanced it. It cannot however be entirely ruled out, and it is hard to suppress the impression that some at least of his critics have rejected it on grounds which have more to do with their own theological position than with the evidence of the texts, or with the rich biblical meaning of 'remembrance'. However strange may appear to us the thought that God needs to be reminded of anything, this way of speaking is certainly quite common in the Old Testament and can also be traced in Jewish prayers of around Jesus' day, including some which call upon God to 'remember' (i.e. to send) the Messiah. Jeremias' suggestion may therefore be correct in spite of the criticisms of it. Even if it is, however, the calling on God to remember Jesus would still also carry with it the 'remembrance' of him by his people in the sense we have just described, and that sense deserves to be emphasised as well.

Much of what we have said about the word over the bread applies equally to that over the cup. Here too something already charged with religious meaning is given further new meaning in the light of Jesus himself. We need not repeat all of that once more, but may concentrate on the new elements in this saying, which in Betz' reconstruction runs:

This cup is the new covenant in my blood.

The distinctive new feature here is the word 'covenant'. We have already seen that this is probably another way of describing Jesus himself, drawn, like the word over the bread, from the Servant passages in Isaiah. It is thus broadly similar in its force to what was said about the bread: Jesus is the content and meaning of the cup given to be drunk. But 'covenant' opens up further aspects of that meaning.

The term 'covenant' appears frequently in the Old Testament. The root meaning of the Hebrew word *berith* is probably best rendered as 'obligation': in making a covenant, one puts oneself under an obligation, enters into a commitment; or, in other cases, imposes obligations upon another person. A covenant can thus be a unilateral promise, or it can be a bond of agreement and alliance between two parties. In the second case, the parties may stand on an equal footing vis-à-vis each other, or one may be the superior of the other – in which case it is the superior who takes the initiative and dictates the terms of the covenant, which the inferior then accepts. The Old Testament knows of covenants between individuals, between nations and rulers, and between God and his people. The history of Israel in particular was marked out by a series of covenants made by God with Abraham, with Israel at Sinai, and with David – as well as by the promise in Jeremiah 31.31-34:

> Behold the days are coming, says the Lord, when I will make a new covenant with the house of Israel and the house of Judah, not like the covenant which I made with their fathers when I took them by the hand to lead them out of Egypt, my covenant which they broke, though I was their husband, says the Lord. But this is the covenant which I will make with the house of Israel after those days, says the Lord: I will put my law within them, and I will write it upon their hearts; and I will be their God, and they shall be my people ... they shall all know me, from the least of them to the greatest, says the Lord; for I will forgive their iniquity, and I will remember their sin no more.

When Jesus calls himself the 'new covenant' and his own blood, or death, the means of making the covenant, he is saying that in him God is laying the foundation for a new alliance with his people and calling them into it. The covenant itself rests upon God's decision: 'I will be your God, and you shall be my people.' It will be brought into being by his own death, through which God will 'forgive their iniquity' and 'remember their sin no more.' The cup which he gives is itself a pledge of the covenant in him: those who take and drink it acknowledge by doing so that the covenant includes themselves. So the cup, like the bread, stands for Jesus himself as the covenant gifted and established by God; it offers the disciples their share in it; and it does not merely picture what will happen, but already declares and ratifies it to them.

This means in particular that the Last Supper has the character of a *promise* and a *commitment* on God's part. It is not merely Jesus who gives the cup, nor does it speak only of his death in and by itself. It is the token of forgiveness and reconciliation and the pledge of the covenant itself. Ultimately it rests on the fact that, as Hebr. 10.23 puts it, 'he who has promised is faithful,' that God does not break his covenant. The Eucharist too is therefore a covenant-meal, a receiving afresh of God's promise in Jesus. This lies at the very heart of the Reformed theology of the sacrament, though even in the Reformed tradition it has sadly often been lost to sight, or even more sadly distorted by a transformation of the biblical understanding of God's covenant into something quite different – a kind of commercial contract or bargain which men make with God, and in which they can be sure of his love for them only if they satisfy certain 'conditions'.[6] But a real and proper sense of the covenant as God's committing of himself to us in Jesus Christ underlies the definition of a sacrament which, as we shall later see, Calvin and other Reformers offered: 'a sign given to confirm a promise'. So too in the old days in the Church of Scotland it was common for the minister, after breaking the bread, to set one piece on either side of the cup, thus symbolising the pattern of the sacrifice in which God established his covenant with Abraham, when the sacrificial offerings were divided in two, and God made a smoking fire-pot and a flaming torch pass between them (Gen. 15). The same sense finds expression in the frequent use of the words of Psalm 116 as a call to prayer in Presbyterian eucharistic worship:

What shall I render to the Lord for all his bounty to me?
I will lift up the cup of salvation and call on the name of the Lord;
I will pay my vows to the Lord now in the presence of all his people.

What these words convey is the reaffirmation of the covenant, the glad response to the faithfulness of God.

The note of promise associated with the covenant also reminds us again of the fact that the Eucharist does not only have to do with what *has been*, but also with what *will be*. The covenant leads on into the future: 'I will be your God and you will be my people.' What God establishes and extends in Jesus is a new identity and a new future for his own people; the covenant is the promise of the coming kingdom. In giving the cup to his disciples and describing it as he does, Jesus says, 'This is myself, and in me the promise of the Father. Take it, drink it, and receive your own place in the covenant I will make, the covenant which I am.'

The Last Supper itself and these few words of Jesus are thus richly packed with meaning, of which here we have been able to draw out only some of the central fibres. But there is one more question that must be raised before we go on to look at some of the other main New Testament passages dealing with the Eucharist. Can the Last Supper itself be regarded as a *sacrificial meal*? Do the bread and wine there have particular sacrificial significance? In view of the debate about Eucharist and sacrifice which has raged since the Reformation, this is a question which cannot be passed by; and indeed, the Passover connexion itself raises it, for as we have seen, the Passover was a sacrifice, though not a sacrifice for sin. For this reason the blood of the lambs slaughtered in the temple was poured out around the altar, and thus given to God; but, unlike the blood of sin-offerings, it was not smeared on the horns of the altar. Nevertheless, the offering at the Passover included the two elements which are broadly characteristic of cultic sacrifice in general: the giving of one part to God, and the sharing by the worshippers in the other part. Can the same be said of the bread and wine as Jesus used and reinterpreted them?

A positive answer to this question must depend in part on whether Jesus' own death is itself seen as an offering to God of a sacrificial kind. If it is, then it can also be held that the bread and wine constitute the sacrificial meal which that offering makes possible. As we have already noticed, and shall shortly see again, Jesus' death was from very early on understood in this way, and the Eucharist accordingly interpreted as a sacrificial meal. So Paul could say in I Cor. 5.7 that 'Christ our Passover has been sacrificed,' and speak of the Eucharist itself as a sacrificial meal in I Cor. 10.14-22. But was this understanding already there at the Last Supper? Jeremias believes that it was – that Jesus understood himself in terms of the Passover lamb, and explained his approaching death in that way as a paschal offering. But if the line of interpretation which we have taken from Betz is correct, the ideas in Jesus' mind seem rather to have been those of the Servant, the covenant, and the forgiving of sins, and none of these is intimately connected with the sacrificial aspect of the Passover. It therefore seems safer to conclude that Jesus himself did not necessarily have in mind this conception of the significance of his death. In that case the new elements introduced by him into the celebration do not necessarily have the corresponding sacrificial associations.

This is not to say that the understanding of Jesus' death in sacrificial terms drawn from the Jewish cult was improper or mistaken. But it may have been the product of subsequent reflection – reflection which can be traced in Paul, which influences the later institution narratives, and which finds its fullest theological development in the Epistle to the Hebrews. Such reflection therefore probably needs to be kept in its proper secondary place, and not allowed entirely to dominate the scene, as has sometimes happened both in eucharistic theology and in wider thinking about the meaning of the cross. If Jesus' death is interpreted exclusively as a sacrifice to God, or if the Eucharist is understood *tout court* as 'the Christian sacrifice', both may be liable to serious distortion.

3

THE EUCHARIST IN PAUL AND JOHN

Apart from the institution narratives themselves, the two main New Testament passages bearing upon the meaning of the Eucharist are I Cor. 10-11 and John 6. There are of course many other texts which would have to be drawn into any comprehensive study of all that the New Testament has to say on the matter. For our purposes, however, it is better to use the limited space available to concentrate on the major discussions and the broad lines of understanding which they open up for us.

1. *Eucharist, Sacrifice and Participation according to Paul*

We have already looked at Paul's version of the Last Supper in I Cor. 11.23-26, but the greater part of the tenth and eleventh chapters has to do directly or indirectly with the Eucharist in connexion with issues troubling the Corinthian congregation. At least two problems appear to have lain in the background. One was whether Christians could take any part in pagan sacrifices – a question made all the more pressing by the fact that the meat sold in the markets would normally have been ritually slaughtered by pagan priests. The other had to do with the way in which the Eucharist was being celebrated in the Corinthian church. It is less clear what further depths of controversy may also have been stirred up, or who exactly the people causing the trouble in Corinth were. Many modern interpreters have seen in them Christians from the Palestinian church who were undermining Paul's influence. Others have more recently discerned in Paul's comments hints at some form of gnosticism, or at a belief that the Eucharist was a magical rite which automatically guaranteed life and salvation. Certainly there seem to have been deep divisions in the community, as Paul himself makes clear in I Cor. 1.10-17, and the way in which he introduces the question of 'spiritual food and drink' at the beginning of chapter 10 does suggest that he may have had 'magical sacramentalists' in mind.

In 10.1-13, Paul looks back to the events of the Exodus from Egypt and the wandering of the Israelites through the desert in order to draw conclusions for his own day and for the situation in Corinth:

I want you to know, my brothers, that our fathers were all under the cloud, and all passed through the sea, and all were baptised into Moses in the cloud and in the sea, and all ate the same spiritual (*pneumatikon*) food and all drank the same spiritual drink. For they drank from the spiritual Rock which followed them, and the Rock was Christ. Nevertheless with most of them God was not pleased, for they were overthrown in the wilderness. Now these things are warnings for us, not to desire evil as they did. Do not be idolaters as some of them were ... Now these things happened to them as a warning, but they were written down for our instruction, for on us the end of the ages has come. Therefore let anyone who thinks that he stands take heed lest he fall ...

The 'fathers' had been baptised 'into Moses', and they had enjoyed food and drink which was real – the manna and the water struck by Moses from the rock – but at the same time 'spiritual'. It is difficult to find an adequate translation for the word *pneumatikos*. In some ways 'supernatural' may be a better rendering, but it too is not wholly satisfactory. Behind Paul's use of it stands the contrast he so frequently draws between 'flesh' and 'spirit', between the 'old Adam' and Christ the 'second Adam', between human life under the law, under sin and under condemnation and the new life opened up in Jesus Christ. Christians are called to be 'spiritual', not in the sense of ceasing to be 'physical', but in that of living their lives in a new way in the power of the Spirit of Christ. This same spiritual nourishment had already been available to the Israel of old: they had eaten and drunk from Christ himself, for he was the Rock. In one sense, Paul is here clearly speaking allegorically, and probably using traditions of rabbinic interpretation which had already seen in the manna a foretaste of the messianic feast, and had also described the rock struck by Moses as following the people in their journey through the wilderness. But – and this is essential to his meaning – he is not merely wishing to be understood allegorically, but also quite realistically. The fathers had all really received real food and drink which was at the same time spiritual because it was supplied by Christ. This is the whole point of the lesson he is intending to teach. They had really received these things, but yet because of their disobedience and their idolatry, God had been displeased with them. This supplies the connexion with what he wishes to emphasise concerning the Eucharist. It is spiritual food and drink, but merely receiving it is not enough, if the recipients then proceed to behave after the fashion of the children of Israel.

The force of this argument, and its direct bearing upon the Eucharist, become more fully apparent in the following verses where he comes to speak of the Eucharist and of contemporary idolatry. So he continues in vv. 14-22:

> Therefore, my beloved, shun the worship of idols. I speak as to sensible people; judge for yourselves what I say. The cup of blessing which we bless, is it not a participation in the blood of Christ? The bread which we break, is it not a participation in the body of Christ? Because there is one bread, we who are many are one body, for we all partake of the one bread. Consider the practice of Israel; are not those who eat the sacrifices partners in the altar? What do I imply then? That food offered to idols is anything [particularly distinctive or significant in itself], or that an idol is anything [real]? No, I imply that what pagans sacrifice, they offer to demons and not to God. I do not want you to be partners with demons. You cannot drink the cup of the Lord and the cup of demons. You cannot partake of the table of the Lord and the table of demons. Shall we provoke the Lord to jealousy? Are we stronger than he?

The key ideas here are those of 'sharing' or 'participation' (koinōnia), of 'partner' (koinōnos), and of 'partaking' (metechein). These are all extremely strong terms: they describe such a sharing in someone or something that one is bound to and united with him or it. What Paul is saying is that in the Eucharist we really participate in the body and blood of Christ, and so in him and in his death for us; but if we also wish to take part in idolatrous worship, this sets up an impossible conflict. While the pagan gods as such do not exist, the demons do, and pagan worship is in fact offered to and bound up with real demonic powers, so that through it people are bound to the demons in the same way as in the Eucharist they are united with Christ. Hence the one is incompatible with the other: if one attempts to do both, one can only 'provoke the Lord to jealousy' — just as Israel had done in the wilderness.

Paul's train of thought here does of course sound rather strange to modern readers who for the most part do not quite know what to make of this talk of 'demons', of dubious or positively evil spiritual powers at work in pagan worship. There arise here all kinds of matters which we cannot explore: whether, for example, the demons are real or not; if so, how they are to be understood and spoken of today; how far Paul's attitude to non-Christian worship should be determinative for the Christian approach to people of other faiths in the modern world. Serious though these questions are, our concern at this point must rather be to enter into and appreciate Paul's view of things in order to grasp what, within that view, he also says about the Eucharist. In it he discerns the same strong participation in the spiritual reality bound up with it, Jesus Christ himself. And just how realistically he understands

that participation comes out very loud and clear a little later on, in
11.27-30:

> Whoever, therefore, eats the bread or drinks the cup of the Lord
> in an unworthy manner will be guilty of the body and blood of
> the Lord ... For 'anyone who eats and drinks without discerning
> the body eats and drinks judgment upon himself. That is why
> many of you are weak and ill, and some have died.

We shall return below to this passage; but for the moment it serves to
underline how strong a sense of real sharing in Christ and in his death
shapes Paul's conception of the Eucharist: the participation is so real and
so powerful that it rebounds on those who receive unworthily, and turns
the Eucharist into a curse rather than a blessing.

One cannot read very far in modern literature upon the Eucharist
and upon Paul's interpretation of it without finding that his 'sacramental
realism', as it may justly be called, has proved embarrassing to many
commentators whose own view of the Eucharist was rather different.
Some, like Lietzmann and Bultmann, resolve the difficulty by ascribing
this note to Hellenistic influence; but Paul's realism is as much Jewish as
Hellenistic, indeed more so, and corresponds to the Jewish outlook of
which we spoke in the last chapter in connexion with the Passover.
Others attempt in various ways to reinterpret Paul's thought in a fashion
which quite drastically dilutes his meaning.[1] On the other hand, some
Roman Catholic commentators have been tempted to seize rather too
quickly on Paul's words here as justifying the doctrine that the bread and
wine are transubstantiated into the very body and blood of Christ.[2] This
founders on the fact that Paul draws such a clear parallel between the
Eucharist and pagan sacrifice, and links both by referring as well to the
Jewish cult. It is not some unique characteristic of the Eucharist as such
that he has in mind, but rather the conviction that *any* sacrifice or
sacrificial meal binds the participants to the spiritual or supernatural
powers, divine or demonic, which are associated with it. If one should
be careful not to read too little into what he says, one must be equally
careful not to read in too much.

In this part of Paul's discussion, then, two distinctive notes can
be recognised which do not appear to have been present in the same
way in the early tradition concerning the Last Supper itself. Firstly,
the Eucharist is interpreted here quite explicitly as a sacrificial meal,
analogous to both Jewish and pagan sacrifices. Second, as the references
to 'the body' and 'the blood' in both 10.16 and 11.27 show, Paul
interprets the bread and wine as Christ's *body* and *blood* rather than as his
person and *covenant*, though in his institution narrative itself, 'body' and
'covenant' are still the two central terms. This throws into relief the
distinctiveness of the institution formula which he preserves; but it also

reveals in his interpretation the influences which were to feed into the later forms of the narrative in Mark and Matthew.

Yet a third note, equally central for Paul, but already implicit in the institution narrative, is to be heard in the words of 10.17, on which we have not so far commented: 'Because there is one bread, we who are many are one body, for we all partake of the one bread.' Here we can see another side of Paul's 'realism': the Eucharist binds those who share it into a single 'body'. This is the point on which he is anxious to build in 11.17-34, where he comes to speak of the abuse of the Eucharist in Corinth:

> But in the following instructions I do not commend you, because when you come together it is not for the better but for the worse ... When you meet together, it is not the Lord's Supper that you eat. For in eating, each one goes ahead with his own meal, and one is hungry while another is drunk. What? Do you not have houses to eat and drink in? Or do you despise the church of God and humiliate those who have nothing? What shall I say to you? Shall I commend you in this? No, I will not.
>
> For I received from the Lord, what I also handed on to you, that the Lord Jesus on the night ... For as often as you eat this bread and drink the cup, you proclaim the Lord's death until he comes.
>
> Whoever, therefore, eats the bread or drinks the cup of the Lord in an unworthy manner will be guilty of the body and blood of the Lord. Let a man examine himself, and so eat of the bread and drink of the cup. For anyone who eats and drinks without discerning the body eats and drinks judgment upon himself. That is why many of you are weak and ill, and some have died ...
>
> So then, my brothers, when you come together to eat, wait for one another. If anyone is hungry, let him eat at home lest you come together to be condemned.

The Corinthian church obviously met regularly, most probably on Sundays, for a common meal which included, or was supposed to include the Eucharist. Paul insists, however, that it is anything but that: whatever they may imagine, they are not in fact 'eating the Lord's Supper'. The reason is that the meal is not in fact being shared, but has become an occasion of selfishness on the part of those who possess more food and drink: they proceed to enjoy themselves while others are left without anything. So the poor are humiliated and 'the church of God', the gathering of God's people, is treated with contempt. Paul calls the Christians of Corinth back very sharply to the real meaning of the Supper of the Lord by retelling the story of the Last Supper, insisting that the Eucharist is grounded in Jesus' death (which makes any purely selfish enjoyment utterly out of place), and that the 'body' must be recognised. 'Body' here seems to have a double reference. On the one hand it means the body (and therefore also the death) of Christ, which some in Corinth are so abysmally failing to take seriously; on the other, it also means the whole congregation, for it too is the body of Christ. To 'despise the church of God' is also to fail to discern the body at the centre of the Eucharist, and the guilty parties in Corinth are charged by him on both counts. Their 'celebration' contradicts the whole meaning and character of the Eucharist, and Paul demands that its pattern be changed. Hunger should first be satisfied at home, and the Lord's Supper performed in a proper fashion.

It is very probable that this kind of abuse in Corinth (and, we may suspect, elsewhere as well), and the steps Paul took to deal with it, were in the end responsible for the separation of the Eucharist from the meal with which it had originally been joined. The surviving evidence is very sketchy, and the development cannot be traced in any detail, but the problems of controlling common meals of this kind may well have been at least one factor in it. At any rate, by the second century the Eucharist and the Agape seem to have fallen apart. This was perhaps inevitable at the time, but it is also regrettable. As a result, the Eucharist became more and more a purely symbolic meal: instead of being a real meal, or part of a real meal, it became a mere shadow of a meal – unlike the Jewish Passover. This also led to its being seen rather narrowly as a cultic, religious rite, separated off from the wider daily and weekly life in the world of the people of God. Would it not have been far healthier if a genuine shared meal could have continued to be linked with it, so that the sharing in Christ and with each other which it involves would have been shown and seen not to be something purely or narrowly 'religious' in the most restricted sense, but the very form and shape of Christian life? To some extent in recent times the attempt has been made in various experiments to recover something of that broader horizon. These have, however, commonly led to the use of a kind of Agape as a *substitute* for the Eucharist – as when inter-church difficulties prevented the celebration of the Eucharist itself. This is obviously not the same thing, though it is doubtless a step in the right direction.[3]

By drawing out and emphasising this second aspect of the 'body of Christ' as the Christian community, Paul makes even clearer what was already implicit at the Last Supper, both in the sharing of the bread and in Jesus' speaking of the 'covenant'. The Eucharist is not simply given to individuals in isolation: it is by its very nature corporate, and binds those who share in it into a community. It is in the Eucharist above all that the Church receives and rediscovers its own identity as the body of Christ.

In this sense, it is proper to say that the Eucharist has an inherent *ecclesiological* dimension as well as the *christological*. It has to do with the Church as well as with Christ. This is powerfully emphasised in a different way by what may be the oldest extant prayer spoken over the eucharistic bread. It comes from the *Didache* ix, which dates from the first or second century, and runs thus:

> We give thanks to thee, our Father, for the life and knowledge which thou didst make known to us through Jesus thy Son: thine be the glory for ever.
>
> As this broken bread was scattered upon the mountains and was gathered together and became one, so let thy church be gathered together from the ends of the earth into the kingdom; for thine is the glory and the power through Jesus Christ, for ever and ever.

Some three centuries later, the same theme was highlighted from yet another angle by St Augustine in his *Sermon* 272:

> If you wish to understand the words, 'the body of Christ', listen to what the Apostle says: 'You are the body and the members of Christ.' (I Cor. 12.27) If you are the body and the members of Christ, it is *your* mystery that is placed on the Lord's table; it is *your* mystery that you receive . It is to that which you are that you answer 'Amen', and by that response you make your assent. You hear the words, 'the body of Christ'; you answer, 'Amen'. *Be* a member of Christ so that the 'Amen' may be true.

There is of course a necessary order of priority to be observed here. 'The body of Christ' refers first of all to Christ himself, and secondarily to the church which he unites with himself. That the church is his body is a mystery which rests upon him. It is not something that simply lies apparent on the surface of the matter. On the surface, indeed, the church is always liable to look much more like an association of like-minded people banded together for their own religious purposes, like a secretarial bureaucracy, or a ministerial or administrative hierarchy. It is the hidden depth of the church that the Eucharist discloses, a hidden depth that lies in Christ, and only through him in the church itself. If that dimension of depth is not opened up, the Eucharist becomes an act of the church's independent self-affirmation: it is made dependent on the church, and the members of the body displace the head. That in turn undermines the authentic ecclesiological meaning of the Eucharist, substituting an inauthentic one for it. This perennial threat can only be guarded against if the Eucharist is consistently and clearly recognised as the gift of the head to the members rather than the church's way of expressing and realising itself. Only so can its real significance for the church be kept in view.

Overall, then, for Paul, the Eucharist is a means of real union with Christ, union enabled and coloured above all by the meaning of the cross. As such, it has the character and power of a sacrificial meal, which has the nature of bringing about a genuine sharing in the spiritual reality mediated through it. This is at the same time the bond which holds the church together as Christ's body. It is not, however, automatically or magically beneficial: it can be received for judgment rather than salvation if its proper content and meaning are ignored or despised. In all these ways, Paul's conception of the Eucharist is strongly realist rather than merely symbolic. At the same time, the reality at work in it is nothing other than the reality of Christ himself and the power of the cross. It is in these that we share in the bread and the wine, and it is in this sense that they are 'spiritual food and drink'. They are a means of receiving and participating in Christ, and therein lies their energy.

This central emphasis in Paul's account of the Eucharist is thus not dissimilar to what we have found in looking at the Last Supper itself. There already, the bread and wine were offered as a means of real sharing in Christ which bound the disciples to him and made them a fellowship within the new covenant to be sealed by his death. At the same time, new notes have also appeared in Paul. Christ's death is understood explicitly as a sacrifice, and the Eucharist as a sacrificial meal. Particular stress is thus laid on that death, which is absolutely central and fundamental in Paul's eucharistic theology. (It is equally fundamental in his understanding of baptism, which he insists is into *the death of Christ* – Romans 6.3.) The thought, too, that unworthy reception of the Eucharist may be a curse rather than a blessing appears to be a new one in Paul.

These fresh emphases in Paul's theology have often been strongly criticised. His concentration on the cross has been seen as turning the Gospel into something morbid and guilt-ridden: his interpretation of the Eucharist in terms of sacrifice as making it all too similar to pagan worship; and his warning against the dangers of unworthy reception as descending to a sub-Christian conception of God as a capricious supernatural force, as likely to be maleficent as beneficent in his working. Against criticisms of this kind, two general points demand to be made. First, neither in I Cor. 10-11 nor anywhere else do we possess a complete, balanced and rounded statement of Paul's theology of the Eucharist. The emphases he selects and the points he stresses all have to do with a particular troubled situation, and it is only indirectly, in reference to that, that he expresses those aspects of his understanding which bear upon it. The comparison with pagan sacrifices was called forth by the need he saw to warn Christians against them, not by any desire to put the Eucharist on a level with them; the insistence on worthy reception by a patently unworthy abuse of the Eucharist in the Corinthian congregation. Second, Paul tends to be given a great deal more blame than can be justified for the ways in which some of his teachings were taken up and applied in later theology or piety. An excessive concentration on the cross and on ideas of sacrifice did indeed develop in Western Christianity, both Roman Catholic and Protestant, and led to medieval and more recent theories of substitutionary punishment which went far beyond anything in Paul or any other New Testament writer. Similarly, his warnings about unworthy reception have had the most unfortunate results where they have been misunderstood, as in the Scottish highlands, to mean that only those who are sure of their own worthiness can dare to receive the eucharistic bread and wine. That, however, is a world apart from his demand that the body of Christ be discerned and the Eucharist celebrated with due discernment of it. He could put up a strong defence against charges of this sort. They do nevertheless serve to remind us that his emphases could be and have been misconceived and misapplied, and warn us to develop them with caution. This caution is needed in at least the following respects:

1. Paul rightly saw that the death of Jesus is pivotal for the Gospel, and struggled to understand it as profoundly as possible. But the cross must not be separated off from what preceded or from what followed it. The Eucharist is a participation in Christ's death, but not only in his death: it is a sharing in the whole Christ with his whole history, for it is in his totality that he is given for and to us.

2. While Paul's stress on worthy reception is fully justified, the way in which he expresses it could easily give rise to the notion that the Eucharist is dangerous in a magical way, that it contains an unpredictable and ambivalent spiritual power of the kind associated with 'holy things' in many religions. This idea was not in Paul's mind: for him it was Christ himself who is the reality shared in the Eucharist. But ideas of this sort could naturally enough develop; they may already have been in the mind of some in Corinth; and they have certainly arisen in other places since. The best safeguard against them is Paul's own message that no mere 'power' but Christ the Lord himself is at work in it.

3. If, following Paul, we understand the Eucharist by analogy with sacrificial meals, it must at the same time be recognised that he sees it as a sacrifice in the sense of sharing in what has been offered to God rather than as being itself the offering. If, over and above that, the Eucharist is to be seen as in some sense offered to God, the sense of that offering and its relation to the self-offering of Christ will need to be carefully explored.

2. Eating and Drinking the Flesh and Blood: John 6

We have already briefly mentioned the section (vv. 51ff) of this chapter which appears to bear explicitly on the Eucharist. Those verses must now be set against the background of the rest of the chapter, as they represent the culmination of the whole, which all has to do with the central theme of 'bread from heaven'. It has been held by some modern commentators, notably by Rudolf Bultmann in his great commentary on John, that the eucharistic material in vv. 51ff was not part of the original text, but inserted by a later editor who had a sacramental interest not shared by the first author. This view has lost some of its former popularity in more recent study, and there are good reasons for believing that the chapter ought to be taken as it stands as a coherent and unified whole. It is a characteristic of the Fourth Gospel that it regularly circles around its themes, approaching them now from one angle, now from another; and shifts in tone which nevertheless preserve the same underlying emphases can be found throughout. The turning of attention to the Eucharist in vv. 51ff does maintain such a degree of continuity with the previous argument that it can quite reasonably be seen as typical of the author's style.

Two other particular features of the pattern and shape of the chapter may be appealed to in support of this view. As it stands, it is carefully constructed around one of the central Johannine motifs: that Jesus is misunderstood and rejected by those to whom he comes. This is developed and illustrated through the chapter by reference to four progressively shrinking circles: the crowd who wish to make him a king (v. 15), the Jews debating with him in Capernaum (v. 41), some of his own disciples (v. 60), and finally, Judas (vv. 70-71). The eucharistic material in vv. 51ff is the necessary lead-in to the disciples' discontent, and cannot easily be excised without disrupting that pattern. A second observation points to the same conclusion. Although most editions and translations of the text divide it into sections or paragraphs which conceal the fact, we shall see below that there is a remarkable similarity of structure between vv. 35-47 and 48-58: these are two parallel and complementary sections, of the same shape and very nearly the same length. If the verses which Bultmann ascribes to his 'sacramental redactor' are taken out, the architectonic of these parallel sections is destroyed. It is not therefore very plausble to think that that pattern itself was the by-product of editorial interference. It might be more convincing to advance a more radical suggestion than Bultmann's, and cut out the whole of vv. 48-58; for it is conceivable that a second author might have added in an entire new section patterned on the one it was to follow. This however is open to a further objection which deserves to carry considerable weight. Each section is a kind of commentary on one part of the text from Psalm 78.24: 'He gave them bread from heaven to eat,' which is introduced in v. 31.[4] The first concentrates on 'bread from heaven', the second on its being eaten. On this score, the second section is as essential to the whole movement of the chapter as the first. The more radical surgery thus loses its attraction as well. If the chapter in its present form, with this clear structure in the disputed sections, is the work of someone other than the original author of part of it, he has reshaped the material much more than suggestions of mere editing or insertion of odd verses allow, and the chapter as we now have it deserves to be taken as a unity.

The chapter begins (vv. 1-21) with the accounts of the feeding of the five thousand and of Jesus' walking on the Sea of Galilee to join his disciples in the boat. These are presented in a fashion fairly similar to Mark 6.32-52 and the parallels in Matt. 14 and Luke 9 (though Luke, alone of all of these, omits the walking on the water). There are, however, some distinctive slants in John's version. He associates the feeding with the approaching Passover (v. 4). He has of course a special interest in Jewish feasts, and regularly relates episodes in the story of Jesus to them, as in 5.1; 7.2 and 10.22; but he gives particular prominence to the Passover, which he links with the cleansing of the temple in chapter 2, and with the story of the passion which begins at 11.55: 'And the Jewish Passover was near . . .' The reference to it here in the sixth chapter is unlikely to be accidental, or to reflect a merely chronological interest. Rather it hints at the significance of the feeding itself: it is an anticipation of the Christian Passover, of the Eucharist. Indeed, it may be that we should go even further in exploring the possible significance of this mention of the Passover. While John appears in chapter, 2, 6, and 11 to be referrring to three different Passovers (and thus lays the basis for the tradition that Jesus' ministry lasted three years), it has often been remarked on that the first of these, apparently belonging at the beginning of that ministry, is associated with the cleansing of the temple which in the other Gospels is located at the beginning of the week of the crucifixion. On one level (though it is not the only one), the entire Gospel seems to be an extended passion narrative, departing from and circling around the Passover at which Jesus was killed. It may therefore well be that we should expect hints and echoes of the week of the passion throughout, and especially where the Passover is explicitly mentioned. The sixth chapter, coming as it does half way through the account of the ministry of Jesus, is the very place where one might also expect to find reference to the turning-point of the last week, the night of the Last Supper and the betrayal. And as we shall see, these hints are to be found there. It is not wholly fanciful to suggest that this chapter is in fact John's 'institution narrative', concerned throughout with the Eucharist and with the rejection of Jesus, culminating in Jesus' own identification of 'one of the twelve I have chosen' as a devil, an identification which finds its closest Synoptic parallels in the accounts of the Last Supper itself.

Hints at a eucharistic reference are also to be found in other points of detail in the story of the feeding. Where the Synoptic Gospels all say that it was the disciples who raised the question of the hunger of the crowd and suggested that Jesus should send them away, John makes Jesus provoke the issue by asking Philip where bread can be found for so many (v. 5); and where the other Gospels describe the disciples distributing the food, in John this is done by Jesus himself (v. 11). Two small verbal differences may also have some significance in this same connexion. Unlike the other Gospels, which all describe Jesus as looking up to heaven and *blessing* (*eulogein*) God over the bread (Mark 6.41 and parallels), John says that he *gave thanks* (*eucharistein*). The meaning is the same, but this use of *eucharistein* cannot but bring to mind the fact that the Pauline and Lukan institution narratives also use *eucharistein* rather than the *eulogein* of Mark and Matthew. John's use of it here in v. 11 may therefore not be accidental. Again, in v. 12 Jesus orders that the scraps of food should be gathered up 'that nothing may be lost': the point is not made in that way in the other Gospels, which emphasise the quantity of what was left over rather than the need to preserve it. This concern that something or someone 'be not lost' is a typically Johannine theme (3.16; 6.39; 10.28; 17.12; 18.9), but it is normally related to *people*. Here it may well be intended to convey that the bread of the Eucharist itself should not be thrown away casually, but gathered up with reverence. At any rate, there is reason enough in this opening passage to suspect that the feeding is indeed seen by John as connected with the Eucharist, so that the more direct references which come later in the chapter are not altogether surprising.

The immediate result of the feeding of the crowd is that those who have seen it conclude that 'this is indeed the prophet who is to come into the world.' (v. 14) To prevent them from making him a king, Jesus withdraws; the disciples return by boat to Capernaum, and he joins them during the night by crossing the Sea of Galilee to their boat and brings them safely to land. The crowd too make their way there, and on meeting Jesus, ask, to quote literally, 'Rabbi, when did you become thus?' (v. 25) – a typically ambiguous question, capable of meaning either, 'When did you arrive here in Capernaum?' or something rather less banal. Jesus replies by challenging them in vv. 26-27:

> Truly, truly, I say to you, you seek me, not because you saw
> signs, but because you ate your fill of the loaves. Do not work for
> the food which perishes, but for the food which endures to eternal
> life, which the Son of man will give to you, for on him has God
> the Father set his seal.

When the crowd ask what kind of 'work' is then expected of them, he tells them it is 'to believe in the one whom God has sent.' (v. 29)

Realising that they are being challenged to believe in Jesus, they reply:
> Then what sign do you do, that we may see and believe you?
> What work do you perform? Our fathers ate the manna in the
> wilderness; as it is written, 'He gave them bread from heaven to
> eat.' (Ps. 78.24) (vv. 30-31)

This quotation from Psalm 78, referring to the manna described in
Exodus 16, now becomes the text which Jesus explains at length in the
following verses.

He begins by clarifying the text itself. He has been challenged in his
turn to perform a miracle similar to Moses' supplying of bread from
heaven. But, he says, the real bread from heaven was not given by Moses
in the wilderness; it is now being given by the Father (v. 32), 'For the
bread of God is that which comes down from heaven and gives life to the
world.' (v. 33) The people are quite happy with this, and eagerly ask to
be given that bread (v. 34), but are soon to be made less happy by Jesus'
clearer explanation that he himself is the bread. That explanation falls
into the two parallel sections we mentioned above – vv. 35-47 and
48-58.

Each of these passages begins with Jesus saying, 'I am the bread of
life,' and then developing the theme (vv. 35-40; 48-51). Each then
reports a debate among the Jews about his words (vv. 41-42; 52), and
Jesus' answer – which in each concludes with a strong reiteration of the
theme of the whole section (vv. 43-47; 53-58). The structural parallelism
emerges quite clearly if the key points in the two passages are set out side
by side:

vv. 35-47	vv. 48-58
I am the bread of life.	I am the bread of life.
He who comes to me shall not	Your fathers ate the manna in the
hunger, and he who believes	wilderness, and they died. This is
in me shall never thirst.	the bread which comes down from
But I told you that you	heaven, that one may eat of it
have indeed seen me, and	and not die. I am the living
do not believe ... I have	bread which has come down from
come down from heaven ... to	heaven ... And the bread which I
do the will of him who sent	shall give is my flesh for the
me ... For this is the will	life of the world.
of my Father, that every	
one who sees the Son and	
believes in him should have	
eternal life ...	

So the Jews began to mutter
disapprovingly about him
... and said, 'Is this not
Jesus the son of Joseph ...?
How can he now say, "I have
come down from heaven"?'

So the Jews began to dispute
among themselves, saying,
'How can this man give us
his flesh to eat?'

Jesus answered, 'Stop
muttering among yourselves.
No one can come to me unless
the Father who sent me draws
him, and I will raise him up
on the last day ... Truly,
truly I tell you, he who
believes has eternal life.'

So Jesus said to them, 'Truly,
truly I tell you, unless you
eat the flesh of the Son of man
and drink his blood, you do not
have life in you. He who chews
my flesh and drinks my blood
has eternal life, and I will
raise him up on the last day ...
He who chews this bread shall
live for ever.'

The first section is thus concerned with Jesus as the bread *from heaven*, and with the need for faith to recognise him as such; the second with the need for this bread *to be eaten*. Each develops one element of the text from Psalm 78.24: 'He gave then bread from heaven to eat.' The first words of that text, '*He* gave them,' had of course already been stressed by Jesus in v. 32, where he insisted that it was God, not Moses, who gave the manna. Thus the entire passage from v. 32 to v. 58 may be seen as commentary on the words of Psalm 78, a commentary which circles around each of the main elements in it in order to come at the theme from different angles. This is a powerful argument for the unity of the chapter as it stands, and for the authenticity of vv. 48-58 as a whole. We shall come back shortly to the content of these two sections, but must first look on to the shape of the remainder of the chapter.

Thus far the discussion has been with the Jews in the synagogue in Capernaum (v. 59). Many of Jesus' own disciples, however, express their own dissatisfaction with what he has been saying (v. 60), and Jesus criticises their unbelief in terms reminiscent of those in which he had answered the Jews in vv. 35-47 (vv. 61-65) – but does not thereby dissuade a number of them from leaving him (v. 66). The twelve, however, remain with him still, with Simon Peter as their spokesman: 'Lord, to whom shall we go? You have the words of eternal life; and we have come to believe and to know that you are the Holy One of God.' (vv. 68-69) Jesus observes none the less that even then there is among those whom he has chosen 'a devil', that is, Judas (vv. 70-71). It seems that the more clearly and openly Jesus states who he is and what he is about, the more he provokes rejection, so that by the end of this chapter the dark shadow of his betrayal by 'one of the twelve' (v. 71) is gathering over the narrative. In a way, this chapter is an epitome of the whole story of Jesus' ministry as seen and described by John, and this too underlines the significance in the eyes of the author of the themes it handles: Jesus himself is the bread from heaven, and he who eats this bread will live for ever.

Now let us look more closely at the way in which this theme is developed. In vv. 35-47, Jesus lays the emphasis firmly on 'believing in me': 'he who comes to me shall not hunger, and he who believes in me shall never thirst.' (v. 35) 'He who believes has eternal life.' (v. 47) 'For this is the will of my Father, that every one who sees the Son and believes in him should have eternal life; and I will raise him up on the last day.' (v. 40) The Jews have seen him but do not believe (v. 36), and their question, 'Is this not Jesus the son of Joseph . . .?' (v. 42) bears that out again. They look at Jesus and see only a man like themselves, just as when they were fed on the other side of the Sea of Galilee on the previous day, they did not recognise the 'sign', but merely enjoyed the satisfying of their physical hunger (v. 26). But it is belief in Jesus that is 'the work of God' (v. 29) by which they will obtain 'the food that endures to eternal life' (v. 27). This belief which can recognise Jesus as 'from heaven' is itself the gift of God: 'No one can come to me unless the Father who sent me draws him.' (v. 44) 'All that the Father gives me will come to me, and him who comes to me I will not cast out . . . and I will raise him up on the last day.' (vv. 37-40) So, at least by implication, the Jews see Jesus but do not believe because God has not drawn them or given them the faith that can recognise him.

This same theme is taken up again in Jesus' conversation with his disciples in vv. 60-65, after he has gone on in vv. 48-58 to talk of the eating and drinking of his flesh and blood. As one of his remarks in vv. 60-65 is very commonly interpreted as qualifying or even contradicting what was said in vv. 51ff, this later passage demands careful attention:

> Many of his disciples, when they heard it, said, 'This is a hard
> saying; who can listen to it?' But Jesus, knowing in himself that
> his disciples muttered at it, said to them, 'Do you take offence at
> this? Then what if you were to see the Son of man ascending
> where he was before? It is the spirit that gives life, the flesh is of no
> avail. The words that I have spoken to you are spirit and life; but
> there are some of you that do not believe.' For Jesus knew from
> the first who were those that did not believe, and who it was that
> should betray him. And he said, 'This is why I told you that no
> one can come to me unless it is given to him by the Father.'

To those who have seen him but do not recognise him as 'from heaven', he throws down the solemn warning, 'What if you were to see the Son of man ascending where he was before?' There is at least an echo here of the answer he is said in Mark 14.62 and parallels to have given at his trial to the High Priest's question, 'Are you the Christ?' – 'I am; and you will see the Son of man sitting at the right hand of power, and coming with the clouds of heaven.' Those who take offence at his claims will learn too late when they see him 'above' that that is indeed the place from which he came. Then come the words with which special care is needed: 'It is the spirit that gives life, the flesh is of no avail. The words that I have spoken to you are spirit and life; but there are some of you that do not believe.' These put in another way the point that it is only by God's power that people can be made able to recognise and believe in Jesus. The contrast between 'flesh' and 'spirit' here is very similar to what we saw earlier in Paul, and is drawn elsewhere in the Fourth Gospel as well – notably in 1.12-13 ('But to all who received him, who believed in his name, he gave power to become children of God; who were born, not of blood, nor of the flesh, nor of the will of man, but of God.') and 3.6: 'That which is born of the flesh is flesh, and that which is born of the spirit is spirit.' In John as in Paul, the antithesis is not simply between 'spiritual' and 'physical', and certainly not between 'ideal' and 'material', but between the world and realm of the 'flesh', the world of men living by their own power and their own standards, their own perceptions and their own light, separate from God, and the new power of life opened up in Christ which transforms the old world into a new one by the creative energy of God himself. Jesus' own words about himself are themselves 'spirit and life'; they are words which 'the flesh' cannot speak, nor even by itself hear. Where they are heard and believed, God is at work using them as his means of communication and drawing those who believe into the life which in Jesus has broken into the world of the flesh in order to make the children of God out of the children of men. Belief itself is therefore, as Jesus had said earlier, 'the work of God' (v. 29). Therefore, 'it is the will of my Father that every one who sees the Son and believes in him should have eternal life; and I will raise him up on the last day.' (v. 40)

All this needs to be kept in mind as we turn back to vv. 48-58 where Jesus speaks directly of his *own* flesh and blood and their eating and drinking. Here, 'flesh' does not have the same emphasis and associations as in v. 63 with its antithesis between 'flesh' and 'spirit', nor does v. 63 refer to or qualify what has just been said about Jesus' own flesh in vv. 51ff. The whole section in vv. 60-65 is not directly concerned to explain or interpret the immediately preceding verses. Its occasion and theme are the fact that some of the disciples find what is said in these earlier verses intolerable, and therefore *their unbelief.* That is why vv. 60-65 recall so strongly what was said in vv. 35-47, for that section too had concentrated on belief and unbelief. It is the *'flesh' which cannot believe* that v. 63 contrasts with 'spirit'. Jesus' own flesh as the flesh taken by the Word (1.14) is absolutely central to the entire Gospel. It refers to his real, flesh-and-blood humanity, to the fact that the Word of God is not simply an idea or a message or a spiritual energy, but *this man Jesus*. On *that* flesh, salvation itself depends, as either the author of the Fourth Gospel or another in the same circle insisted: 'Every spirit which confesses that Jesus Christ *has come in the flesh* is of God, and every spirit which does not confess Jesus is not of God.' (1 John 4.2-3) If it seems confusing, as well it may, to have 'flesh' used in these rather different ways so close together, it is nevertheless precisely what we might expect from the author of the Fourth Gospel. The same different uses are to be found even closer together in 1.13-14, which first contrasts 'flesh' and birth from it with birth from God, then immediately goes on to assert that the Word 'became flesh'.

Vv. 48-58 begin with a contrast between the bread which can give life and that which does not in the end preserve from death:

I am the bread of life. Your fathers ate the manna in the
wilderness, and they died. This is the bread which comes down
from heaven, that one may eat of it and not die. (vv. 48-50)

In other words, the real bread from heaven will give real and lasting life, and this bread is Jesus himself. V. 51 spells this out even more bluntly:

I am the living bread which has come down from heaven. If
anyone eats of this bread, he shall live for ever. And the bread
which I shall give is my flesh for the life of the world.

As we saw earlier, it is very probable that the last words here are a variant of Jesus' own word over the bread at the Last Supper, but modified by the context, the 'bread of life' theme, and by the fact that the Last Supper is not being directly reported. The allusion was, however, doubtless clear enough to the original readers. Here now the Eucharist, which has in various ways been hinted at earlier in the chapter, is beginning to come more obviously to mind. From this verse on to v. 58, Jesus' words have a double sense: they refer both to himself and to the eucharistic bread and wine. The author, however, never disentangles these senses, nor does he even make clear how they are related. Rather he relies, as so often in his writing, on *double entendre*, gathering different meanings into a single statement that can be and is intended to be taken on more than one level. On the surface, this is purely a discussion between Jesus and the Jews in the synagogue at Capernaum about his physical flesh and blood, the body that is there in front of them. But the Christian readers of the Gospel would recognise a different meaning, and apply the lesson to the Eucharist. This is all the more likely in that the objection which the Jews immediately make can very plausibly be understood as reflecting controversy about the Eucharist around the period from which this Gospel dates – at the end of the first century or the beginning of the second. According to the *Letter to the Smyrneans* of Ignatius of Antioch, written around that same period, and connected, as the Johannine group seem to have been, with western Asia Minor, some Christians 'absent themselves from the Eucharist and from prayer because they do not confess that the Eucharist is the flesh of our Saviour Jesus Christ, which suffered for our sins, and which in his goodness the Father raised.'[5] Behind the question put by John in the mouth of the Jews may well lurk the challenge of others known to him in contemporary Christian circles. 'How can this man give us his flesh to eat?' is very similar to what Ignatius may well have been hearing: 'How can the eucharistic bread be the flesh of Jesus?' Neither of these questions 'how?' is given a direct answer by Jesus in the following verses. Instead, he repeats, what he has already said in even blunter and more concrete fashion:

> Truly, truly I tell you, unless you eat the flesh of the Son of man and drink his blood, you do not have life in you. He who chews my flesh and drinks my blood has eternal life, and I will raise him up on the last day. For my flesh is true food and my blood is true drink. (vv. 53-55)

This does not explain how his flesh and blood can be eaten, or drunk, but insists that they must be. Just as he who believes 'has eternal life, and I will raise him up on the last day' (v. 40), so too, 'he who chews my flesh and drinks my blood has eternal life, and I will raise him up on the last day.' But no more explanation of the one process can be offered than of the other. The faith that can recognise in the man Jesus the bread from heaven is the gift and work of God, it is of the spirit and not the flesh. In the same fashion, John seems to imply, it is the gift and work of God that have made the flesh and blood of Christ real food and drink for us, and enable these to be received in the Eucharist. That this is indeed the tendency of his thought is further suggested by the closing words of this section, in which Jesus offers the nearest thing to an explanation of what he is saying:

> He who chews my flesh and drinks my blood abides in me and I in him. As the living Father sent me, and I live through the Father, so too he who chews me shall also live through me. This is the bread which has come down from heaven, not as the fathers ate, and died. He who chews this bread shall live for ever. (vv. 56-58)

Here we are presented with two of the threads that run through the whole Fourth Gospel: the union of Jesus Christ with the Father, and also with those who belong to him. In Jesus the life that is God's and from God has taken human form and expression, actualising itself in human existence; and through him it has been opened up as the source of life for others. This life, it should be added, is not conceived of as a kind of power which, so to speak, *emanates* or *spreads out* from God through Jesus, as it were moving further and further away from its point of entry into human history. Rather it is a life which is *shared* by Jesus with the Father, and which others receive part in *by union* with Jesus, with his person and history. He is the bread from heaven for us only as we feed on him and live out of him; and this feeding on him is represented and mediated through the eucharistic bread and wine. It is also to be understood quite concretely, and not spiritualised away – as the repeated use of the Greek *trōgein* ('chew') dramatically illustrates.

There is thus in John a degree of 'sacramental realism' similar to what we have found in Paul, and built on similar foundations. Like Paul, John believes that in and through the Eucharist there is a real sharing in Christ himself: so much is obvious from the way he uses eucharistic language in these verses. Like Paul, too, he believes that such a sharing in Christ is precisely what the Christian faith is all about, so that his understanding of the Eucharist fits without tension into that wider christological horizon. Again like Paul, he is far from seeing the Eucharist as something magical which can confer benefit by the mere physical act of eating and drinking if there is no recognition or discernment of Jesus Christ himself in his real identity as the bread from heaven for us: the emphasis on believing in Jesus throughout the chapter makes that abundantly clear. It may be that he does go a step further than Paul in stressing the importance of receiving the Eucharist: 'unless you eat the flesh of the Son of man and drink his blood, you do not have life in you.' (v. 53) This should probably not be taken as meaning that participation *in the Eucharist* is necessary for salvation, but as a serious warning against those who undervalue or reject it, and with it misconceive the nature of their participation in Christ himself. It is also probably of some significance that John deals with the Eucharist only in the rather indirect and allusive fashion we have noticed. He develops no distinct 'doctrine of the Eucharist' as such, but concentrates on *Christ himself*. Here he certainly puts the centre of gravity in the proper place, and in much the same way as the other eucharistic passages in the New Testament.

Where John differs from Paul, it is in the angle from which Jesus himself is primarily seen. Paul tends to focus attention on his death on the cross, and we have seen how that colours his exposition of the Eucharist. That emphasis is certainly there in John, but he also inclines to emphasise throughout that in Jesus' whole life the divine power was already at work, and so to see in the cross and resurrection the climax and completion of the entire movement of his life. It is not surprising therefore that he seems to see the Eucharist itself chiefly as a means of sharing in the *life* which is in Christ and which he gives to us by his own death. This is only a difference in emphasis, and ought not to be over-stressed. Nevertheless, it means that John underlines an aspect of the meaning of Christ and of the Eucharist which was already there in the Last Supper, but which in Paul seems to be receding into the background. It is one which has not always been kept in view in the West, which has tended to be 'Pauline' rather than 'Johannine' while the Eastern theology has commonly tended in the opposite direction. It is however necessary for a balanced understanding of the Eucharist that it be given its place.

What has just been said may seem to run counter to the point made in the first chapter – that the Johannine language of *flesh* and *blood* reflects the end result of a development in which attention had moved from Christ's person and covenant and come to concentrate increasingly on his death, understood as a sacrifice. Certainly John's overall theology of the Eucharist does not entirely fit into that scheme. The language he uses, however, is likely enough to reflect tendencies and developments other than those which he himself gives prominence, and the shift from 'body' to 'flesh', though as he develops it it has its own special Johannine colouring, does cohere with the transition from 'covenant' to 'blood' which we find both in John and in Mark and Matthew. To this extent, his terminolgy may justifiably be looked upon as evidence for a wider development, even if his own main positive lines of interpretation are distinctive.

Finally it is worth noticing that John also preserves the strong eschatological note which we have heard elsewhere in the New Testament passages relating to the Last Supper and the Eucharist. 'I will raise him up on the last day' is a repeated refrain through the central sections of this chapter. The theme is of course cast in a particular Johannine form: the thought is not that the Eucharist is itself an eschatological meal, nor that it is a proclamation of the Lord's death till he comes, but rather that it is the means by which we share in the life of the resurrecton. It is very much along the same lines that Ignatius in another of his letters (*Eph.* 20.2) calls the Eucharist 'the medicine of immortality, the antidote to ensure that we shall not die, but live in Jesus Christ for ever.' No doubt this is a dangerous way of talking, and could easily run back into a magical understanding of the Eucharist itself of the kind against which Paul may have been warning in I Cor. 10. Nevertheless it does throw into relief what was already implied at the Last Supper: that the Eucharist is a pledge of the coming kingdom because it is a sharing in the life given for us and the covenant established in Jesus Christ. As such it is a promise for the future and a token of resurrection.

3. *The Eucharist in the New Testament: A Summary*

Although in the last three chapters we have necessarily concentrated only upon the main New Testament passages relating to the Eucharist, they have supplied us with a good deal of quite varied material. Even within the New Testament, Jesus himself, the meaning of his cross, the Last Supper and Eucharist are seen and interpreted from several angles, and different theological and liturgical influences have helped to shape the accounts we possess. The evidence is fragmentary, diverse and incomplete, and we should not expect to find in it a single comprehensive and systematic 'theology of the Eucharist'. In spite of this variety, however, there is also an impressive overall coherence, and it is possible to detect the broad shape of the New Testament approach to the subject, to identify certain central emphases, and to trace the roots of some problems which were to emerge later. The main points may be summarised as follows.

(1) *The content and meaning of the Eucharist is Jesus himself.* This is the primary force of the 'words of institution' in which Jesus refers to himself by speaking of his 'body' and 'covenant'. Where the emphasis shifted, as it appears to have done, to his 'blood', and so to his death, it is still *his* death; similarly in John, it is because *Jesus himself* is 'the bread from heaven' that the eating and drinking of his 'flesh' and 'blood' are stressed.

(2) *The Eucharist is the means of a real sharing in him, of a genuine union with him.* This is expressed already at the Last Supper in the giving of the bread and the cup: both effect a bond with him. The same perception underlies the theology of both Paul and John. It is axiomatic in their exposition of the Gospel that we share in Jesus Christ himself, in his life, death and resurrection for us, and it is in that horizon that they set the Eucharist. This sharing is not, however, something magical or automatic: it must be discerned and recognised (Paul) and is bound up with the faith which is the gift of God (John).

(3) *The Eucharist also establishes a bond between those who participate in it.* This too is implicit at the Last Supper, and is drawn out further by Paul when he identifies the 'body' as the community of the church. In the Eucharist the church discovers its own identity as the body of Christ, and the many are made one by the sharing of the one loaf.

(4) *The Eucharist directs us both backwards and forwards.* In retrospect, it is 'remembrance' of Jesus Christ; in prospect, it is anticipation of the kingdom of God. In each direction what is involved is not simply that *we* look back to a remote past or forward to a remote future. Rather, we are opened to the past of Christ which bears upon our present, and so we are *made* to remember – and in that remembering, to encounter at the same time the promise of God's future in him.

(5) *The question of the precise connexion between Jesus Christ and the eucharistic bread and wine is not directly posed in the New Testament.* Only in John 6 is there a hint that this has become a problem, and no very explicit answer is given there. The New Testament witnesses do however assume that the connexion is real: in the bread and wine, Jesus gives himself. In the background lies a pattern of thinking which does not draw a sharp line between 'things' and 'meanings'. A material identification of Jesus' physical body and blood with the elements, and a purely 'symbolic' interpretation of the bread and wine, are equally far away from the understanding which Jesus and his disciples would find natural. The bread and the cup are the means by which he offers them their share in his own person, destiny and covenant; they are the instruments of a genuine exchange which he offers and extends as real.

(6) *Relatively little is said in the New Testament about the Eucharist as a 'sacrifice'.* Paul does draw a parallel between it and Jewish and pagan sacrifices. Here he appears chiefly to have in mind the aspect of sacrifice as a shared meal and means of communion with spiritual realities. The other aspect – that of an offering to God – is not clearly associated with the Eucharist. The understanding of Jesus' death as a sacrifice to God does, however, raise the question of whether or how far the Eucharist itself also partakes of that character.

These last two points touch on themes which were eventually to develop into major controversial issues at the Reformation. Another side of the New Testament approach is also significant in the light of later debate and conflict:

(7) *The New Testament does not possess the concept of 'a sacrament', nor is it primarily interested in sacred rites in themselves.* That interest, and the development of the idea of 'sacraments', only came later, as we shall see in the next chapters. The Greek term *mysterion* ('mystery'), which is commonly translated into Latin as *sacramentum*, does indeed appear several times in the New Testament. There, however, its meaning is not that of 'sacred rite', but of 'mystery' or 'secret', and it most usually refers to the hidden things of God which are disclosed in Jesus Christ: it speaks of revelation, not ritual. There is a warning here that demands to be heeded. As time went on, and it became necessary to forge a technical theological vocabulary to name the things of which the Bible speaks, the concept of 'sacraments' was naturally and usefully constructed. Some such concept is needed, just as it was necessary in the fourth century to incorporate the clumsy word *homoousios*, 'of one substance', in the Nicene Creed in order to make quite clear that it is God himself who is present and active for us in Jesus Christ. Such concepts do however need to be controlled for they have a tendency to take on an independent life of their own. Then we may be tempted to proceed by first defining the

terms and then imposing them on the text of the Bible. The danger in the case of 'sacrament' is then that we might start off with some general idea of what a sacrament is, and then squeeze the Eucharist, baptism, and perhaps other things as well into that framework. At least two serious consequences have flowed from this in the history of eucharistic theology. First, there has been a great deal of sometimes artificial debate between different schools of thought as to how 'sacrament' should be defined, frequently accompanied by some disagreement about how many sacraments there might be. If it is not recognised – and it has not always been – that much depends here on what one *means* by 'sacrament', the discussion is more likely to generate heat than light. Second, and even more seriously, the specific nature and character of particular 'sacraments' – whether the Eucharist, or baptism, or other ceremonies, such as ordination or marriage – can be thoroughly obscured by the domination of the discussion by this or that general conception of what a sacrament is or ought to be. However the idea of a sacrament is defined and applied, it must be used in a way that permits the things which are called 'sacraments' to stand out and be recognised in their own colours and with their own distinctive shape and meaning. If 'the sacraments' become an independent subject of theological interest, there is a serious threat to the very things which are thus described. Nor is that all, for there is a more serious danger still. This is that the central 'mystery', Jesus Christ himself, may be lost to sight in concentration on the sacraments as such.

PART TWO
THE ROMAN CATHOLIC AND REFORMED INTERPRETATIONS

4

THE EUCHARIST IN THE EARLY CENTURIES

After lingering for so long around the New Testament evidence –
though it could indeed have been studied in much more detail and at
much greater length still – we must now quicken our pace and begin to
move rather more rapidly over the following centuries. In the next two
chapters we shall look in turn at the way in which medieval thinking
shaped what is still the broad outline of Roman Catholic eucharistic
theology, and at the alternative understanding developed in the course
of the Reformation. The issues involved in the conflicts of the sixteenth
century did not, however, suddenly arise out of thin air in the late middle
ages. Their roots run back to the New Testament itself, and can be seen
running through the early centuries of the history of the church. So it is
to the development in understanding and interpretation of the Eucharist
in those early centuries that we first turn.

This era, from the second to the fifth century or so, saw Christianity
rise from its beginnings as an obscure splinter group within Judaism to
expand, consolidate and become established as the official religion of the
Roman Empire. It brought the fixing of the official New Testament
canon; the establishment of a church order and organisation centred in
particular on the office of bishop, and with powerful centres of authority
and influence in the great metropolitan sees such as Rome, Alexandria
and Constantinople; the conflict with sundry heresies and schisms which
brought about the crystallisation of catholic orthodoxy, expressed in
such formulae as the Nicene Creed; the formation of a large and
complex body of Christian theology through the work of a great
number of bishops, philosophers and teachers; and alongside that, the
growth of the great liturgies of the ancient church. A full study of the
eucharistic theologies which were worked out to greater or less degree in
that immensely fruitful age would have to take account of a huge
quantity of theological and liturgical material and set it against its
background. Here we can undertake nothing remotely so ambitious, but
simply pick out some key themes which shed light on the development
and on what was to follow it.

A good place to begin is the oldest reasonably full description of the
Eucharist, given by Justin Martyr in his *First Apology* lxv-lxvi, written in
Rome around the middle of the second century.[1]

65.2 When we have ended the prayers, we greet one another with a kiss.

65.3 Then bread and a cup of water and of mixed wine are brought to him who presides over the brethren, and he takes them and offers praise and glory to the Father of all in the name of the Son and of the Holy Spirit, and gives thanks at some length that we have been deemed worthy of these things from him. When he has finished the prayers and the thanksgiving, all the people present give their assent by saying, 'Amen.'

65.4 Amen is Hebrew for 'So be it.'

65.5 And when the president has given thanks and all the people have assented, those whom we call deacons give to each one present a portion of the bread and wine and water over which thanks have been given (*eucharistēthentos*), and take them to those who are not present.

66.1 And we call this food 'thanksgiving' (*eucharistia*); and no one may partake of it unless he is convinced of the truth of our teaching, and has been cleansed with the washing for forgiveness of sins and regeneration, and lives as Christ handed down.

66.2 For we do not receive these things as common bread or common drink; but just as our Saviour Jesus Christ, being incarnate through the word of God, took flesh and blood for our salvation, so too we have been taught that the food over which thanks have been given by a word of prayer that is from him, from which our flesh and blood are fed by transformation, is both the flesh and blood of that incarnate Jesus.

66.3 For the apostles in the records composed by them which are called gospels, have handed down what was commanded them: that Jesus took bread, gave thanks, and said, 'Do this for my remembrance; this is my body'; and likewise he took the cup, gave thanks, and said, 'This is my blood'; and gave to them alone.

This account tells us a great deal, especially about the way in which the Eucharist was being celebrated a century or so after Paul wrote to the Corinthians. It makes it clear that – at least in Justin's circle – the Eucharist had been clearly separated from the Agape and come to stand as a distinct service by itself. The celebrant is not any member of the community, but 'the president' – in all probability the bishop or a priest appointed by him, for Justin goes on a little later to say that this person is also responsible for distributing the offerings of the people to help 'orphans and widows, and those who through sickness or any other cause are in need, and those in prison, and strangers sojourning among us.' (lxvii.7) He thus seems to have a general responsibility for the affairs of the community. Fifty years before, Ignatius had insisted, 'No one should do anything in the church apart from the bishop. Let that be considered a valid Eucharist which is under the bishop or one whom he has delegated.'[2] While our information is scanty, it is very likely that from the earliest period the Eucharist was conducted by the recognised leader of the community; and with the spread of the system of monarchical episcopacy in the first and second centuries, that authority naturally came to be vested in the bishop and those whom he had appointed. The principle that the Eucharist must be celebrated by an ordained minister or priest continues to be maintained to this day in most major churches, although some Protestant traditions have departed from it. Within the family of Reformed churches, the congregational branch has come to make a place for lay celebration, but the presbyterian, generally speaking, has not. The *Westminster Confession* in ch. xxvii.4 specifically states that neither baptism nor the Supper 'may be dispensed by any but a minister of the Word, lawfully ordained.' Restriction of participation in the Eucharist to baptised believers has equally remained a general (if not universal) practice, and is in accord with both Roman Catholic and Reformed teaching to the present time.

The cup described by Justin contained wine mixed with water – as it still does in the Roman Catholic and some other churches. The original reason for this may have been the simple fact that in the ancient world wine was generally diluted with water; but this mixing soon came to be seen as recalling the blood and water which flowed from Jesus' side when pierced by the spear after his death on the cross. Justin also tells us that portions of the bread and wine were taken to those who were not present. This practice too continues to the present day in a variety of forms, and is not uncommon in the Church of Scotland – though it is something the *Westminster Confession* forbade (xxix.3) along with the reservation and veneration of the sacrament in the church (xxix.4) – which of course is still standard in the Roman Catholic, Eastern Orthodox and some Anglican churches, but not in the Reformed. Apart from these significant details, what is especially important for our enquiry is the way in which Justin speaks of the bread and wine themselves as 'the flesh and blood of the incarnate Jesus'. His description is very much in line with what we found in the Fourth Gospel in the previous chapter; and, like the Gospel, he does not offer much by way of further elucidation, except to make more explicit the connexion with the incarnation which in John 6 is left to be grasped by the reader. With Justin, however, we stand on the threshold of further reflection on the matter.

Before we pursue that topic further, let us first jump forward to a slightly later writer than Justin who gives a form of prayer to be used over the bread and the cup, and thus fills out a little further the picture which Justin offers. In his *The Apostolic Tradition*, written around 215, Hippolytus gives a specimen prayer which is probably his own composition, but doubtless reflects the pattern with which he was familiar in the Roman church in his own day. This translation of ch. iv describes the celebration of the Eucharist by a newly consecrated bishop:[3]

4.1 *And when he has been made bishop, all shall offer him the kiss of peace, greeting him because he has been made worthy.*

4.2 *Then the deacons shall present the offering to him; and he, laying his hands on it with all the presbytery, shall say, giving thanks:*

4.3 The Lord be with you.

And all shall say:

> And with your spirit.
> Up with your hearts.
> We have them with the Lord.
> Let us give thanks to the Lord.
> It is fitting and right.

And then he shall continue thus:

4.4 We render thanks to you, O God, through your beloved child Jesus Christ, whom in the last times you sent to us as saviour and redeemer and angel of your will;

4.5 who is your inseparable Word, through whom you made all things, and in whom you were well pleased.

4.6 You sent him from heaven into the Virgin's womb; and, conceived in the womb, he was made flesh and was manifested as your Son, being born of the Holy Spirit and the Virgin.

4.7 Fulfilling your will and gaining for you a holy people, he stretched out his hands when he should suffer, that he might release from suffering those who have believed in you.

4.8 And when he was betrayed to voluntary suffering that he might destroy death, and break the bonds of the devil, and tread down hell, and shine upon the righteous, and fix the limit, and manifest the resurrection,

4.9 he took bread and gave thanks to you, saying, 'Take, eat; this is my body, which shall be broken for you.' Likewise also the cup, saying, 'This is my blood, which is shed for you;

4.10 when you do this, you make my remembrance.'

4.11 Remembering therefore his death and resurrection, we offer to you the bread and the cup, giving thanks because you have held us worthy to stand before you and minister to you.

4.12 And we ask that you would send your Holy Spirit upon the offering of your holy Church; that, gathering them into one, you would grant to all who partake of the holy things (to partake) of the fullness of the Holy Spirit for the confirmation of faith in truth;

4.13 That we may praise and glorify you through your child Jesus Christ, through whom be glory and honour to you, to the Father and the Son with the Holy Spirit, in your holy Church, both now and to the ages of ages.

(Amen.)

The whole movement of this prayer is from thanksgiving to praise, and the greater part of it is taken up with recital and affirmation of what God has done in Jesus Christ. Just as the Jewish thanksgiving for bread was not a prayer for blessing *on the bread*, but one of praise *to God* who gives food, so too here attention is not concentrated chiefly upon the bread and the wine, nor indeed on what the speaker and the congregation are doing, but on what *God has done*. So the creation of the universe through the Word, his incarnation, life, death and resurrection, are ringingly proclaimed, and the words of institution then follow. Then come the moments in the prayer which were later to be technically labelled *anamnesis* ('remembrance' – paragraph 11) and *epiclesis* ('invocation' – paragraph 12). In *anamnesis*, the church looks back to Christ and sets its own offering of bread and wine in the context of that remembrance; in *epiclesis*, it asks for the gift of the Holy Spirit to take hold both of the elements and of the worshippers and so, gathering them together and strengthening their faith, to make them able to worship God through Jesus. These two moments are thus integrated within the overall pattern which centres on the mighty acts of God in Christ. We shall see later how subsequent liturgical development in the West tended to fragment and disrupt this framework. The emphasis came to lie increasingly on what the church and the priest were doing, and on the consecrated elements themselves; and this in turn evoked the strong reaction of the Reformers who attempted to restore the earlier centre of gravity with its objective focus in Jesus Christ himself – an enterprise in which more modern Roman Catholic theological and liturgical reform has also been deeply engaged.

Now to return once more to Justin's insistence that the bread and wine are not 'common' but 'the flesh and blood of the incarnate Jesus'. His language seems to suggest that it is because 'thanks have been given by a word of prayer that is from him' that the bread and wine are in some way changed. And this is stated with all directness by Justin's younger contemporary, Irenaeus of Lyons. In his *Against the Heresies*, written in the last quarter of the second century, he speaks of the Eucharist several times. Two brief extracts show how he understood it: in both, he appeals to the Eucharist in arguing against opponents who believe that the resurrection is purely 'spiritual':

> How can they assert that the flesh is dissolved in corruption and does not receive life, this flesh that is fed from the body and blood of the Lord? Let them either change their views, or refrain from making the offerings we have been describing. For our belief is consonant with the Eucharist, and the Eucharist confirms our belief. We offer to God what is his own, properly proclaiming the communion and unity of flesh and spirit. For just as the bread from the earth receives the invocation (*epiclesis*) of God, and is then no longer common bread, but Eucharist, consisting of two things, an earthly and a heavenly, so too our bodies after sharing in the Eucharist are no longer corruptible, but have the hope of resurrection to enternity. (IV.xviii.5)

> Whenever, then, the mixed cup and the bread that has been made receive the word of God, the Eucharist becomes the body of Christ, and by it the substance of our flesh is nourished and sustained. How can they claim that the flesh is incapable of receiving the gift of God which is eternal life, when it has been fed from the body and blood of the Lord, and is a member of him? (V.ii.3)

It is significant here that Irenaeus is not setting out to prove something about the Eucharist as such, but arguing *from* it. The people whose opinions he is attacking were a variety of Christian and semi-Christian gnostic teachers and sects who in the second century came to constitute a serious threat to the integrity of Christian belief. Their tenets and systems of belief varied very considerably, but several connected tendencies were broadly typical of most gnostic groups. They inclined to draw a very sharp distinction between the physical and the spiritual, and to regard this material world as something which was at best unimportant, at worst positively evil. It was regarded not as the creation of the true, supreme God, but as the work of an inferior deity or the consequence of a cosmic accident. Man they believed to be a spark of divinity imprisoned in a fleshly body; and the way of salvation brought release from this prison through inner, spiritual illumination imparted by secret, esoteric knowledge (*gnosis*). The gnostics thus had a good deal of difficulty with the Old Testament, speaking as it does of this world as God's good creation, and generally distinguished more or less sharply between the God of the Old Testament and the Father of Christ. So, for example, Marcion – one of Irenaeus' prime targets – contrasted the 'just God' of the Old Testament with the good and loving God of the New. Most gnostics also looked on Jesus in a more or less docetic fashion: that is, they saw him, certainly, as Saviour, but they meant by this that he was

the revealer of divine truth and wisdom, but not a man of flesh and
blood who really suffered and died on the cross. Consistently with all
this, they had little time for the Jewish and Christian belief in the
resurrection *of the flesh*. In one form or another, ideas of this kind seem to
have a perennial appeal, and they surface regularly in the church and in
Christian theology as well as elsewhere. This lends the struggle of the
early church with them an abiding significance and relevance.

Against gnosticism, Irenaeus and the main line of early Christian
teaching insisted powerfully on the unity of the Old and New
Testaments, stressing that this physical world is God's own creation, and
that salvation has to do with the whole person, not merely with an
'immortal soul'. Jesus himself was a real man, and his real humanness, his
life, suffering, death and resurrection are the centre and foundation of
the Gospel and the ground on which faith and confidence in God can
rest. It is as part of this general argument that he appeals in the terms we
have quoted to the Eucharist. There, material things, bread and wine, are
used to unite us to Jesus Christ because our very bodies are to be raised
and renewed by God. At the same time, they are not *merely* material, for
they are taken up into the movement of God's redemptive activity and
used as its instruments. Through the *epiclesis* and the word of God, they
become 'heavenly' as well as 'earthly': the cup mixed and the bread
made by human hands become Eucharist, the body and blood of Christ.
In them the heavenly and the earthly are held together in a way which
reflects the union of heaven and earth in Jesus Christ himself, and points
to the restoration of human beings in what Irenaeus loves to call 'the
image and likeness of God'. Thus from beginning to end, the material
and the physical has its own place in God's scheme of creation and
salvation.

Irenaeus thus draws out a little further still the implications of the
approach to the Eucharist which we have noticed in the Fourth Gospel
and in Justin. While he does not offer any more detailed explanation of
how the bread and wine 'become' the body and blood of Christ, the
horizon of understanding which he opens up for us was bound
eventually to lead to further attempts to clarify more precisely the
'change' in the elements by which they are made 'heavenly' as well as
'earthly'. The change itself is very commonly asserted by Christian
writers from his time onwards, as, for example, by Cyril of Jerusalem in
his *Catecheses*, delivered in the middle of the fourth century:[4]

> Since then he himself has declared and said of the bread, 'This is
> my body,' who shall dare to doubt any longer? And since he has
> affirmed and said, 'This is my blood,' who shall ever hesitate,
> saying that it is not his blood? He once turned water into wine, in
> Cana of Galilee, at his own will, and is it incredible that he should

have turned wine into blood? That wonderful work he miraculously wrought, when called to an earthly marriage; and shall he not much rather be acknowledged to have bestowed the fruition of his body and blood on the children of the bridechamber? Therefore with fullest assurance let us partake as of the body and blood of Christ: for in the figure of bread is given to you his body, and in the figure of wine his blood, that by partaking of the body and blood of Christ you might be made of the same body and the same blood with him. For thus we come to bear Christ in us, because his body and blood are diffused through our members ... Contemplate therefore the bread and wine not as bare elements, for they are, according to the Lord's declaration, the body and blood of Christ; for though sense suggests this to you, let faith stabilise you. Judge not the matter from taste, but from faith be fully assured, without misgiving, that you have been granted the body and blood of Christ. (*Mystagogical Catechesis* IV.1-3, 6)

In the next lecture, where he is describing the pattern of the eucharistic service, Cyril adds a further explanation:

Then having sanctified ourselves by these spiritual hymns [by which he means the eucharistic prayer of thanksgiving, praise and affirmation which he has just outlined], we call upon the merciful God to send forth his Holy Spirit upon the gifts lying before him; that he may make the bread the body of Christ, and the wine the blood of Christ; for whatsoever the Holy Spirit has touched is sanctified and changed. (*Myst. Cat.* V.7)

While there is not yet here any very precise theory of the nature of the 'change' in the elements, Cyril does appear to hold that the power of Christ, and in particular, the *epiclesis* of the Holy Spirit, bring about a miraculous alteration. In this, he expresses in especially clear form what was the general view of the matter in his day. Towards the end of the fourth century, John Chrysostom was to speak of a 'transformation' (*metarruthmizein*) and a 'transmutation' (*metaskeuazein*) of the elements,[5] while in the West, Ambrose of Milan said that Christ's words 'have power to change the character (*species*) of the elements'.[6] Nor did all the writers of the fourth century content themselves with the simple assertion that the elements are 'changed'. One of them, Gregory of Nyssa, offered what is probably the first attempt to explain more closely how this change should be understood.[7] The core of Gregory's argument is that food – such as bread and wine – is nourishment for the body, and therefore potentially body. Just as Christ himself had a human body which was the body of the Word incarnate in him, so too the food that he ate was potentially the body of the Word even before he ate it.

The same divine power that made his human body holy, and the means of our salvation, can also transmute the eucharistic elements immediately into that body, and so enable them to become the source of spiritual life for us. This is certainly a somewhat strained 'explanation', but it was to have a long history in Eastern Orthodox teaching. This is how it was put three centuries later by John of Damascus in his *De Fide Orthodoxa* – a work which covered most of the main heads of theology, and drew heavily on the work of earlier teachers, eventually itself becoming a standard text-book in the Eastern Church:

> Just as bread through eating, and wine and water through
> drinking, naturally become the body of him who consumes them,
> and do not become some other body than his previous one; so too
> the bread which is offered and the wine and water are
> supernaturally changed (*metapoiountai*), through the invocation
> and coming-down of the Holy Spirit, into the body and blood of
> Christ; and these are not two bodies, but one and the same. (*De
> Fide Orth.* IV.13)

This remained the general Eastern interpretation until, in the fifteenth century, ideas resembling the very different Western theory of transubstantiation began to spread in the East, where they were at last officially approved at the Synod of Jerusalem in 1672. Another point worth noticing is that John of Damascus identifies the moment of the change as the *epiclesis*. The writers of earlier centuries were not always so precise, and could commonly associate the change either with the *epiclesis* or with the words of Jesus Christ, 'This is my body .. this is my blood,' or sometimes with both. As the centuries passed, however, the East came to focus especially on the *epiclesis*, though it was also disinclined to attempt to tie down or locate the exact moment too precisely. In the West by contrast, it was Christ's words which came increasingly to stand out as *the* key moment of the consecration of the elements, while the *epiclesis* virtually disappeared. This may seem a small technical point, but it had wider ramifications as we shall see later.

Through the early centuries, then, it is not hard to trace the development from insistence that the elements somehow 'are' the body and blood, through rather vague ideas of 'miraculous change', to attempts to explain the change in some more comprehensible fashion. In the West, the extension of this movement was to lead in the high middle ages to the doctrine of transubstantiation, and then to the rejection of that doctrine by the Reformers. But there were other very significant lines of development in the early period, and two in particular are relevant here. One attempted to grasp and express the character of the Eucharist in terms more 'symbolic' or 'spiritual' than 'realist', while another concentrated attention on the Eucharist as a sacrifice. These approaches and the one just outlined were by no means mutually exclusive; it is not uncommon to find all of them in a single writer. But each has its distinctive importance in the early church and as preparing the way for later theology. We shall look first at the 'symbolic' approach which helped to produce the developed concept of 'sacraments', then turn to the 'sacrificial' emphasis.

We have seen how the eucharistic realism of a man like Irenaeus was very much bound up with his rejection of any gnostic attitude to the material creation. Other Christian teachers were also to distance themselves from the gnostics, but at the same time to guard against what they feared was a too materialistic understanding of salvation. The leading representatives of this approach at the end of the second and into the middle of the third century were the Alexandrians, Clement and Origen. They characteristically stressed the *spiritual* meaning of the Gospel, of the words of the Bible, of the eucharistic elements. So while they too spoke of the Eucharist as an eating and drinking of the body and blood of Christ, they inclined to interpret this more metaphorically than Irenaeus, and to see it as referring to the nourishing of the soul by the Word who was incarnate in Christ. So Clement could say that Jesus' words at the Last Supper are to be understood allegorically: 'my flesh' stands for the Holy Spirit, and 'my blood' for the Word himself;[8] and that those who partake of the Eucharist 'in a more spiritual manner' receive as 'the flesh and blood of the Word' 'the apprehension of the divine power and essence' by which their souls are fed.[9] This distinction between a deeper, more spiritual understanding and reception of the Eucharist and a simpler, more widely held one, is also made by Origen:

> Let the bread and the cup be understood by simpler people
> according to the general teaching about the Eucharist. But those
> who have learned a deeper comprehension ought also to observe
> what the sacred proclamation teaches concerning the nourishing
> Word of truth. (*Commentary on John* XXXII.24)

Part at least of the force of this distinction between a simpler and a profounder understanding of the Eucharist can be gleaned from another of Origen's discussions:

> That which is 'sanctified through the word of God and prayer' (I
> Tim. 4.5) does not of its own accord sanctify the person who
> receives it. Otherwise it would sanctify the one who eats the
> bread of the Lord unworthily, and no one because of this food
> would become 'ill or weak' or 'fall asleep' (I Cor. 11.30). Even in
> respect of the bread of the Lord, the benefit for the receiver
> depends on his sharing in the bread with a pure mind and a clear
> conscience. We are not deprived of any good merely by not
> eating of the bread sanctified by the word of God and prayer, nor

do we abound in any good by the mere eating ... In respect of the
prayer which is added to it, it becomes profitable 'according to
the proportion of faith' (Ro. 12.6), and is the cause of spiritual
discernment in the mind which looks to its spiritual advantage. It
is not the material bread that profits the person who eats the bread
of the Lord, and does so not unworthily: rather it is the word
which is spoken over it. (*Commentary on Matthew* XI.14)

So Origen distinguishes very clearly between the material elements and
the spiritual reality of Christ the Word of God, and insists that what
matters is not simply the physical eating of the bread, but the reception
of the Word, of Christ, in faith.

Origen's concern is certainly valid, and the points that he makes are
sound so far as they go; but they do raise further questions. Is he in
danger of driving such a wedge between the physical and the spiritual
that they can no longer really be held and seen together? What, on his
view, is the real value of the Eucharist as opposed to hearing and
believing the Word proclaimed to us? Further attention needs to be
given to the connexion between the elements and the spiritual reality if
these questions are to be answered. This attention was given to the
matter in particular by the man who more than any other shaped the
course of Western theology – St Augustine, whose main work was done
in the opening decades of the fifth century. He worked out a concept of
'a sacrament' which could serve to explain the connexions which in
Origen and others lacked adequate grounding. As we cannot travel very
far through western theology without meeting Augustine's influence,
and as his eucharistic theology in particular was to be enormously
significant for both Roman Catholic and Reformed thinking, we must
give him a little more attention than the others we have mentioned –
though we can still only select a few of the central aspects of his thought.

The term *sacramentum*, 'sacrament', was already in common use in
the church by Augustine's day. It was one of the standard translations of
the Greek *mysterion*, 'mystery', and had a variety of senses. It could refer
to the 'mystery' of Christ, to sacred rites in general, or to the Eucharist
or baptism in particular. In the background also lay other meanings of
the word in Latin usage. *Sacramentum* was the name for the oath
administered to a Roman soldier on enlistment in the army; it could also
refer to a sum of money deposited in a temple as a bond pending the
settlement of a legal dispute. In general, a *sacramentum* could thus be
either a solemn religious observance or a sacred or devoted object. What
Augustine did was to reflect further on the way in which particular
things or actions can have this extra dimension of sacred meaning. The
clue to his starting point can perhaps be traced in a comment made,
almost by the way, by his revered older contemporary, St Ambrose of

Milan. In his *De Sacramentis* VI.3.4, Ambrose comments on the horror felt by the disciples in John 6 at the idea of eating the flesh of Jesus:

> And so, to prevent others from saying that they are going to leave him because of abhorrence of actual blood, and so that the grace of redemption should continue to be available, for that reason you are given the sacrament in a similitude, to be sure – but you obtain the grace and power of the reality.

With this may also be compared Cyril of Jerusalem's comments about baptism, where a similar contrast is drawn between 'figure' and reality:

> O strange and inconceivable thing! We did not really die, we were not really buried, we were not really crucified and raised again, but our imitation was but in a figure, while our salvation is in reality. Christ was actually crucified, and actually buried, and truly rose again; and all these things have been granted to us that we, by imitation communicating in his sufferings, might gain salvation in reality. (*Myst. Cat.* II.5)

It is this distinction and connexion between the 'figure' or 'similitude' and the 'grace and power of the reality' that Augustine sets out to clarify.

First of all, Augustine insists:

> Men can be bound together in the name of no religion, whether true or false, unless they are bound together by some sharing of visible signs or sacraments. (*Contra Faustum* xix.11)

In other words, external, visible, public observances are necessary for any religion if it is not to be something purely private and individual. At the same time, however, Augustine is also clear that these observances have a deeper aspect, and that this is essential to their character as 'signs or sacraments'. 'Although it must of necessity be celebrated in visible form, it must nonetheless be understood invisibly.'[10] Therefore, 'The sacrament is one thing, the power of the sacrament, another thing.'[11] What, then, is the connexion between these two levels? In the light of his general understanding of a sacrament as a 'visible sign', Augustine traces a twofold link. First, as a 'visible sign', a sacrament must in some way *resemble* what it signifies:

> If the sacraments had not a kind of likeness to those things of which they are sacraments, they would not be sacraments at all. From this likeness, further, they are generally given the names of the things themselves. So the sacrament of the body of Christ is, in a sense, the body of Christ, and the sacrament of Christ's blood is Christ's blood ... (*Ep.* 98.9)

Second, over and above this resemblance, the sign must also be *identified* as a sign by a *word* spoken about it. This makes the sacrament itself a 'visible word'. So, as he put it, in words which were to ring down the centuries, in section 3 of his eightieth *Tractatus* on the Gospel of John, *accedit verbum ad elementum et fit sacramentum etiam ipsum tamquam visibile verbum*: 'The word comes to the element and it becomes a sacrament, itself a kind of visible word.' It follows from this that genuine sharing in the sacrament is a matter of apprehending and participating in the invisible reality which is, so to speak, manifested in it, rather than something purely external, merely visible, simply physical:

> 'He who eats of this bread will not die.' (Joh. 6.50) But that means the one who eats what belongs to the power of the sacrament, not simply to the visible sacrament; the one who eats inwardly, not merely outwardly; the one who eats the sacrament in the heart not just the one who crushes it with his teeth. (*In Ev. Joh. Tract.* XXVI.12)

So to eat the body of Christ is to believe in Christ in one's heart; and Augustine can even say, '... there is no necessity of chewing and digesting. Believe, and you have eaten (*crede, et manducasti*).'[12]

Consistently with this general conception of a sacrament, Augustine is repeatedly at pains to stress the distinction between the 'sign' and the 'spiritual meaning', between the 'sacrament' and the 'power' or 'reality' of the sacrament. He insists that Jesus' words about the eating and drinking of his flesh and blood are 'figurative',[13] and offers this paraphrase of his meaning:

> Interpret what I have said in a spiritual sense. It is not the body which you see that you are going to eat; you will not be drinking the blood which those who crucify me are to shed. I have entrusted you with something sacramental which, when spiritually understood, will give you life. Although it must of necessity be celebrated in a visible form, it must nonetheless be understood invisibly. (*Enarr. in Ps.* 98.9)

He underlines this same distinction further when he discusses the meaning of Paul's warning against unworthy reception of the Eucharist. He takes that warning very seriously, but insists that what the unworthy receive for their destruction is *only the sacrament*, not the *reality*, for 'the reality itself, of which this is the sacrament, is for every one who partakes of it the means of life, but never of destruction.'[14] It is a real question whether he has not here moved some considerable distance beyond Paul, who does not make or presuppose exactly this sort of distinction. What can be seen here is in fact another central aspect of Augustine's general sacramental theology – the thought that sacraments, even apart from the reality which they signify, have a certain secondary power and effectiveness of their own. This comes out very clearly in his discussion of baptism in his *De Baptismo*, where he argues that baptism administered by heretics or schismatics is indeed *valid* but *ineffective* and even *dangerous* unless or until the baptised person returns to the fold of the one true church. Only then does the 'brand-mark' of the Lord which has really been set upon him become powerful for his salvation. So he maintains:

> The baptism which is consecrated by the words of Christ in the Gospels is holy even when it is administered by the polluted to the polluted, no matter how shameless and unclean they may be. This holiness is itself incapable of contamination, and the power of God supports his sacrament, whether for the salvation of those who make proper use of it, or for the condemnation of those who abuse it. (*De Baptismo* III.15)

This 'secondary objectivity' of the sacraments, as it may be called, certainly rests upon the divine power and command which underlie the sacraments themselves, but it is clearly also distinguishable from the *spiritual reality* as such.

What then is that invisible spiritual reality which is apprehended and received in faith? In a word, it is Jesus Christ himself; but here again, Augustine separates out two senses in which Christ might be recognised and received, and holds that only one of these two senses is applicable:

> In respect of his majesty, his providence, his ineffable and invisible grace, his own words are fulfilled, 'Lo, I am with you always, even to the end of the world.' (Matt. 28.20) But in respect of the flesh he assumed as the Word, in respect of that which he was as the son of the Virgin, of that wherein he was seized by the Jews, nailed to the tree, let down from the cross, enveloped in a shroud, laid in the sepulchre and manifested in his resurrection, 'you will not have him always' (cf. John 12.28). And why? Because in respect of his bodily presence he associated with his disciples for forty days; and then, having brought them forth for the purpose of seeing him rather than of immediately following him, he ascended into heaven, and is no longer here. He is there indeed, sitting at the right hand of the Father; and he is here also, never having withdrawn the presence of his glory. In other words, in respect of his *divine* presence we always have Christ; but in respect of his presence *in the flesh* it was rightly said to his disciples, 'Me you will not have always.' In this respect, the church enjoyed his presence only for a few days; now it possesses him by faith, without seeing him with the eyes. (*In Ev. Joh. Tract.* L.13)

This element in Augustine's eucharistic theology, with its sharp distinction between Jesus' physical presence and that of his divine power, raises problems which were to be of some importance in later debate and controversy. Medieval and Roman Catholic theology agreed that the physical location of the humanity of Christ is 'in heaven', but came to argue in addition for the real presence of the 'substance' of his body and blood under the eucharistic elements. Calvin and the Reformed tradition also located Christ's humanity in heaven, but replaced the doctrine of 'substantial presence under the elements' with the teaching that the Holy Spirit unites us with Christ in spite of the 'distance' between our place and his at the right hand of the Father. Luther and his followers took yet another path, maintaining that Christ's human nature shares in the qualities and attributes of his divinity by the 'communication of attributes' (*communicatio idiomatum*), and is therefore omnipresent: 'in, with and under' the bread and the wine the *man* Jesus is present, as he is present universally, and they then reveal his presence as there *for us*. Roman Catholic and Reformed teaching here both follow Augustine, but develop his thought further, while the Lutheran seeks to some extent to shift the pattern of thinking. All to some degree at least point to a crucial difficulty in Augustine's position. It risks drawing such a sharp and clear divide between Jesus' humanity and divinity, his physical presence and the outreach of his divine power, and with it, between the reality and the sacramental sign, that it is not in the end apparent that he has really succeeded in overcoming the problems we noticed above in Origen. This is perhaps the fundamental problem to be faced by any approach to the Eucharist via the category of 'sign': there is always the danger that the two sides thus correlated, the physical and the spiritual, visible and invisible, may appear to fall apart – or, what is little better, to be held together only in a quite arbitrary fashion.

Augustine himself did not entirely succeed in facing and coping with this danger because his own thought was deeply coloured by his early study of Plato and later Neo-platonist thought. It was a commonplace in that philosophical tradition that the world which we perceive is a copy of invisible realities which are discerned by the mind rather than by the eye. In a way, therefore, the whole universe could quite easily be understood to be 'sacramental' in Augustine's sense, and everything in it seen as the visible reflection of invisible things. Against this background, it was natural enough for Augustine to work out his particular conception of 'a sacrament' and to overlook its weaknesses. The bond between the two sides could, as it were, be taken for granted; and so it has been repeatedly through the centuries in the West, where Augustine's understanding of a sacrament as 'the visible sign of invisible reality' has lodged itself deep in the foundations of Christian thinking, and come to serve as the almost invariably unquestioned starting-point for reflection upon 'the sacraments'. What then is all too easily lost to sight is the fact that the bond between visible and invisible on which everything turns in Christian theology is not that supplied by a 'sacramental universe', but is rather Jesus Christ himself. There is *the* link between God and man, heaven and earth, the divine and the creaturely, and, we must add, the spiritual and the material. And it is there too that the 'sacramentality' of the Eucharist, or of anything else, must be grounded if it is not to be both arbitrary and precarious. To this extent, a good deal of Augustine's heritage in Western sacramental theology needs to be critically re-thought and deepened, and only so can the divergences between the different traditions influenced by him begin to be overcome.

To draw this brief survey to an end, we must now say a little about the third strand of thinking in the early church which was mentioned earlier – that which speaks of the Eucharist as a 'sacrifice'. The emphasis here is not, as it had been in St Paul, on the Eucharist as a *sacrificial meal*, a means of communion; rather it is upon the Eucharist as an *offering* to God. If in the lines just sketched the focus of attention was on the Eucharist as a gift *from* Christ, now it is on a movement in the reverse direction, *from man to God*, on *giving* rather than *receiving*.

The background to this emphasis is not to be looked for primarily in the New Testament accounts of the Eucharist, but rather in a wider general recognition that in the church we offer to God – we offer ourselves, our worship, our prayers, our thanks, our whole lives as, in Paul's words, 'a living sacrifice, holy and acceptable to God, which is your spiritual worship.' (Rom. 12.1) Very early on, this 'Christian sacrifice' came to be polemically contrasted with those offered by the Jews, and passages in the Old Testament attacking the cult were taken up and interpreted afresh as prophesying its replacement by Christian worship. One of the most influential and widely used of these was the first chapter of Malachi, especially vv. 10-11:

> I have no pleasure in you, says the Lord of Hosts, and I will not
> accept an offering from your hand.[11] For from the rising of the
> sun to its setting, my name is great among the gentiles and in
> every place incense is offered to my name, and a pure offering; for
> my name is great among the gentiles, says the Lord of Hosts.

As early as the *Didache*, these words from Malachi are to be found applied to the Eucharist:

> On the Lord's day, gather together and break bread and give
> thanks (*eucharistēsate*), confessing your sins, that your sacrifice may
> be pure. Everyone who has a quarrel with his neighbour should
> not meet with you until they are reconciled, so that your sacrifice
> may not be defiled. For this is the sacrifice spoken of by the Lord,
> 'In every place and time offer me a pure sacrifice. For I am a great
> King, says the Lord, and my name is marvellous among the
> gentiles.' (*Did.* xiv)

A fuller statement of the same outlook is given by Irenaeus in *Adv. Haer.*

IV.xvii.5; he has been speaking of what God required of the people of Israel:

> From all this it is quite clear that it was not sacrifices and holocausts that God required from them, but faith, obedience and justice for the sake of their salvation. So God taught them his will in Hosea: 'I desire mercy rather than sacrifice, and knowledge of God more than holocausts.' (Hos. 6.6) But our Lord too gave them the same warning, saying, 'If you had understood what this means, "I desire mercy and not sacrifice," you would never have condemned the innocent.' (Matt. 12.7) So he testified of the prophets that they had proclaimed the truth, but convicted them [i.e. the Jews] of their own guilt. But again, he also instructed his own disciples to offer to God the first-fruits of his creation, not as if God were in need of them, but so that they should not be unfruitful or ungrateful. He took bread of the natural creation, and gave thanks, and said, 'This is my body.' Similarly he declared the cup, belonging to the same natural creation as we do, to be his blood, and explained it as the new oblation of the new covenant. This oblation the church receives from the apostles, and throughout the entire world offers it to God who supplies as our nourishment the first-fruits of his gifts in the new covenant. It was of this that Malachi thus prophesied, 'I take no pleasure in you, says the Lord omnipotent, and I will not accept an offering from your hand . . .' (Mal. 1.10-11) By this he clearly means that the former people will cease to offer to God, but in every place a sacrifice will be offered to him, and that a pure one, while his name is glorified among the gentiles.

At its core, the 'sacrifice' of which Irenaeus speaks is the offering of thanks and praise to God, an offering which is made in the presenting to him of the bread and wine, the 'first-fruits of the natural creation', and the prayer of thanksgiving over them. It is not that God needs them, but 'that we should not be unfruitful or ungrateful.' So he can also say elsewhere, 'We make our offering to him, not as if he stood in need of anything, but giving thanks to his sovereignty and sanctifying his creation.'[15] Sacrifice, thanksgiving and consecration are ultimately one and the same -- as they were in Jewish grace before meals, and as we also saw them to be in Hippolytus' eucharistic prayer, composed a generation or so after Irenaeus wrote.

This association of Eucharist and sacrifice was, however, capable of being developed further through the exploration of the connexions that might be traced between *this* offering and the sacrifice of Christ himself. This could lead to the conviction that in the Eucharist Christ himself is in some way offered to God. Moves in that direction can be recognised in this same early period. Around the year 200, Tertullian of Carthage calls the Eucharist a 'sacrifice' which is 'made through the priest to God',[16] and refers to celebrations in which it was offered to God on behalf of the dead.[17] A little later, Origen calls the Eucharist 'the memorial which makes God propitious to men'.[18] Here it certainly appears that the Eucharist is being drawn into the closest possible connexion with the self-offering of Christ and interpreted in that light as a 'sacrifice of propitiation'. One of the earliest very clear statements of this understanding is to be found in Cyprian of Carthage, who was martyred in 258:

> If Christ Jesus, our Lord and God, is himself the high priest of
> God the Father, and first offered himself as a sacrifice to the
> Father, and commanded this to be done in remembrance of
> himself; then assuredly the priest acts truly in Christ's place (*vice
> Christi vere fungitur*) when he reproduces what Christ did, and he
> then offers a true and complete sacrifice in the church to God the
> Father (*id quod Christus fecit imitatur, et sacrificium verum et plenum
> tunc offert in ecclesia deo patri*), if he begins to offer as he sees Christ
> himself has offered. (*Ep.* LXIII.14)

Both the sacrificial understanding of the Eucharist and the tone in which the *priest* is spoken of can already be seen here to have the character which would shape centuries of theology and devotion: the Christian minister is a priest, a representative of Christ the great high priest, and his central role in the church is to offer the true and complete sacrifice which imitates and reproduces Christ's own. How deeply anchored this perception of the matter came to be in the early church can be shown by what Cyril of Jerusalem said about it a century or so after Cyprian's death: After describing the *epiclesis* and the 'change' in the passage we quoted earlier, he goes on:

> Then, after the spiritual sacrifice is perfected, the bloodless service
> upon that sacrifice of propitiation, we entreat God for the
> common peace of the church, for the tranquillity of the world;
> for kings; for soldiers and allies; for the sick; for the afflicted; and,
> in a word, for all who stand in need we all supplicate and offer
> this sacrifice. Then we commemorate also those who have fallen
> asleep before us . . . believing that it will be a very great advantage
> to the souls for whom the supplication is put up while that holy
> and most awful sacrifice is presented . . . (we) offer up Christ,
> sacrificed for our sins, propitiating our merciful God both for
> them and for ourselves. (*Myst. Cat.* V.8-10)

Not perhaps surprisingly, this passage from Cyril has come in modern controversy to be something of a favourite with Roman Catholic writers, while Protestants have looked upon it in a rather different light. Depending on one's point of view, it can be seen either as proof of the early church's support for medieval eucharistic theology with its understanding of the sacrifice of the Mass, or as proof of how fast and far the early church travelled away from the biblical understanding of the matter. These are questions to which we shall come later. For the moment it is enough to observe that – however it be evaluated – there has been a significant development of the idea of the Eucharist as a sacrifice by the time we reach Cyril. And this inevitably raised further issues to which profounder thinkers than he were to direct their minds in the second half of the same century. In what sense is the Eucharist this kind of sacrifice? In what relation does it stand to the sacrifice of Jesus Christ? Does it add to what he has done, or is it in any way an independent or distinct 'offering to God', or must it somehow be seen as integrally bound up with Christ's own giving of himself? While these questions were rarely posed so directly by the writers of the early church, they can be seen to underlie things which came to be said and taught about the Eucharist.

In attempting to cope with these issues the theologians of the later fourth century worked out and applied two key ideas in particular. One of these was that Jesus Christ himself is the priest who makes the eucharistic offering; the other, that the Eucharist is a visible representation of his intercession before the throne of the Father in heaven. An especially clear expression of the first – and one which was to have a vast influence on subsequent eucharistic theology – is to be found in John Chrysostom, who was for a few years patriarch of Constantinople, and who died in 407:

> Now too Christ is present. He who adorned that table [i.e. of the Last Supper] is the same who now adorns this. It is not man who makes the gift of the oblation to become the body and blood of Christ, but Christ himself, who was crucified for us. The priest stands, fulfilling the original pattern, and speaks these words; but the power and grace come from God. 'This is my body,' he says. This affirmation transforms the oblations; and as the command, 'increase and multiply', spoken once, extends through all time and gives to one human nature the power of reproduction, so too the statement, 'This is my body,' uttered once, makes complete the sacrifice at every table in the churches from that time until now, and even till Christ's return. (*De Proditione Judae* I.6)

By this, Chrysostom does not mean that the sacrifice of Christ is somehow *repeated* in the Eucharist, but rather that because that one unique sacrifice has been made once and for all, it stretches out to include every celebration of the Eucharist within itself. So he can explain elsewhere:

> We offer every day, making a memorial of his death. This is one
> sacrifice, not many. And why? Because it was offered once ... We
> always offer the same person ... the same oblation: therefore it is
> one sacrifice ... By the same token, the offering of the sacrifice in
> many places does not of course mean that there are many Christs.
> Christ is everywhere one, entire in this place and in that, one
> body ... and so there is one sacrifice. Our high priest is he who
> offered the sacrifice for our purification. We offer now what was
> offered then, an inexhaustible offering ... We offer the same
> sacrifice; or rather, we make a memorial of that sacrifice. (*Homily
> on Hebrews* XVII.3)

As Chrysostom understands the matter, then, the primary actor in the
Eucharist is Christ himself, and the action is that of his unique and
inexhaustible sacrifice which has already been made. The Eucharist in
each celebration is drawn back into that sacrifice and receives its own
meaning from it. Priest and people are the instruments of the action of
Christ: 'He who did this at the Last Supper is the very same who now
performs the act. We rank as ministers [i.e. as servants performing a
delegated task on their master's authority, in his name and on his behalf];
it is he who consecrates and transmutes.'[19]

A similar sense of the centrality and primacy of the action of Jesus
Christ is expressed in the West around this same date by Ambrose, who
also develops the second line of reflection mentioned above – that the
Eucharist is a visible representation of Christ's own heavenly
intercession. Two quotations may serve to illustrate his interpretation:

> We have seen the high priest coming to us; we have seen and
> heard him offering his blood for us. We priests follow, as well as
> we can, so that we may offer sacrifice for the people. Though we
> can claim no merit, we are to be honoured in this sacrifice; for
> although Christ is not now visibly offered, yet he is himself
> offered on earth when his body is offered. Moreover it is clear that
> he himself offers in us, since it is his words that sanctify the
> sacrifice which is offered. (*In Psalm.* 38.25)

> Here is the shadow and the symbol; there is the reality – the
> shadow in the Law, the symbol in the Gospel, the reality in
> heaven. Formerly a lamb was offered, and a calf; now Christ is
> offered. But he is offered as a man, accepting suffering; and he
> offers himself as priest, so that he may forgive our sins – here in
> symbol, in reality there, where he intercedes for us as an advocate
> before the Father. (*De Officiis* I.238)

The second of these excerpts presents us with the theme, common in the
church fathers, of the 'heavenly altar' before which Christ eternally
pleads his sacrifice upon the cross. In much modern discussion it has been

suggested that this theme in particular can offer a way round the impasse in which Roman Catholic and Protestant thinking have often found themselves – the one linking the Eucharist very closely with Christ's own sacrifice, the other tending to distinguish sharply between them. The continuing intercession of Christ for us can be seen as offering a bridge between the cross and the Eucharist. The suggestion is not without merit and importance, and by countering what can sometimes be a rather too narrow conception of 'the sacrifice of Christ', it is able to help to widen the horizon of understanding and to overcome some at least of the established divergences in approach. At the same time, however, the idea of the heavenly altar as developed by the early fathers on the basis of the Epistle to the Hebrews does tend to have the same kind of Platonist colouring, and to be open to the same challenges, as Augustine's concept of 'a sacrament'. The connexion between the heavenly reality and the earthly sign needs to be more solidly grounded. So too does that between the heavenly intercession of Christ and his offering of himself 'once and for all' on the cross. These things are all rather more hopefully held together and more promisingly integrated in the perspective opened up by John Chrysostom. What he suggests to us is that the Eucharist itself is a form by which Christ makes us participate in his unique self-giving which centres in the cross. There is the focus alike of his intercession in heaven and of the celebration of the Eucharist, and both need to be carried back to that point and opened up from it, as the centre on which both turn. Along these lines the conflicts about Eucharist and sacrifice which have grown up since the middle ages are more likely to be constructively resolved.

5

THE SHAPING OF MEDIEVAL EUCHARISTIC
THEOLOGY

The broad lines of what is still today the official Roman Catholic understanding of the Eucharist were laid down in the middle ages, and received classic definition at the Council of Trent, which met from 1545 to 1563. By then, the Protestant Reformation was well under way, and Trent consolidated the answering movement within the Roman Catholic Church which is generally called the Counter-Reformation – 'counter', not simply in the sense of being directed against the Protestant Reformation, but in that of being a corresponding process of reform and renewal within the Roman Church itself. It was however much too late to restore the unity of the whole body of Christians in the West – though at the start of the Council some at least still had hopes of that – so that in retrospect Trent stands for the hardening of the divisions opened up in the previous decades. This has had the unfortunate consequence that for centuries thereafter Roman Catholics and Protestants have inclined to define their positions by opposition to each other. When teaching is forged in the fires of conflict, hardly any other outcome can be expected. In substance, however, the eucharistic teaching of Trent was that of the medieval church, more formally articulated in answer to the Reformers' criticisms. It can therefore be treated as the conclusion and climax of the medieval development, over against which the Reformers developed their rather different theologies of the Eucharist.

Three of the documents of the Council of Trent are of special relevance to the Eucharist: the *Decree on the Sacraments*, with its canons on sacraments in general, dated 3rd March 1547; the *Decree on the Holy Sacrament of the Eucharist*, with its canons, dated 11th October 1551; and the *Doctrine concerning the Sacrifice of the Holy Sacrament of the Mass*, also with its canons, dated 17th September 1562. These deal respectively with the three themes which we have seen emerging in the early centuries: the nature of a sacrament, the presence of Christ in the Eucharist and the change in the elements, and the sacrificial character of the Eucharist. In each of these areas the middle ages brought further significant developments, and each became controversial at the

Reformation and has remained so to the present day. In this chapter we shall take them one by one in order to trace the broad lines of the emergence of medieval eucharistic theology.

First, however, some other general developments must be mentioned which had a profound influence on the shaping of thought about the Eucharist throughout this period. These were very largely negative in character and harmful in their effects. But it is as well also to observe that it is by no means only Roman Catholic theology which is open to the criticisms we shall suggest. Some of the more dubious elements in the medieval heritage are still very much alive and well in the churches of the Reformation too, and Protestants need to remember that the medieval history is also theirs, no matter how critically they wish to stand over against it. Only as the churches on both sides of the divide that opened up at the Reformation come together to reflect critically on that common history can they hope to work through its inheritance to a new and deeper mutual understanding.

The first of these developments has to do with some unfortunate consequences of the Arian controversy in the fourth century. It was Arius' teaching that was condemned by the Council of Nicea in 325. He held that Jesus was not really or fully God, but a 'divine being', created by God to be his agent in the work of creation, and then sent as a man to be our Saviour. Against him, the orthodox position was clarified by the description of Jesus Christ as 'true God of true God, begotten, not made, being of one substance (*homoousios*) with the Father', as the Nicene Creed put it. A century and a quarter later, the Council of Chalcedon (451) spoke of Jesus Christ as fully God and fully man, having 'two natures in one person'. As against Arius and those who inclined to his views, these clear statements were certainly necessary: only if God and man were recognised as really united and reconciled in Jesus Christ himself can the heart of the Gospel be preserved from dilution. The unfortunate by-product of this insistence was however that Christian thought and devotion tended increasingly to focus so much on the divinity of Jesus that his real humanness was easily lost to sight. He came very often to be seen and depicted as a remote figure of unutterable majesty, the *Christos Pantocrator* of so many Byzantine mosaics, armed with the book of judgment and the authority to condemn, rather than as the one who has identified himself with us in our human existence, who has taken our weakness upon himself, and who has gone before us as our pioneer, representative and advocate with the Father. Particularly at the level of popular piety, a terrifying gulf opened up between him and us, a gulf which demanded to be bridged. What then tended to fill it was the church, the system of the sacraments by which grace was dispensed, and the merits of the saints. This is something with which Protestants at least are well familiar. But the increasing sense of the remoteness of Christ in his divinity had another consequence whose effects were if anything deeper and more insidious, and have infected Protestant belief and practice fully as drastically as Roman Catholic.

This further consequence was, quite simply, a loss of the awareness that it is in, through and with Jesus Christ that we are able to worship God. Instead, the centuries following the Arian controversy brought a shift which can be clearly traced in the liturgical language of the church from emphasising prayer, worship and offering *through* and *with* him towards stressing the addressing of prayer *to* him. Both emphases were to be found in the early church, and each has its place. (The conclusion of Hippolytus' eucharistic prayer which we quoted in the last chapter is an excellent example.) But as the first retreated from view, prayer and worship came more and more to be seen as *our* action rather than as *his*. *We* worship, the *church* worships, and he is the object of worship rather than its leader. Only in very recent times has the disastrous impact of this shift in perspective begun to be diagnosed, and it must be said that the Roman Catholic Church in its liturgical changes since the Second Vatican Council has taken major steps towards reversing it. By contrast, the implicit assumption behind a good deal of Protestant worship, not least in the Church of Scotland, still appears to be that worship is an activity of the church and of Christians, but not of Christ himself. The result is much the same as in the centuries after Arius: the church becomes in effect a substitute for Christ, and we are thrown back on our own pitifully inadequate resources in attempting to worship God. This makes it exceedingly difficult, to say the least, to retain the sense of participation in Christ and what he has done for us which is fundamental to the meaning of the Eucharist.[1]

The second development is in some ways closely bound up with the first and contributed to the same trend. In the fourth century, Christianity became the established religion of the Roman Empire; and in the same century, the Empire itself was finally divided into two parts – the East with its capital at Constantinople, and the West with its centre in Rome. Gradually the Christian East and West grew further and further apart, and the church in the West became more and more characteristically Roman in its ethos and outlook. With the collapse of the Western Empire under the pressure of invasions from the north in the fifth century, the Roman Church became the effective legatee of the old Empire, the bearer of culture and civilisation, with its own hierarchical pattern of administration, its own laws and its own courts. The Roman genius had always been for law and organisation, and that genius lived on in the church of the West. This led to the emergence of several of the characteristic features of that church – its strong emphasis on the centrality of Rome in the life of the whole church, its insistence that the church bears authority in the world as the representative of Christ, and a strongly juridical tone in its theology and teaching. Not only did there grow up a vast and complex body of canon law, including many elements, such as the concept of 'natural law', inherited from ancient Roman thought: theology itself took on a decidedly legalistic cast, concerned to give precise definitions and authoritative rulings. In all these ways, what can perhaps best be called a 'Roman ecclesiastical consciousness' came into being – a consciousness whose roots can be traced back to the second century, but which reached its peak a thousand years later in the famous Bull *Unam Sanctam* of Pope Boniface VIII (18th November 1302):

> We are compelled at the urging of faith to believe and to hold one holy church which is catholic and apostolic . . . out of which there is neither salvation nor remission of sins . . . which represents the one mystical body, whose head is Christ, and Christ's is God. In her is 'one Lord, one faith, one baptism.' For in the time of the flood there was one ark of Noah, prefiguring the one church . . . which had in Noah a single captain and ruler . . .
>
> Of this one, single church there is one body and one head . . . namely Christ and Peter the Vicar of Christ and the successor of Peter; for the Lord said to Peter himself, 'Feed my sheep.' . . . If then the Greeks or others say that they were not entrusted to Peter and his successors, let them admit that they cannot be of the sheep of Christ; for the Lord says in John that there is 'one sheepfold and one single shepherd'.
>
> We are told by the sayings of the Gospels that there lie in the power of the church and the Vicar of Christ two swords, that is, the spiritual and the temporal . . . but the second is exercised on behalf of the church, the first by the church, the one by the hand of the priest, the other by that of kings and armies . . . But one sword must be subordinate to the other, the temporal to the spiritual power . . . For we must admit that spiritual power excels any earthly power in dignity and nobility as clearly as spiritual things surpass temporal . . . Therefore if an earthly power errs, it will be judged by the spiritual; if a lower spiritual power errs, it will be judged by its own superior; if the supreme spiritual power errs, it can only be judged by God alone, not by man; for the apostle testifies, 'The spiritual man judges all things, but is himself judged by none.'
>
> Further, this authority, though it has been given to a man and is exercised by a man, is no mere human power but divine, given to Peter by the mouth of God, both to him and to his successors

... Therefore whoever resists this power thus ordained by God 'resists the ordination of God himself' ...

Finally we declare, state and define, that it is an absolute necessity for salvation for every human creature to be subject to the Roman Pontiff.

Very much more is involved in this Bull than simply the climactic assertion of the claims of the papacy – though that is, not surprisingly, the matter on which Protestants naturally seize. But it is not for that reason that we have quoted it at such length. What is of wider and deeper significance is the way in which the church itself is depicted as a legally constituted body, established by God in Jesus Christ, and exercising his divinely delegated authority in the world. This is something which was by no means abandoned at the Reformation: the spirit of *Unam Sanctam* flourished like the cedars of Lebanon in more than one Protestant church, including the Church of Scotland. Andrew Melville stood very much in the tradition of Boniface when he informed the young King James VI that 'there be twa kings and twa kingdoms in Scotland' and left the monarch in no uncertainty at all as to which kingdom had the pre-eminence. The same trumpet-note is sounded in no uncertain fashion in the *Solemn League and Covenant* of 1643 and in the *Westminster Confession*, §§ 23 and 30. The pitfall which awaits any church seeking to understand itself in these terms is that of casting the Gospel and theology too much in the mould of law, and of treating the church itself as if it could be adequately defined in terms of constitutional legality. Obviously law has its place in the church as in any organised body of people; but if it is not kept within its proper limits, the loss of sight of the ends which it ought to subserve can only distort the whole. Authoritarian legalism is a perennial temptation to the church, both Roman and Reformed; and it can be seen working powerfully in *Unam Sanctam*. It is no accident that at the same time and as part of the same view of the church, Christ himself is depicted essentially as one who exercises and has delegated authority and power, rather than as the one who has taken our place under the 'curse of the law' in order to redeem and set us free. His authority is in fact being interpreted in terms that are all too worldly, and so too is the spiritual power of the church. The special relevance of this to the Eucharist is that it encourages a tendency to look upon the Eucharist and other rites as forms in which this delegated authority and power are exercised by the church, and to define them in legal rather than evangelical terms. Such a tendency can indeed be detected in the development of medieval sacramental theology.

Third must be mentioned a cluster of shifts and changes which took place in the celebration of the Eucharist itself in the centuries between the early church and the high middle ages. From the fourth century onwards, the eucharistic liturgy grew more and more complex. This complexity was especially marked in the eucharistic prayer or, as it came to be called, the canon of the Mass. The pattern of the early prayer, as Hippolytus' form shows, was relatively simple and contained three main elements: thanksgiving and affirmation, *anamnesis* and *epiclesis*. By around 700 the canon of the Mass had grown very much longer and taken on a very different shape. The *epiclesis* virtually disappeared, while throughout the prayer there was repeated reference to the Eucharist as *the offering of the church*, with the fervent request that this offering would be acceptable to God. Overall, the canon by this stage is only with difficulty recognisable as descending from the kind of prayer known to Hippolytus. The centre of gravity has shifted from what God has done or is being asked to do to what the church is doing.

At the same time, the celebration of the Mass in these centuries was coming increasingly to be seen as the concern of the clergy rather than of the whole congregation, who were steadily reduced to the role of spectators. From the sixth century there developed the practice of private Masses, said by the priest alone. In the era of Charlemagne and his successors, the liturgy was standardised throughout the Western church, and the Mass came everywhere to be said in Latin. When this process began in the latter part of the eighth century, many local languages were still close enough to Latin for the people to be able to follow; but as their own tongues grew further and further away from Latin, it became increasingly difficult, and finally quite impossible, for them to participate with any real comprehension. The situation was hardly improved by the practice, which seems to have begun in the eighth century, of reciting the words of the canon very quietly because of their immense sanctity; and by 900 the priest was no longer permitted to say them aloud. In the same period it became common for the priest to include further private prayers in the liturgy, and this served further to characterise the celebration as his rather than the people's. Attempts were made to overcome the distance thus opened up between him and them by introducing other signals to inform them of what was happening. So the elevation of the host – the raising of the bread above the priest's head so that it could be seen by the congregation – which had earlier come in other places in the liturgy, came in the middle ages to follow immediately after the consecration of the elements by Jesus' words, 'This is my body . . .' By around 1200, too, this moment came to be marked by the ringing of a bell. In effect, however, while this did allow the people to know when the central moment in the celebration had been reached, it powerfully reinforced the passivity of their role as mere spectators of a rite being performed by the priest.

Other practical changes led in the same general direction. From as early as the fourth century it appears that at least some laypeople were in the habit of attending at the Eucharist, but not of regularly taking communion. Complaints about this are made, for example, by John Chrysostom[2] and Ambrose.[3] One reason was no doubt the influx of converts whose Christianity owed more to the new-found respectability of what was now the established religion than to any very deep conviction. Another was probably reverence and awe before the mysterious sacrament. The custom of non-participation in communion grew more and more common as the generations passed, until in 1215 the Fourth Lateran Council found it necessary to insist that the faithful should communicate at least once a year. That is a striking indication of how far the laity had come to feel that the Eucharist was essentially a sacerdotal matter. In addition, by about 1200, it had become normal practice to give only the bread but not the cup to lay communicants. In spite of protests – especially from John Hus and his followers – the Council of Constance in 1415 defended this restriction in its *Decree on Communion solely under the Species of Bread*, as also did the Council of Trent in its *The Doctrine concerning Communion under either Species and by Children* (DS 1198-1200 and 1725-1734).[4] The main points made by these councils were that as the whole Christ is present under the bread, nothing is lost by not receiving the cup as well; and that there were sound practical reasons for withholding the cup from the laity, even though this was admittedly a departure from primitive practice. These arguments had a certain force – at any rate within the horizon of medieval sacramental theology to which we shall shortly come – but could scarcely conceal the fact that a very substantial alteration had in fact been introduced into the eucharistic celebration, and one which underlined the distinction between priest and people in an emphatic way. The Reformers, like Hus before them, were to insist that this change was far more serious than the medieval church admitted; and in very recent times the Roman Catholic Church itself has shown signs of a partial conversion to the same view.

The overall result of these theological and liturgical developments was a shift in one consistent direction. The Eucharist came increasingly to be seen as that action of the church, and specifically of the priest, in which an offering is made to God in virtue of a power given to the church by Jesus Christ and exercised by his appointed representatives. The sharp distinction between clergy and laity reflects a deeper structural shift in understanding and perception in consequence of which the church and its priesthood are seen as a kind of extension of Jesus Christ himself – an extension which threatens to become a substitute for him. All this must be kept in mind as we go on to look more closely at medieval eucharistic and sacramental theology along the three lines already indicated – sacrament, presence and sacrifice.

1. The Nature and Number of the Sacraments

The foundations of western theology of the sacraments had been laid by Augustine above all; but for many centuries after his death it remained undeveloped and indeed somewhat confused. For a long time there was no universally accepted definition of 'a sacrament', nor even formal agreement as to how many sacraments there might be. That a sacrament was a visible sign of invisible reality, that it carried spiritual power, that baptism and the Eucharist in particular were sacraments – so much was indeed generally accepted. But there was room for a great deal of variation in belief and opinion beyond that basic core, and different writers and authorities down to the twelfth century subscribed to a variety of views about what a sacrament was and how many sacraments should be recognised.

From the middle of the twelfth century, however, the pattern of medieval sacramental teaching suddenly came together, as with many other topics, as part of the great flowering of medieval scholastic theology. The catalyst and turning point was the work of Peter Lombard. In the fourth book of his *Sentences* (*c.* 1150), he taught that there were in fact seven sacraments, and that what they all have in common as sacraments is that they both symbolise and convey a gift of divine grace. This understanding was further worked out and systematised by others, and most notably by Thomas Aquinas, who died in 1274. The fullest and most masterly exposition of it is given in his *Summa Theologica* III, *quaestiones* 60-90. In the year of his death, the Council of Lyons formally affirmed as a matter of official teaching that there are indeed seven sacraments.[5] A particularly clear outline of what thus became established as the belief of the church in the West is to be found in the *Decretum pro Armeniis* of the Council of Florence, meeting in 1439. This is a lengthy document, dealing in turn with each of the seven; but for our purposes it will be enough to quote from the opening section which deals with the sacraments in general:

> There are seven sacraments of the New Law, namely baptism, confirmation, Eucharist, penance, extreme unction, orders and marriage; which are very different from the sacraments of the Old Law. For the latter did not cause grace (*non causabant gratiam*), but only signified that grace would be given through the passion of Christ; but these sacraments of ours both contain grace and confer the same on those who worthily receive them (*et continent gratiam et ipsam digne suscipientibus conferunt*).

The first five of these were ordained for the spiritual perfecting of each individual in himself, the last two for the government and multiplication of the whole church. For by baptism we are spiritually reborn; by confirmation we are increased in grace and strengthened in faith; reborn and strengthened, we are nourished by the divine food of the Eucharist. If we fall into sickness of the soul through sin, we are spiritually healed through penance; and healed both spiritually and physically, so far as that is for the benefit of the soul, through extreme unction. Through orders, on the other hand, the church is governed and spiritually multiplied, while through marriage it is physically increased.

All of these sacraments consist of three elements, namely things as the matter (*materia*), words as the form (*forma*), and the person of the minister conferring the sacrament with the intention of doing what the church does. If any of these is lacking, the sacrament is not completed.

Among these sacraments there are three, baptism, confirmation and orders, which imprint on the soul an indelible character (*character indelebilis*), that is, a kind of distinctive spiritual mark. Therefore they are not repeated on the same person. The remaining four do not imprint a character, and permit of repetition. (DS 1310-1313)

To this we may add some of the thirteen canons on the sacraments approved by the Council of Trent in 1547, as these serve to highlight certain other points which the *Decretum pro Armeniis* does not stress. The formulation of these canons of course reflects the particular controversies of the Reformation, but they faithfully reproduce the tendency of earlier teaching.

1. If anyone should say that the sacraments of the New Law were not all instituted by Jesus Christ our Lord; or that there are more or fewer than seven, namely baptism, confirmation, Eucharist, penance, extreme unction, orders and marriage; or that any of these seven is not a true and proper sacrament: let him be anathema.

3. If anyone should say that these seven sacraments are equal among themselves in such a way that none of them is in any way of greater dignity than another: let him be anathema.

6. If anyone should say that the sacraments of the New Law do not contain the grace which they signify, or that they do not confer grace itself on those who put no obstacle in the way, as if they were merely external signs of a grace or righteousness received through faith, and particular marks of Christian

profession by which among men the faithful are distinguished from unbelievers: let him be anathema.

8. If anyone should say that grace is not conferred objectively by the performance of the rite (*ex opere operato*) through the sacraments of the New Law themselves, but that only faith in the divine promise is sufficient for grace to follow: let him be anathema. (DS 1601 ff.)

The working-out of this comprehensive understanding of the system of the seven sacraments was one of the outstanding achievements of the medieval church, and in it, the church's view of itself is given magnificently clear and confident expression. It is the divinely ordained and instituted ark of salvation, the organised community of the faithful, governed by Christ through his representatives, and mediating divine grace through the sacraments which are themselves related to the key stages and moments in the life of the individual and of the whole community of the church. The nature of a sacrament itself is systematically and precisely defined, and a coherent classification given of all seven. Protestant theology has on the whole inclined to be less than enthusiastic about this entire development; and in view of the extent to which the Reformers found it necessary to break with it, that is hardly astonishing. Nevertheless, its imposing strength, cohesion and comprehensiveness command respect. It is hard to conceive of a more impressive or more powerful synthesis; and it still supplies the ground-plan of modern Roman Catholic sacramental teaching. Critics do well to appreciate its strength and attractiveness as well as its questionable aspects: the two are indeed very closely connected, for it is precisely in its strengths as a theological system that its weaknesses also lie.

The heart of the whole is the description and definition of a sacrament as a *cause of grace*, in which grace is contained and by which it is objectively conferred. The idea of grace came to occupy a position of remarkable centrality in medieval theology and combined with the Aristotelian conception of causality to construct the very core of this sacramental teaching. It is this combination above all which marks off high medieval theology of the sacraments from that of earlier centuries, and gives it its distinctive character.

The term *gratia* and the Greek equivalent *charis* had already had a long history in Greek and Roman thought, and in the early church. Among their basic meanings are those of thanks; of a gift; of a special beauty or some particularly pleasing quality – much the same senses as are still preserved in various uses of 'grace' in English. In the New Testament, however, *charis* takes on a further special reference: it is used of the *graciousness of God towards us in Jesus*. Here it has an active sense: grace is not so much a thing or a quality in itself as the way in which God approaches us. *Charis* is in effect defined afresh, centred upon the person of Jesus. To speak of the grace of God is to speak of him. This conception of *charis* soon, however, sank back below the level of conscious awareness in the church, and 'grace' came to be understood less in terms of the gracious, personal presence and action of God, and more as a kind of 'thing' which God gives. In the early church, this development only proceeded a certain distance: grace did not become the focus and foundation of theology. In the middle ages, however, it did assume this further centrality. Grace then came to be understood as a supernatural power infused by God into the soul, and distinctions were drawn, for example, between 'habitual grace' and 'actual grace' – the first referring to supernatural qualities imparted by God, the second to the action of God himself upon the soul, moving it to will, know or act.[6] Grace was thus thought of as coming from God and set in action by him, but as nevertheless distinct from God himself. It was seen as the source and nourishment of the spiritual life of the soul, the life which is weakened and can even be destroyed by sin, but which a fresh gift of grace can once again restore. In a real sense, the doctrine of grace in this form was the living heart of the theology of the church in the West in the middle ages, and it has largely remained so in the Roman Catholic church down to modern times.

At the same time, this grace of God was seen as stemming from Jesus Christ, and as mediated through the church and the sacraments. This helps to explain the emphasis which came increasingly in the middle ages to be placed upon Christ's *institution* on the one hand of the church and the papacy, and on the other of the seven sacraments. That was seen as the guarantee of their authenticity and the key to their power to mediate grace. In this horizon, too, one can begin to comprehend the immense insistence of the medieval teaching upon the fact that grace is objectively *there* in the sacraments, that it is available, that it is truly received through them for the supernatural life of the soul. It is here that the language of 'cause' was pressed into service. It did not mean that the sacraments as such *create* grace; for that creativity lies in God alone, and it is by him and from him that grace is given. It meant rather that they are the *means*, the *instruments* by which God works and gives grace. God in Jesus Christ has ordained the sacraments; he has given them their objective validity; he works through them. It is for this reason that they were said to be effective *ex opere operato*, through the performance of the objective rite, rather than *ex opere operantis*, through the activity of the person performing it, for that person is himself an instrument in God's hand.[7] This is relevant to a point made in the *Decretum pro Armeniis*, one which was already then ancient tradition and remains deeply embedded in Roman Catholic sacramental teaching to the present: that all that is necessary on the part of the 'minister' of the sacrament, provided that he is qualified and empowered to dispense it, is that he should 'have the intention of doing what the church does'. His personal holiness or unholiness does not and cannot make the sacrament invalid. The sacraments possess an inherent objective validity, power and effectiveness, grounded on the facts that they are God's chosen means of dispensing grace and given and practised in the church, not merely by individuals acting on their own account. Church and sacraments are bound up in a single whole which is of divine providence and empowering, and in which men, women and children are enabled to draw on the resources of divine grace for their renewal and salvation.

There is, however, another side to the matter which must also be noted. Not everyone is empowered and qualified to dispense every sacrament. Baptism, indeed, may theoretically at least be given by a pagan, and the sacrament of marriage is administered mutually by the couple (provided they are baptised). But the others may only be dispensed by a priest or, in certain cases, a bishop; otherwise they are invalid. The validity *ex opere operato* rests on the condition that the dispenser is qualified by ordination or consecration to give the sacrament. That qualification is part of the structure of the objective reality of the sacrament: it has indeed nothing to do with the *personal quality* of the celebrant (provided the requirement of proper intention is met), but has everything to do with his *office* and *status*. In other words, the doctrine of the *ex opere operato*, though pointing chiefly to the objective working of God, carries with it the ideas of *priestly and episcopal power*: where that power is lacking, the objective sacrament cannot be performed. In this sense, the doctrine serves not simply to point to the objective action of God, but also to anchor that action in the activity of his chosen instruments, the priests and bishops of the church. The channels of the divine grace cannot be by-passed!

Another point relating to the matter of the 'institution' of the sacraments by Christ is also of some importance. Although it was felt in medieval discussion to be absolutely vital that the seven sacraments had all been ordained by him, both the medieval church and the Council of Trent left open the question of the precise fashion in which this must have been done. Some theologians held that an explicit command of Christ could be traced somewhere in the New Testament for each and every one of the seven; others argued that this was not really necessary so long as each of the seven could in some fashion be traced back to Jesus or the apostles. The very fact that the sacraments were being celebrated in the church, and had been for time immemorial, was itself a compelling argument, at least within the medieval horizon. More recent Roman Catholic thinking has explored the rather different theme that the church itself is the primary sacramental reality instituted by Christ, and that the sacraments are such in virtue of their character as expressions of the life and nature of the church. The Reformers on the other hand tended generally to follow the stricter interpretation of 'institution' as referring to an explicit command, and at least partly for this reason came eventually to restrict the number of true and proper sacraments to two alone – baptism and the Eucharist. The criticism has sometimes been made of them that in this they were simply following the narrower conception of 'institution' found in some of their medieval predecessors; and the charge is not entirely without justification. At the same time, however, their cutting down of the number of the sacraments had a deeper ground in their reorientation of the idea of 'sacrament' as such, as we shall see in the next chapter.

The medieval concern to express and hold to the objective availability of divine grace in the sacraments finds its counterpart in the special case of the Eucharist in the way in which the objective presence of the body and blood of Christ was emphasised. This brings us to our second key theme: the eucharistic presence of Christ and the doctrine of transubstantiation which was worked out in the middle ages to clarify the nature of his presence.

2. *Transubstantiation and the Real Presence*

We saw in the last chapter how talk of a change in the bread and wine had become common by the fourth century, and had led in the East to the explanation of the change which was sketched by Gregory of Nyssa and followed by John of Damascus and later Eastern Orthodox theology. The West was much slower in dealing with this question, partly at least because of the influence of Augustine and his very clear distinction between the *sacramentum*, or *signum*, and the *virtus sacramenti*, and also between the eucharistic elements and the physical body of Christ in heaven. Among the faithful at large, however, it is likely that the elements were thought of as being transmuted in some fairly literal sense, and debate on the issue was bound sooner or later to erupt. This eventually came about in the ninth century when the abbot of Corbie, in France, Paschasius Radbertus, around 832 wrote his *Liber de Corpore et Sanguine Domini*. This offered a combination of what might be termed 'popular realism' with Augustine's sacramental theology.

According to Radbertus, after the consecration of the elements the flesh and blood of Christ – and this means that very flesh and blood which was born of Mary, suffered on the cross and rose from the grave – is present in them, albeit under the 'figure' (*figura*) of bread and wine (i.2). Certainly, the bread and wine are not changed in physical appearance, in taste, or in any external fashion; but faith discerns an internal alteration (i.5), for 'The substance of the bread and wine is effectively (*efficaciter*) changed internally into the flesh and blood of Christ.' (viii.2) Radbertus adds two very important qualifications. First, this does not mean that Christ himself is 'torn by the teeth', but rather that he wills 'that in a mystery this bread and wine . . . should be created his very flesh and blood.' (iv.1) It is not that his body becomes bread, but that bread becomes his body. Second, while all who receive the Eucharist partake of the *sacramenta altaris*, the 'sacraments of the altar', one may spiritually eat the flesh and drink the blood of Christ, while another does not (vi.2). Thus, following Augustine, he does distinguish between the physical body of Jesus Christ and the flesh and blood 'created' in the Eucharist, and also between the sacramental *figura* and the spiritual eating and drinking. It is not clear in Radbertus himself whether he can really and consistently succeed in holding this side of the matter together with his main positive concern; but his importance is that, however unclearly, he has begun the process of reflection on a change in the 'substance' of the elements. His work evoked a variety of reactions, the most important coming from one of his fellow-monks of Corbie, the confusingly similarly-sounding Ratramnus.

Ratramnus was asked by the Emperor Charles the Bald whether Radbertus' views were to be accepted, and in particular whether 'that which in the church is consumed in the mouth of the faithful becomes the body and blood of Christ in a mystery or in reality (*in mysterio an in veritate*)?' In his own work *De Corpore et Sanguine Domini* he divided this question further into two: (a) whether there is present in the consecrated elements something which faith alone can recognise, something secret and veiled in mystery; (b) whether that something is the very body of Christ which was born of Mary, suffered, died, was buried, rose, ascended into heaven and sits at the right hand of the Father (v). His answer to the first question is an unqualified affirmative:

> That bread which through the ministry of the priest is made the
> body of Christ appears one thing externally to the human senses,
> but proclaims itself another to the minds of the faithful.
> Externally, the form of the bread which it previously was is
> presented, its colour is seen, its flavour tasted. But internally
> something far and away more precious, more excellent, is
> intimated. (ix)

To this extent, Ratramnus also is prepared to speak of a 'change' (*mutatio*), and he is convinced that what the bread and wine become is the body and blood of Christ (xv). But to the second question – whether this is the same body that was born, died and ascended – his answer is negative:

> There is a difference between the spiritual flesh which is consumed

in the mouth of the faithful and the spiritual blood which is daily
presented to believers to drink, and the flesh which was crucified
and the blood which was poured out. (lxxi)

The elements 'become' Christ's flesh and blood in the sense that he gives
nourishment through them, because 'under the cover of material things
the divine power secretly dispenses salvation to those who faithfully
receive them' (xlviii). 'According to their invisible substance, that is the
power of the divine Word, they are the true flesh and blood of Christ.'
(xlix) So while Ratramnus is prepared to speak of the elements as being
changed into the body and blood, it is not Jesus' physical body that he
understands by this. He aligns himself more clearly than Radbertus with
the line of thought represented by Augustine, and to that extent is
opposed to the tendencies in popular thought and piety to which
Radbertus gives slightly more scope. The differences between
Radbertus and Ratramnus should not however be exaggerated: they
have to do with emphases rather than with a wholesale confrontation
between a purely 'realist' and purely 'spiritual' interpretation. They do
however indicate the shape of things to come and anticipate the next
major stage in the debate – the case of Berengarius of Tours, who died in
1088.

Berengarius held to the views of Ratramnus, whose work he, like
many of his day, wrongly ascribed to John Scotus. He was involved in a
series of disputes with the ecclesiastical authorities – including Lanfranc
of Bec, the later Archbishop of Canterbury, Cardinal Humbert, and
even Pope Gregory VII, who had originally sympathised with him and
sought to protect him. Berengarius held very firmly to the distinction
between the *sacramental sign* and the *sacramental reality*, insisting that it is
only in a spiritual sense, and not in any way a physical one, that the body
and blood of Christ are consumed. In 1059 and again in 1079 he was
compelled to recant and made to sign statements categorically affirming
the views he had attacked. The 1059 formulation emphasises in the
strongest and crudest terms imaginable the real eating and drinking of
the very body and blood:

I Berengarius . . . anathematise every heresy, especially that of
which I have been accused, which attempts to argue that the
bread and wine which are placed on the altar are after
consecration solely a sacrament and not the true body and blood
of our Lord Jesus Christ; and that these cannot be handled by the
hands of the priests, or broken or crushed by the teeth of the
faithful, except in a sacrament alone. I agree . . . that the bread and
the wine . . . are not merely a sacrament, but also the true body
and blood of our Lord Jesus Christ; and that they are sensibly –
not merely in a sacrament, but in truth – handled by the hands of

the priests and broken and crushed by the teeth of the faithful . . .
(DS 690)

The 1079 confession then concentrates on the identity between the eucharistic body and the original body of Christ:

I Berengarius believe . . . that the bread and wine which are placed
on the altar are substantially changed (*substantialiter converti*)
through the mystery of the sacred prayer and the words of our
Redeemer into the true and proper and lifegiving flesh and blood
of Jesus Christ our Lord, and that after consecration they are the
true body of Christ which was born of the Virgin . . . and the true
blood of Christ which flowed from his side; and this not only
through the sign and power of a sacrament, but in the
authenticity of their own nature and in the truth of their own
substance (*in proprietate naturae et veritate substantiae*). (DS 700)

With these confessions, the language of 'substantial change' – though its precise meaning is as yet not wholly clear – comes to be officially approved and indeed demanded, as does the close identification of the consecrated elements with the genuine body and blood. This sets the scene for further and more sophisticated exploration of the matter in the next centuries.

Peter Lombard carried thought a stage further in his *Sentences* IV.2, where he considered four possible senses in which the change might be conceived: (a) the bread becomes the body of Christ in the same kind of way as meal is changed into bread; (b) what was formerly bread is transformed into body; (c) the bread is destroyed and replaced by the body; (d) the bread remains, and the body is also with it. He rejected all but the second of these: (a) the bread is not altered in a way analogous to any natural process of change; (c) it is not simply destroyed and replaced by something else; (d) it does not remain as bread after the change has taken place. Rather, it is changed from bread into body, and its reality, its substance, is now that of the body rather than of bread. About this date, in the middle of the twelfth century, the term 'transubstantiation' was coming into use to describe this kind of change. It was used by the Fourth Lateran Council in 1215 in its *Definitio contra Albigenses et Catharos* (DS 802), and again by the Council of Lyons in 1274 (DS 860). By then, however, it had received further and closer analysis, above all by Thomas Aquinas.

Aquinas' teaching on transubstantiation is summarised in the *Summa Theologica* III, *quaestiones* 75–77, which deal in turn with the changing of the substance of the bread and the wine into that of the body and blood of Christ, the mode of Christ's eucharistic presence, and the problem raised by the fact that the 'accidents' of the bread and the wine remain in existence in spite of the change of their substance. Basic to the entire discussion are the distinctions between *material, substance* and *accidents*. *Material*, first, is the physical stuff of which everything is composed. Thomas, following Aristotle and other Greek thinkers, believed this to be made up of the four elements of earth, air, fire and water which are the constituents, in varying combinations, of every material thing. *Substance*, on the other hand, is quite different. We might imagine that it must mean the same as material, but it does not – which is of considerable importance for its use in eucharistic theology. The substance of anything is what gives it its identity as whatever it is – bread, stone, table, human being, or whatever. A substance is not therefore something *physical*: it is that which gives anything its form and character, and which is recognised by the mind when it grasps and discerns them, and with them the identity of the thing itself. At the same time, a substance is objectively real: it is not merely a construct of the mind of the observer. Finally, everything possesses its own particular qualities, which may and do vary from one individual instance to another – colour, shape, size, taste, place and so on. These are the *accidents*, and together they constitute the *species*, the 'appearance' or specific, visible or tangible form of the thing. The *accidents* are thought of as inhering in the substance, rather like pins in a pincushion; and it is the combination of substance, accidents and material which adds up to compose any particular object.

With the help of this language, honed and sharpened with immense precision, Aquinas brought a new clarity to the statement of the doctrine of transubstantiation. The substance of the bread and the wine is changed into the substance of the body and blood of Jesus Christ, but the accidents of the elements remain. What is now present 'under' the *species* is a transformed substance which faith discerns. What seems still to be bread is in fact no longer bread, for its inner reality has been altered. But this is in no way a physical change; it involves no alteration in the material any more than in the accidents. The change is *only* in respect of substance, and 'is perceptible neither by sense nor by imagination, but only by the mind, which is called "the eye of the soul"' (*qu.* 76, *art.* 7) – and then only with the further aid of faith, for no created intellect, not even that of the angels, is capable of apprehending this substance by its own natural powers (ibid.). In faith, however, there is made possible a real recognition of the substance of the body and blood of Jesus Christ.

From this it follows further that the mode of Christ's presence – or rather, of the presence of his body and blood: we shall return to this distinction in a little – is not of any normal kind. In the usual way of things a substance is present only along with its own accidents which inhere in it; but here we are presented with a mere substance, but not with all the accidents normally associated with flesh and blood. This means in particular that the substance of the body and the blood is not *localised* 'in' the elements; for spatial dimensions themselves belong to the category of accidents, not of substances (*qu.* 76, *art.* 5). Nor can only a *part* of the substance be present in the bread and wine, for a substance *qua* substance is not divisible into parts: rather, the *whole* substance of the body is present in each and every tiniest fragment of the bread, and of the blood in every minute drop of the wine (*qu.* 76, *art.* 3). Thus the body and the blood are not present in the elements 'as if in a place', nor can they be properly said to 'move' when the consecrated elements are carried from one place to another (*qu.* 76, *art.* 6), nor indeed are they 'broken' or 'poured' when these things are done to the bread and the wine. So Thomas is able to quote Berengarius' 1059 confession, but to interpret it in a sense rather closer to Berengarius' own original belief than to the opinion he was being forced to avow:

> It cannot be said that the very body of Christ is itself broken; first of all because it is incorruptible and impassible; secondly because it is completely present under any individual part of the bread . . . which is of course contrary to the nature of that which is broken . . . Just as the sacramental *species* are a sacrament of the body of Christ, so the breaking of the *species* in this way is a sacrament of the passion of the Lord, which took place in the true body of Christ . . . That which is eaten in its own *species* is also broken and chewed in its own *species*. But the body of Christ is not eaten in its own *species*, but in a sacramental one . . . And so the very body of Christ is not broken except in a sacramental *species*. And it is in this way that the confession of Berengarius is to be understood: that the breaking and grinding with the teeth are to be referred to the sacramental *species*, under which the body of Christ truly is.
> (*qu.* 77, *art.* 7)

It is worth remarking at this point that, so far as Thomas is concerned, the original body of Christ is located in heaven and remains there: that is where the substance *and accidents* of the body are together 'in a place' (*qu.* 75, *art.* 2). The body is not in any sense 'transported' from heaven to the altar. Instead, the connexion is established through the miraculous transformation of the substance of the elements into the substance of his body and blood, and substances are not localised in space.

It has only been possible here to offer the sketchiest outline of the main points in Aquinas' account, which is vastly more detailed and complex that this summary might suggest. Enough has perhaps been said, nonetheless, to show that the doctrine of transubstantiation as he formulated it is very different indeed from any crude theory of a physical alteration of bread into body or wine into blood. He in fact succeeded, within the horizon of thought in which he was working, in massively shifting the emphasis away from quasi-material transmutation, and offering a restatement of the tradition stemming from Augustine which distinguished so clearly between the visible sacrament and the spiritual reality. On any reckoning, his theory of transubstantiation was an enormous intellectual achievement. This must be said; but so too must other things more critical; for the theory is in fact exposed to very serious criticisms, some of which must be mentioned, both as highlighting difficulties with this entire pattern of thought and as illustrating some further aspects of the theory.

The first problem is that it involves not only one but two distinct miracles. Only by a miracle can the substance of the bread and the wine be changed into that of the body and the blood; but that is not all. A further miracle is required to explain how the accidents of the bread and wine, the sacramental *species*, still remain in being after their original substance has been transformed. Accidents inhere in their substance: they cannot support themselves, but need a 'subject' to which they can belong, and this is the substance. But that substance is no longer there. Nor, Aquinas insists, can they inhere now in the substance of Christ's body and blood: that is present as *mere* substance, 'nor is it possible that the body of Christ, which is glorious and impassible, should be changed to take on qualities of this kind.' (*qu.* 77, *art.* 1) Christ is not changed into bread! Only the power of God can maintain these now unsupported accidents in being without any substance to be their subject. When one has followed the theory thus far, it becomes hard to suppress the question whether something must not have gone wrong further back in the chain of reasoning if such a loose-ended conclusion is the result. No doubt God *could* do what is here suggested, but that is not really the question. The issue is, rather, how many miracles a theologian (or indeed a church) is entitled to assume in order to sustain a theological hypothesis.

A second difficulty – or rather, a whole series of difficulties – have to do with the way in which Aquinas employs the concept of 'substance' itself. Within the framework of Aristotelian philosophy, the fundamental definitions of and distinctions between material, substance and accidents could be accepted and used. By and large, however, we no longer think in that framework today. The idea of a substance, of the essential identity of something as somehow underlying its outward form and apprehended by the mind, and contrasted with the accidents discerned by the senses, is one which it is exceedingly hard to maintain. In particular, the notion that a substance is a non-physical, non–localised entity – and it is upon this above all that Aquinas' use of the concept relies – is not only extremely sophisticated and abstract, but open to serious philosophical challenge. One can indeed if one wishes talk in this way; but it is debatable whether one is in fact talking about something *real*.

This has admittedly been a persistent issue in philosophy from the time of Plato and Aristotle; it erupted afresh in the middle ages in the controversy between nominalism and realism; and it is still alive today. That the debate has gone on so long is doubtless an indication that there is some truth on either side; but the position on which Aquinas builds is hard to accept just as it is stated. Even if it is adopted, however, there is a further major difficulty to be faced.

Aquinas uses the distinction between substance and accidents to allow for the existence of a substance apart from its accidents, and of accidents apart from their substance. Not only is a miracle required in each case: the categories are in fact being torn out of the philosophical framework within which they belong, and applied for a quite different purpose. The question here is whether or how far they can any longer plausibly retain their meaning; for the distinction between them belongs within a metaphysical and epistemological theory which holds that the two do not in fact subsist in isolation from each other, whereas just such an independent subsistence is demanded by the theory of transubstantiation. The Aristotelian horizon is being drastically interfered with – not overall, nor by any radical re-thinking of its foundations, but by the exploiting of certain inbuilt distinctions at one point where the pattern of thought on which they depend is being contradicted. There is therefore here a *prima facie* incoherence which cannot simply be passed over as insignificant.

A third area of questions relates to a fact touched on earlier: that according to the theory it is not, strictly speaking, Christ himself who is 'present' under the sacramental *species*. Under the bread is the substance of his body, and under the wine the substance of his blood. In order to move from there to the position that the whole reality of Christ himself, body, soul and divine power, is given in the Eucharist, Aquinas has to introduce a further doctrine – that of *concomitance* (*qu. 76, art. 1*). Because the whole Christ is linked to and bound up with his body, the whole Christ is wholly received when the substance of his body is received, and this by the power of genuine 'concomitance'. The same applies to the wine, under which is, strictly speaking, only the substance of his blood. So transubstantiation needs this supplementation by the theory of concomitance if it is not to leave us, so to speak, with the mere body and blood of Christ rather than his whole person and saving power. A similar concern was expressed in a rather different fashion some years earlier by Pope Innocent III in his letter *Cum Marthae circa* in 1202:

> A careful distinction must be made between three distinct things which are in this sacrament, namely the visible form, the truth of the body, and the spiritual power. The form is of bread and wine, the truth of flesh and blood, the power of unity and love. The first

is 'sacrament and not reality'. The second is 'sacrament and reality'. The third is 'reality and not sacrament'. But the first is sacrament of both realities. The second is sacrament of the one reality, and the reality of the other. The third is the reality of both sacraments. (DS 783)

Leaving aside Innocent's identification of the central 'reality' as 'unity and love' rather than Christ himself – though this is revealingly characteristic of the medieval tendency to shift attention from Christ himself to the grace which flows from him – we can recognise here the same essential concern as in Aquinas. 'Body and blood' are not enough: the central reality at the heart of the Eucharist lies deeper. And this is certainly correct, and very much in harmony with what we have found in the New Testament passages. The fact that these further steps in the argument have to be constructed is however a warning that the focus of the theory risks being placed on the wrong question by concentrating too much on the link between bread and wine and flesh and blood. Such an approach is all too likely to issue in an eccentric and strained interpretation of the presence of Christ.

To some degree, the force of these criticisms can be weakened by another observation. Aquinas is interpreting and expounding the same profound truth that the New Testament itself holds out to us: that in the Eucharist Christ gives himself to us, and gives us part in himself. The problems, it may be said, stem from the inherent mystery of the theme, and even the incoherences in the exposition rightly remind us of the inability of the human mind fully to grasp or express the deep things of the faith. They warn us that theology, even the theology of a towering intellectual giant such as Aquinas was, is still an activity of men, whose thought will always fall into antinomies when it grapples with the reality of God. This is a point of capital importance, and one which some over-confident Protestant criticisms of Roman Catholic thinking too often and too readily overlook. There is a kind of Protestant polemic against Rome which is all too superficial and rationalistic, far too quick to seize on inconsistencies in argument without looking beyond them to see what is struggling for expression. (And this in turn, it must be said, commonly encounters an equally superficial Roman Catholic reaction.) Given the correctness of this general defence of Aquinas, however, one can still move on in either of two rather different directions. One may hold that in spite of all the problems which it may raise, the doctrine of transubstantiation is essentially valid: at the heart of the eucharistic celebration there takes place a miraculous metaphysical change which the label of transubstantiation may serve in some fashion to describe. Or one may conclude, more radically, that not only Aquinas' conclusions, but the whole way in which the question had come to be posed in the theological development which preceded him, and from which he took both the idea of a 'change of substance' and the word 'transubstantiation', must be seen as an attempt, but *only* an attempt, to struggle with a truth which may and should be approached along other lines. By and large, Roman Catholic theology has traditionally adopted the first of these approaches, while Reformed thought has chosen the second.

This section may now be concluded by some quotations from the *Decree on the Eucharist* of the Council of Trent. These do not include all the elements in Aquinas' theory, but rest very much upon it. So the fourth chapter offers this statement 'On Transubstantiation':

> Since Christ our Redeemer declared that to be truly his body which he offered under the *species* of bread, this has always been believed in the church of God; and this holy Synod now affirms it afresh: through the consecration of the bread and wine there takes place a conversion of the whole substance of the bread into the substance of the body of Christ our Lord, and of the whole substance of the wine into the substance of his blood. This change is suitably and properly called transubstantiation by the holy catholic church. (DS 1642)

This is what Trent, in the first chapter of the same decree, describes as the 'real presence' of Christ, though making the same distinction as Aquinas and others had earlier seen between the 'natural' presence of Christ at the right hand of the Father and his real but sacramental presence upon the altar. The chapter is entitled, 'On the Real Presence of our Lord Jesus Christ in the most holy Sacrament of the Eucharist', and begins thus:

> In the first place, this holy Synod teaches and openly and simply professes, that in the bountiful sacrament of the holy Eucharist after the consecration of the bread and wine, our Lord Jesus Christ, true God and true man, is truly, really and substantially contained under the *species* of those things which the senses perceive. Nor is there any contradiction between these things, that the Saviour himself sits always at the right hand of the Father in heaven according to his natural mode of existence, and that he should nonetheless also be present sacramentally in his own substance in other places by that mode of existence which, although we can scarcely express it in words, we can conclude is possible for God, and ought most constantly to believe. (DS 1636)

Finally, we may note that it is on this real presence, enabled by transubstantiation, that Trent grounds the superiority of the Eucharist over all other sacraments. This it does in the third chapter of the same decree in these words: the other six sacraments 'only have the power of sanctifying when someone makes use of them; but in the Eucharist the author of sanctity himself is present even before it is used.' (DS 1639) The

Eucharist is the shining jewel of surpassing excellence and singular glory, the heart of the church and the centre of the whole pattern of the seven sacraments. Here is given the objective presence of the Lord himself, on which all else depends.

3. *The Sacrifice of the Mass*

So far we have been discussing the medieval understanding of the Eucharist as a sacrament, a means of grace, a form of Christ's presence. In all this the emphasis lies on *what is given to men* in the Eucharist, on a movement *from* God, in Christ, to those who receive. This, however, is only one side of the matter. It was complemented, as the medieval theologians saw it, by an answering movement *from* man to God. The Eucharist was not only sacrament but also sacrifice; as sacrament, it was to be *received*, but as sacrifice, it was to be *offered*.[8] This brings us to the third main strand of interpretation of the Eucharist in the middle ages and at Trent.

The doctrine of the Eucharist as sacrifice in this era does not in fact show quite the same degree of fresh development as that of the real presence. This does not mean that the doctrine was regarded either as insignificant or as questionable. It was more or less universally accepted, and there was little need either to extend or to defend it. Only rarely do we find it touched upon in major statements by Popes or councils before the Reformation, and then only briefly – as, for example, in the *Definitio contra Albigenses et Catharos* of the Fourth Lateran Council in 1215, to which we have already referred as sanctioning the term 'transubstantiation'. The relevant section runs simply:

> There is one universal Church of the faithful, outside which no-one can be saved at all, in which Jesus Christ himself is both priest and sacrifice; (for) his body and blood are truly contained in the sacrament of the altar under the *species* of bread and wine, the bread being transubstantiated into his body by divine power, and the wine into his blood. (DS 802)

This condensed sentence does, however, highlight two prime features of this understanding of the Eucharist. First, *it is Christ himself who is both priest and sacrifice*. Second, *the emerging doctrine of transubstantiation is coming to bear directly upon the sacrificial interpretation*. While the two motifs of presence and of sacrifice are distinct and complementary, they also interact; and in this way the fuller articulation of the theory of the real presence comes to give a fresh colouring to the conception of sacrifice. The Eucharist is the offering to God of the Christ who is present under the *species* of the consecrated bread and wine. The first of these points has often been overlooked by Protestant critics of medieval teaching, while the second has perhaps not always been sufficiently recognised by Roman Catholic apologists. Both need to be taken into account.

We have already noticed that the thought of the Eucharist as a sacrifice was already strongly established by the fourth century, and mentioned how theological and liturgical trends in subsequent ages led to a particular concentration upon the Mass as the offering of the church or of the priest. In the twelfth century, however, when Peter Lombard came to consider whether 'what the priest does is properly called a sacrifice or immolation', his answer was very much along the lines of his predecessors eight hundred years before, stressing the uniqueness of Christ's own sacrifice on the cross, and describing the Eucharist as a memorial and representation in sacramental form:

> What is offered and consecrated by the priest is called a sacrifice and an immolation because it is a memorial and a representation of the true sacrifice and holy immolation made upon the altar of the cross. Christ died once upon the cross, and there he was immolated in his own self; and yet every day he is immolated sacramentally, because in the sacrament there is a recalling of what was done once. (*Sentences* IV.xii)

Among the authoritative texts which Lombard quotes in support of this account is an excerpt ascribed by him to Ambrose. In fact, it is from the same passage in John Chrysostom's *Homily 17 on Hebrews* that we cited in the previous chapter. Part of Lombard's version of it runs:

> In Christ the saving victim was offered once. Then what of ourselves? Do we not offer every day? Although we do offer daily, that is done for the recalling of his death, and the victim is one, not many ... because Christ was immolated once ... the same reality, remaining always the same, is offered; and so this is the same sacrifice. Or would you say that because the sacrifice is offered in many places, therefore there are many Christs? No, but there is one Christ in all these places, fully present here and fully present there. And just as what is offered in all the places is one and the same body, so there is one and the same sacrifice. Christ offered a victim, and we offer the self-same now; but what we do is a recalling of his sacrifice. Nor is the sacrifice repeated because of any inadequacy in it (since it is what perfects mankind), but because of our own; for we sin daily.

Here in the position sketched by Peter Lombard, drawing on Chrysostom, we may trace the essential shape of the medieval sacrificial interpretation of the Eucharist. It is not an addition to the sacrifice of Christ, nor is it a repetition of it; for the sacrifice has been completed once and for all upon the cross. The Eucharist is, rather, a sacramental sharing in that sacrifice. In the sacrament, the sacrifice itself is present –

the same that was offered to God on Calvary – for Christ himself is present, both as victim and as priest; and the priest on earth acts *in persona Christi*, as Christ's representative,[9] through whom Christ himself works. So, against the attacks of the Reformers upon the Mass, the Council of Trent in framing the *Doctrine concerning the Sacrifice of the Holy Sacrament of the Mass* could affirm in the second chapter, 'That the Visible Sacrifice is Propitiatory for the Living and the Dead':

> For there is one and the same victim, and the same one who offered himself then on the cross now offers through the ministry of the priest; only the mode of offering is different. For the fruits of that offering in blood are received most richly through this bloodless offering: in no way is it the case that this offering in any manner derogates from that. (DS 1743)

The same point is made in the encyclical *Caritatis studium*, sent by Pope Leo XIII in 1898 to the Roman Catholic bishops in Scotland. This was particularly directed against the criticisms of Roman Catholic doctrine made in the 1560 *Scots Confession*, and so bears directly on our topic:[10]

> The sacrifices employed in the Old Testament long before Christ was born prefigured the sacrifice made on the cross; and after his ascension into heaven that same sacrifice is continued (*continuatur*) in the eucharistic sacrifice. Therefore those err exceedingly who reject (the eucharistic sacrifice) as if it diminished the truth and power of the sacrifice which Christ made, nailed to the cross, 'offering himself once and for all to expiate the sins of many' (Hebr. 9.28). Entirely perfect and complete was that expiation for mortal men; nor is it any other, but this itself, which is in the eucharistic sacrifice ... which does not bring any bare similitude or mere memorial of the reality, but the truth itself, albeit under a different *species*. Therefore the effectiveness of this sacrifice ... flows entirely from the death of Christ. (DS 3339)

In tracing this outline, however, we have not yet exhausted the full scope of the medieval understanding of the matter. The view of the Eucharist as Christ's own single sacrifice opened up a further perspective in which the offering of the priest and of the church, though in principle wholly dependent upon Christ's self-offering, could nevertheless take on a distinct role of its own and come to be interpreted as sacrificial in its own right. This was certainly encouraged by the liturgical emphasis upon the offering made by the priest; and it was further supported by the articulation of the doctrine of transubstantiation – for the priest who makes the offering is at the same time he who speaks Christ's words by which the miraculous change is effected. So it was scarcely surprising that the celebration of the Eucharist came to be seen as a sacrificial offering in its own way, over and above the sacramental sharing in

Christ's own sacrifice. This emerges with all possible clarity in some of the things Aquinas has to say in *Summa Theologica* III about the Eucharist as sacrifice:

> This sacrament is simultaneously both sacrifice and sacrament: it has the nature of a sacrifice to the extent that it is offered, but that of a sacrament to the extent that it is consumed. Therefore it has the effect of a sacrament in him who consumes it; but the effect of a sacrifice in him who offers, or in those for whom it is offered ... To the extent that it is a sacrifice, it possesses the power to make satisfaction (*vim satisfactivam*). But in satisfaction more weight is placed upon the attitude of the person offering (*affectus offerentis*) than upon the measure of the oblation ... Therefore although this oblation in its own measure suffices to make satisfaction for every sin, yet it becomes a means of making satisfaction (*fit satisfactoria*) for those for whom it is offered, or even for the person offering, according to the measure of their devotion, and not (necessarily) for all their sins. (*qu.* 79, *art.* 5)

The sacrifice is effective to make 'satisfaction' to God, and so to obtain forgiveness, in proportion to the faith and devotion of him who makes it, or those for whom it is made. Aquinas distinguishes very clearly between that side of the matter and the *objective* value of what is offered – the sacrifice of Christ himself. His motive can well be appreciated. He is anxious to stress that the Eucharist is not in itself an automatic means of forgiveness. What is significant, however, is that the language of sacrifice and satisfaction is being used in direct connexion with the actions and attitudes of those who celebrate the Eucharist. It is not only or solely Christ's sacrifice; it is *also* the sacrifice of those who offer it, and is effective in proportion to their devotion. As such, it makes satisfaction to God – a satisfaction which is certainly ultimately grounded upon that offered by Christ, but nevertheless remains distinguishable from his, and capable of being analysed and weighed on its own.

The further implications of this distinction between sacrament and sacrifice, and between Christ's sacrifice and ours, come to light a little later in Aquinas' argument:

> As I have already said, this sacrament is not only a sacrament; it is also a sacrifice. For to the extent that in this sacrament the passion of Christ is represented ... it has the nature of a sacrifice; but to the extent that in this sacrament grace is invisibly transmitted under the visible *species*, it has the nature of a sacrament. Therefore this sacrament is of benefit to those who consume it both by the mode of sacrament and by that of sacrifice ... But to others who do not consume it, it is of benefit by the mode of sacrifice, to the extent that it is offered for their salvation ...

Consuming belongs to the nature of a sacrament; but offering belongs to the nature of a sacrifice. So from the fact that one person, or several, consume the body of Christ, no assistance accrues to others. Similarly, too, the effects of this sacrament are not multiplied by the fact that the priest consecrates several hosts in one Mass; for there is only the one sacrifice. There is no more power in many consecrated hosts than in one, since under all and under one there is only the whole Christ. So too, even if someone consumes many consecrated hosts in one Mass, he will not have a greater share in the effects of the sacrament. But in several Masses, the oblation of the sacrifice is multiplied; and therefore the effects of the sacrifice and the sacrament are multiplied. (*qu.* 79, *art.* 7)

It is the fact that the consecration-*and-offering* can be repeated that makes several Masses more effective than one; the *sacramental* reality, the presence of Christ, is the same in each case, and as full in one as in many. And it is as *sacrifice*, not as *sacrament*, that the Eucharist is of benefit even to those who do not partake – if it is offered for them.

In this way, Aquinas offered a theological ground for what was already the deeply rooted conviction of the medieval church – that the celebration of the Mass and the offering of the sacrifice was in itself a meritorious and beneficial action. This encouraged the saying of the Mass with all possible frequency in order that maximum benefit be obtained both for the living and also for the dead, who could also be helped by it, provided that they were not in hell, but undergoing purification in purgatory. This pattern of belief and practice combined with the doctrine of transubstantiation to produce the synthesis against which the Reformers would so vehemently react, but which the Council of Trent restated in the passage of the *Doctrine concerning the Sacrifice of the Holy Sacrament of the Mass* from which we have already quoted, but may now cite more fully:

Since in this divine sacrifice which is enacted in the Mass that same Christ is contained and bloodlessly immolated who on the altar of the cross offered himself once for all in blood; the holy Synod teaches that that sacrifice is truly propitiatory; and through it comes about that if we come to God with a true heart and a right faith, with fear and reverence, contrite and penitent, 'we shall obtain mercy and find grace in timely help' (Hebr. 4.16). For the Lord, placated by this sacrifice, granting grace and the gift of penitence, remits even great crimes and sins. For there is one and the same victim, and the same one who offered himself then on the cross offers now through the ministry of the priest; only the mode of offering is different. For the fruits of that offering in blood are received most richly through this bloodless offering: in

no way is it the case that this offering in any manner derogates
from that. Therefore it is duly offered, according to the tradition
of the apostles, not only for the sins, penances, satisfactions and
other needs of the faithful who are alive, but also for those who
have died in Christ, but are not yet fully purified. (DS 1743)
It is noticeable that this statement carefully avoids giving the impression
of any independent or even distinct sacrifice made by the church or by
the priest. That, however, leaves open the question whether without
some such conception the concluding sentences can be sustained. They
appear still to presuppose what was more openly argued by Aquinas –
that each particular celebration of the Mass is, as Luther was to describe
it, 'a good work and a sacrifice', with its own distinct measure of power
to make satisfaction, and not merely a sacrifice in the secondary and
derivative sense of sharing in the one sacrifice made once for all. At the
very least, there remains here an unresolved question.

*   *   *   *   *

The position taken by the Council of Trent on all the main points
we have outlined in this chapter is neatly summarised in the so-called
Tridentine Confession of Faith, published by Pope Pius IV in his Bull,
Iniunctum nobis, of 13th November 1564, a year after the Council had
completed its work. The key sentences on the sacraments and on the
Eucharist run thus:
    I confess also that there are truly and properly seven sacraments of
    the New Law instituted by Jesus Christ our Lord and necessary
    for the salvation of the human race (although not all are necessary
    for each individual), namely baptism, confirmation, Eucharist,
    penance, extreme unction, orders and marriage; and that they
    confer grace . . . And I receive and accept the received and
    approved rites of the catholic Church in the solemn
    administration of all of the said sacraments.
        I confess equally that in the Mass there is offered to God a
    true, proper and propitiatory sacrifice for the living and the dead;
    and that in the most holy sacrament of the Eucharist there is truly,
    really and substantially the body and blood of our Lord Jesus
    Christ, together with his soul and divinity; and that a conversion
    takes place of the whole substance of the bread into the body, and
    of the whole substance of the wine into blood, which conversion
    the catholic Church calls transubstantiation. I also avow that even
    under a single *species* the whole and complete Christ and the true
    sacrament is eaten. (DS 1864; 1866)

6

THE EUCHARIST IN THE REFORMATION

Just as the medieval understanding of the Eucharist and the sacraments fits into the wider horizon of the medieval church and its theology, so too must the Reformation reorientation of eucharistic and sacramental thinking be seen against its own background. Where before, the mediation of grace through the sacraments of the church was the central concern, now it became the Word of God displayed in the Bible as the message of salvation through Christ alone, of justification by grace through faith. Such a shift in perspective could not but put numerous aspects of church structure, life, tradition and teaching under radical question. Within the reform programme, the medieval sacramental system, the theory of the priesthood and the doctrine of the Mass rapidly became a primary target; for there the Reformers diagnosed with particular sharpness the practical displacement of Christ by the church, of the Word of God by human inventions. This they set out to correct by a recovery of the message and intention of Scripture in a renewed theological vision.

1. *Luther on Sacrament, Presence and Sacrifice*

The first full-scale assault came in two of Luther's great writings of 1520, the *Appeal to the Ruling Class of German Nationality* and *The Pagan Servitude of the Church*.[1] The *Appeal* consisted chiefly of a long series of proposals for reform which Luther wished to persuade the young, newly elected Emperor Charles V to have debated at a general council. First, however, he had to demolish 'three walls' with which 'the Romanists have very cleverly surrounded themselves' (p. 112). The first, which is our concern here, was the claim that the secular power had no authority to interfere in spiritual matters, because the spiritual power was superior to it. (The other two ascribed to the Pope alone the competence authoritatively to interpret Scripture, or to summon a general council.) In seeking to breach this wall, Luther denied any essential difference between clergy and laity, stressed the 'priesthood of all the baptized', rejected the 'fiction' that ordination imprinted an 'indelible character', and reduced the difference between religious and secular occupations to one of function.

For all Christians whatsoever really and truly belong to the religious class, and there is no difference between them except in so far as they do different work. . . . This applies to us all, because we have one baptism, one gospel, one faith, and are all equally Christian. . . . The fact is that our baptism consecrates us all without exception, and makes us all priests. . . . If we ourselves as Christians did not receive a higher consecration than that given by pope or bishop, then no one would be made priest even by consecration at the hands of pope or bishop. . . .

It follows that the status of a priest among Christians is merely that of an office-bearer; while he holds the office he exercises it; if he be deposed he resumes his status in the community and becomes like the rest. . . . Yet the Romanists have devised the claim to *characteres indelebiles*, and assert that a priest, even if deposed, is different from a mere layman. . . . All these are human inventions and regulations. . . . Therefore those now called 'the religious', i.e. priests, bishops and popes, possess no further or greater dignity than other Christians, except that their duty is to expound the word of God and administer the sacraments . . .
(pp. 113-116)

This frontal attack on the current theology of the priesthood is of twofold importance. First, such a radical critique of the theory of orders could not but shake the foundations of the entire sacramental theology, in which that theory was embedded and of which it was a constitutive element. Second, the questioning of the distinction in anything other than function between a priest and a layman undercut the whole conception of the sacrifice of the Mass and the distinctively sacrificial role of the priest. The question of the nature of the priesthood or ministry has a direct bearing on the issue of Eucharist and sacrifice – and vice versa.

The Pagan Servitude brought a wider-ranging critical analysis of all seven medieval sacraments, four of which – confirmation, ordination, marriage and extreme unction – Luther found to be no genuine sacraments at all. The principle he applied to distinguish between authentic and inauthentic sacraments may be summed up as follows: in effect it points to a fresh understanding of what a sacrament is. First, God deals with us in no other way than by his *Word of promise*, which calls forth and can only be heard in *faith*. Second, God commonly also attaches a *sign* as a mark of his promise. Third, only a sign which has been explicitly *given by God* as such a sign of his Word of promise can properly be called a sacrament:

The church has no power to initiate and institute divine promises of grace, as is the case when the Romanists pretentiously claim that anything instituted by the church has no less authority than what has been ordained by God, since the church is governed by the Holy Spirit. For the church was born by virtue of her faith in the word of promise, and by that promise she is both fed and maintained. In other words, she was instituted by God's promise, and not God's promise by her. (pp. 308-309)

More is involved here than simply cutting down the number of the sacraments by a stringent application of the criterion of divine or dominical institution. A 'sacrament' itself is now being understood as something different from the medieval definition – no longer a sign and cause of grace marking and nourishing a crucial stage in the life of the individual or the church, but a sign of the divine promise given to and directed towards faith. In other words, a sign of the promise which is Jesus Christ himself, and in him, the justification of the ungodly, the forgiveness of sins. Luther was quite clear about the difference from the older understanding:

... it cannot be true that there resides in the sacraments a power capable of giving justification, or that they are the 'signs' of efficacious grace. All such things are said to the detriment of faith, and in ignorance of the divine promises. ... Now, if a sacrament were to give me grace just because I receive the sacrament, then surely I should obtain the grace, not by faith, but by my works. I should not gain the promise in the sacrament, but only the sign instituted and commanded by God. (p. 264)

It is also in *The Pagan Servitude* that Luther develops his criticisms of eucharistic theology and practice. Here he discerns a 'threefold enslavement' of the sacrament – the withholding of the cup from the laity, the imposition of the doctrine of transubstantiation as an article of faith, and the teaching that the Mass is 'a good work and a sacrifice'. It is with the second and third that we have mainly to do here; of the first it is enough to note that Luther took it, too, extremely seriously, indeed regarded it in practice as a worse and more serious abuse than the doctrine of transubstantiation, because it impaired the 'substance and completeness' of Christ's institution, arrogated to the priests what belonged to all as if they were 'lords and not servants', in short, placed the teaching of the church over the command of its Lord and made the faithful suffer under 'the tyranny of Rome' (pp. 223-224).

On transubstantiation and sacrifice it is worth quoting the well-known key passages rather more fully. First, transubstantiation:

Some time ago, when I was studying scholastic theology, I was greatly impressed by Dr Pierre d'Ailly, cardinal of Cambrai. He discussed the fourth book of the *Sententiae* very acutely, and said that it was far more likely, and required the presupposition of fewer miracles, if one regarded the bread and wine on the altar as real bread and wine, and not their mere accidents – had not the church determined otherwise. Afterwards, when I saw what was the kind of church which had reached this conclusion, namely, the Thomist, or Aristotelian church, I gained more courage. At last, after hesitating between conflicting opinions, I found peace in my conscience in accepting the earlier opinion, viz., that the true flesh and the true blood of Christ were in the true bread and true wine, and this not otherwise, nor less, than the Thomists regard them as under the accidents.

His first complaint is thus directed against what he feels to be an untenable philosophical implication of the theory; his second against its dogmatic definition by the church, in which the church has simply over-reached itself:

I adopted this view, because I saw that the opinions of the Thomists, even though approved by pope and council, remained opinions still, and would not become articles of faith even if decreed by an angel from heaven. For what is ascribed without a basis of Scripture or a proven revelation, may be held as an opinion, but is not to be believed of necessity. . . . I would therefore allow anyone to hold whichever opinion he prefers . . . so that no one may fear being called a heretic if he believes that the bread and wine on the altar are real bread and wine . . . because no particular view is a necessary article of faith. (pp. 224-226)

Luther goes on to criticise the theory of transubstantiation as inherently absurd and as twisting the meaning of the words of Scripture (p. 227). He asks why it should not be possible for the body of Christ to be maintained 'within the substance of the bread as truly as within its accidents', and offers the illustration of red-hot iron which contains in every part both iron and fire (p. 228). 'Why cannot the glorified body of Christ be similarly found in every part of the substance of the bread? . . . Why not hiss these ingenious enquiries off the stage, and hold to the words of Christ in simple faith, satisfied not to understand what takes place, and content to know that the true body of Christ is there by virtue of the words of institution?' (pp. 228-229) Or:

When I fail to understand how bread can be the body of Christ, I, for one, will take my understanding prisoner and bring it into obedience to Christ; and, holding fast with a simple mind to His words, I will firmly believe, not only that the body of Christ is in the bread, but that bread is the body of Christ. . . . What if the philosophers do not grasp it? The Holy Spirit is greater than Aristotle. . . . Thus what is true in regard to Christ is also true in regard to the sacrament. It is not necessary for human nature to be transubstantiated before it can be the corporeal habitation of the divine, and before the divine can be contained under the accidents of human nature. Both natures are present in their entirety, and one can appropriately say: 'This man is God'; or 'This God is man'. Though philosophy cannot grasp it, yet faith can. The authority of the word of God goes beyond the capacity of our mind. Thus, in order that the true body and the true blood should be in the sacrament, the bread and wine have no need to be transubstantiated, and Christ contained under the accidents; but, while both remain the same, it would be true to say: 'This bread is my body, this wine is my blood', and conversely. That is how I would construe the words of divine Scripture. I cannot bear their being forced by human quibbles and twisted into other meanings. (pp. 230–231)

While Luther's criticisms of the doctrine of transubstantiation, and of the church which had presumed to make it an article of faith, were to become part of the common stock of Reformation argument, his particular view of the 'real presence of the true body and blood *in* the true bread and true wine', and the arguments with which he backed it up, came to be highly controversial, and eventually constituted the major point of difference between the traditions of Lutheran and Reformed theology. Before we come to that controversy, it may therefore be useful to summarise the main lines of Luther's position as we have just quoted it. First, he finds the theory of transubstantiation philosophically nonsensical and biblically ungrounded in its claiming that only the accidents, not the substance of the bread and wine remain after their consecration. Second, he is nonetheless willing to let it stand as a theological opinion – but not as an article of faith. Third, his primary appeal is to the words of institution, which are to be heard and accepted 'in simple faith', not philosophised about and quibbled over, and certainly not changed in meaning just because we may have difficulty in understanding or accepting them as they stand. Fourth, he holds as firmly as his medieval predecessors to the real presence of the true body and blood within the true bread and wine, and that 'by virtue of the words of institution' – which are the words of Christ himself, and carry their own authority with them. Fifth, while he does not attempt to offer a *philosophical* explanation of how this can be, as Aquinas had done, he does supply a *christological analogy*: as Jesus Christ is true God and true man, so that we can properly say, 'This man is God' or 'This God is man', so too in the Eucharist we have together the true body and true bread, so united that we may also say, 'The body of Christ is this bread' or 'This bread is the body of Christ'. All in all, it is fair to say that Luther affirms the *intention* of the doctrine of transubstantiation, but rejects it as an inadequate, indeed misconceived *explanation*, and that his chief resentment is against its imposition as an article of faith binding the conscience of believers, not at all against the virtual identification of the eucharistic bread with the body of Christ and the wine with his blood. For him, the word, 'This is my body', is the very heart of the matter – as subsequent events were to confirm.

By contrast, his tackling of the 'third enslavement' is much more radical, and confronts the medieval tradition head-on:

> The third shackle imposed upon this sacrament is by far the most wicked abuse of all. The result of it is that there is no belief more widely accepted in the church today, or one of greater force, than that the mass is a good work and a sacrifice. And this abuse has brought in its train innumerable other abuses; and these, when faith in the sacrament has completely died away, turn the holy sacrament into mere merchandise, a market, and a business run for profit. This is the origin of the special feasts, the confraternities, intercessions, merits, anniversaries, and memorial days. Things of this kind are bought and sold in the church, dealt in and bargained for; the whole income of priests and monks depending on it. (p. 231)

It is not, however, merely commercial abuse that Luther denounces, but the underlying conception of the matter which alone makes such abuse possible – the view of the Mass as sacrifice and of the priest as one who is uniquely empowered to offer it:

> All of them imagine that they are offering Christ himself to God the Father, as a fully sufficient sacrifice; and that they are doing a good work on behalf of all whom they wish to help. . . . We must therefore make a clear distinction between testament and sacrament on the one hand; and, on the other, the prayers which we offer at the same time. . . . Prayer can be extended to comprehend as many people as I choose; the mass covers none other than him who exercises his own faith, and then only in so far as he exercises it. Nor can the mass be given to God or to other men; rather God bestows it on men through the agency of the priest; and men receive it through faith alone, apart from all works or merits. (p. 247)

So Luther snaps the nerve of the connexion Aquinas had sought to establish between *sacrament* and *sacrifice*. He distinguishes between the *Mass received in faith* and *prayers which we may offer for others*, insisting that the Mass can *only* be received from God, not offered to him, and is therefore in no sense a 'work'. It is a 'testament' and a 'sacrament', but not a 'sacrifice'. He is well aware that in saying this he is opposing the language of the current liturgy – he quotes 'these gifts, these offerings, these holy sacrifices', 'this oblation', the request 'that this sacrifice will be accepted as was Abel's' and the description of Christ as 'the victim on the altar' – and 'the many sayings of the holy Fathers, and the whole custom of the church as observed throughout the world' (p. 248), but is equally clear as to his ground:

> We must resolutely oppose them all with the words and example of Christ. . . . For if we do not hold firmly that the mass is the promise, or testament, of Christ, as His words plainly show, we shall lose the whole gospel, and all its comfort. We must not allow anything to prevail contrary to these words, not even if an angel from heaven were to teach otherwise. These words contain nothing about a good work or sacrifice. . . . Hence, as it is a self-contradiction to speak of distributing a testament, or accepting a promise on the one hand, and on the other, of offering a sacrifice, so it is a self-contradiction to call a mass a sacrifice; for a mass is something we receive, but a sacrifice is something we offer. But one and the same thing cannot be both received and offered at the same time, nor can it at once be given and accepted by the same person. . . . (pp. 248-249)

Here, then, we have the platform that Luther established at the start of the Reformation on the themes of sacrament, presence and sacrifice. But this is only the beginning of the story of eucharistic theology (and controversy) in the sixteenth century among the Reformers. By and large, everything that Luther rejected in the medieval theory was rejected by the others as well; but not all could rest satisfied with his positive position. In particular Calvin, in spite of his profound admiration and sympathy for Luther, found it necessary to oppose his doctrine of the real presence in the form in which it was maintained by Luther's confessional successors, while they in their turn came to anathematise the doctrine of Calvin and the Reformed theologians generally. To trace how this came about we must, before coming to Calvin himself, look across from Wittenberg to Zürich, and to the tensions emerging between them in the 1520s.

2. Luther and Zwingli

The Zürich – and from it, the Swiss – Reformation developed out of the preaching of Zwingli in the Grossmünster from early 1519 onwards. He had never been in any sense a disciple of Luther's, and the Zürich movement was effectively independent of the German, though not of course unaffected by what was happening around Luther. It began to gather real momentum only around 1522, and was from the start somewhat different in tone. It was not so much the radical rediscovery of justification by grace through faith that drove it forward – rather, the spirit of an evangelical humanism concerned to hear the Word of God afresh and to reconstruct the life of the church in harmony with it. In certain respects, however, such as church organisation and order of worship, it was more radical and earlier engaged on the task of thoroughgoing reformation than was Luther's; and Zwingli himself had absorbed much more of the spirit of humanist learning and much less of that of medieval piety and scholastic theology than had Luther. All this was to have a bearing on the conflict between them.

Early in 1523, in preparation for the public disputation which became the turning-point of the Zürich Reformation, Zwingli published 67 'Conclusions' as topics for debate. Two of them read:

XVII. Christ is the only eternal high priest. Therefore those who have called themselves high priests have opposed the honour and power of Christ, yea, cast it out.

XVIII. Christ, having sacrificed himself once, is to all eternity a certain and valid sacrifice for the sins of all the faithful. Therefore the mass is not a sacrifice, but is a remembrance of the sacrifice and assurance of the salvation which Christ has given us.

The theme of 'remembrance' had of course had its place, as we have seen, in the medieval interpretation of the Mass as sacrifice. Now, however, 'sacrifice' and 'remembrance' are seen as *opposed* categories. It is one thing to *sacrifice*, another to *remember* a sacrifice already made: that is the sense of Zwingli's contrast. It is not without significance that, where Luther had seized on the terms 'testament' and 'promise', Zwingli picks out that of 'remembrance'. With Luther, the emphasis falls on *Christ's* promise and testament to us; with Zwingli, on *our* remembering of Christ's sacrifice. Both formulations are based on the language of the institution narratives, and both emphases have their validity. But it is symptomatic of the difference between them that Luther should opt for the more objective, Zwingli for the more subjective side of the matter.

Another contrast comes to light a little later in the same year. Zwingli followed the 'Conclusions' with a commentary and defence under the title 'Interpretations of the Conclusions'. Here he also rejected transubstantiation as an invention of the theologians; and while he spoke repeatedly of the eating of the flesh and drinking of the blood of Christ, he interpreted this by reference especially to John 6 as amounting to nothing other than faith, very much as Origen had done in the third century. Thus he applied the Johannine antithesis between 'flesh' and 'spirit' to make 'eating' and 'drinking' amount to the 'spiritual' reality of faith, as opposed to communion in the real flesh and blood of Christ. Luther on the other hand, both in *The Pagan Servitude* and later, was strenuously exercised to deny that John 6 had anything to do with the

Eucharist at all. In this, if the interpretation we have sketched of the Johannine chapter is at all correct, Luther was certainly wrong; but by the same token it must be doubted whether Zwingli had rightly grasped the genuine meaning of the passage. Throughout his theology there runs a pervasive antithesis between 'flesh' and 'spirit', and a stressing of the 'spiritual' over against the 'physical', which owes more to Hellenistic dualism than to the unitary and unifying way of thinking which is present in the New Testament.

One last contrast at this stage of Zwingli's thought should also be mentioned. He speaks, like Luther, of the sacrament as a 'sign'; but it is essential to his understanding that not simply the *elements*, but the *whole action* constitutes the 'sign'. To put it in a nutshell: for Luther, the decisive saying is, 'This is my body.' For Zwingli, it is, 'Do this in remembrance of me.' Or, as Zwingli himself put it in a letter of July 1523 to Thomas Wyttenbach, the body and blood are there in the Eucharist only insofar as the elements are taken and eaten, just as there is no heat in a flint 'unless one strikes the fire from it'. Luther too could and did emphasis the *usus* and *actio*, the 'use' and the 'action', as essential to the nature of the Eucharist, but he could no more reduce the objective presence of the true body and blood to them than he could scale down eating and drinking to believing in Christ.

In all these ways, the differences which were soon to come into the open were already there in embryo in Zwingli's views of 1523. At that time, however, his position was not yet wholly worked out. It was to crystallise between then and 1525, the year in which he finally replaced the celebration of the Mass with a new liturgy of the Lord's Supper, and so set the seal on the Zurich reformation. One point in particular greatly concerned him in the intervening period: how are the words, 'This is my body', to be understood? He was sure that they could not be taken as stating a literal identification of the bread with Christ's body, but was still searching for a clue to their authentic meaning. He knew, for instance, that Luther's former associate and ally, Carlstadt (whose views in some respects resembled Zwingli's own, and whom Luther had in the meantime disowned). interpreted the 'This' as meaning that in speaking the words, Christ had pointed to himself rather than to the bread; but he naturally enough could not find this anything but far-fetched. Probably towards the end of 1524, however, he became acquainted with the exegesis of a Dutchman, Cornelis Hoen, in which he found what he later called 'the pearl of great price – that "is" is to be taken in the sense of "signifies"'. The bread is a symbol of the body, the wine a symbol of the blood, just as the entire eucharistic action symbolises our faith in Jesus Christ sacrificed for us. This now became the controlling centre of his eucharistic theology (the zwinglian 'signifies' over against the lutheran 'is') and paved the way for a new and fuller statement in his *Commentary Concerning True and False Religion* (1525). Here he came to challenge, not only prevailing conceptions of the real presence, but also, much more radically than Luther, the traditional understanding of a 'sacrament'. The main thrust of his argument may be summed up thus:

(a) It is mistaken to understand a sacrament as having any inherent power either to convey forgiveness or to strengthen faith; for this ties the freedom of God's Spirit to human performance.

(b) A sacrament can accordingly only have the character of an *initiatio*, a ceremony of initiation, or an *oppignoratio*, a *publica consignatio*, an oath, a public confession of allegiance. Here, Zwingli takes up again one of the ancient meanings of *sacramentum* in Latin – one which makes a sacrament an *expression*, a 'sign and badge' of faith and commitment. So far as the Eucharist is concerned, this makes it a visible, public affirmation and demonstration of faith. (The case with baptism as *initiatio* is somewhat different, for Zwingli vigorously defended infant baptism as a sign of belonging to the people of God, by analogy with circumcision in the Old Testament, rather than as an expression or demonstration of faith, as the Anabaptists would have it. At the same time, however, he tended to see baptism in fairly formal terms, and felt that the Anabaptists ascribed it altogether too much significance, so that this instance does not outweigh in any significant fashion the elimination of any objective 'being addressed' or 'acted upon' in his redefinition of 'sacrament'.)

(c) The worth and value of the flesh of Christ is not that it is *eaten* by us, but that it was *slain* for us. To 'eat his flesh' is, simply, to believe that he was sacrificed for us (John 6).

(d) The point and purpose of the contrast between 'flesh' and 'spirit' in John 6 is that the Spirit of God raises our hearts above all earthly and material things and brings our faith to bear on Jesus Christ, to the strengthening of our soul and spirit.

(e) The risen and glorified body of Christ is in heaven, where he sits at the right hand of the Father; it cannot at the same time be 'present' on earth in bread and wine. Otherwise his human nature would be utterly unlike any other – which would contradict the burden of the Gospel.

(f) Christ's words of institution have to be interpreted in the light of all these considerations. That is precisely the task and responsibility of authentic faith, which can by no means take them literally. 'This is . . .' means, as elsewhere in the Bible, 'This signifies . . .' Genuine faith is not credulous literalism or superstition; and it must exclude any notion of 'real presence' which involves confusing the divine and human natures of Christ, and so divinises what is and remains creaturely, namely Christ's truly human body and human nature.

Luther soon heard of Zwingli's stance, and was horrified by it. It is, admittedly, doubtful whether he studied it with any real concern to try to understand what Zwingli was after. It sounded to him as if Zwingli were just another *Schwärmer*, a fanatical 'spiritualiser' of the Gospel, dissolving its objective, given truth and solidity into his own delusive and subversive dreams – like Carlstadt or, even worse, Thomas Münzer! He almost immediately fired off a polemic in his *Sermon on the Sacrament of the Body and Blood of Christ against the Enthusiasts* (1526), which led in the following years to a veritable avalanche of tracts from Zwingli, Luther and others.

In the course of the controversy Luther found himself insisting that on the matter of the real presence he and the Roman Catholics stood together over against the 'sects of the Enthusiasts', though he stood by his rejection of transubstantiation. At the same time he built out his christological analogy to the point where it became much more than an *analogy*, rather an *explanation* of how Christ's body and blood could be really present. In virtue of the 'personal union' (*unio personalis*) between his human and divine natures there is in Jesus Christ the 'communication of properties' (*communicatio idiomatum*) by which his human nature shares in all the attributes of the divine. It is therefore 'ubiquitous', omnipresent, in the same way that God is omnipresent, namely non-locally and without extension or dimension *in* space (*definitive*), and so present *at* every point in space – and therefore also in each and every particle of the bread and wine. Different in detail as this is from Aquinas' explanation of transubstantiation, it is strikingly similar in pattern and end-result, the divine omnipresence playing the role which the non-spatial *substantia* fulfilled in Aquinas' account.

At the same time, the doctrine of ubiquity, taken by itself, says both too much and too little to establish the identification of the body of Christ with the bread, which it was Luther's primary concern to maintain. Too much, in that it 'proves' the presence of Christ's human nature *everywhere*, not merely in the consecrated elements; too little, in that the *special* and *particular* connexion and presence in and with the eucharistic bread and wine does not follow from it. *That* Luther supported chiefly by appeal to the authority of the words of institution as the words of the Lord himself; the doctrine of ubiquity was in effect worked up as a subsidiary argument to counter the assertion of Zwingli and others that the body of Christ is ascended to the right hand of the Father, and cannot therefore in any proper sense be 'present' 'in' or 'with' or 'under' the bread and wine. Against them, Luther affirmed that 'the right hand of God is omnipresent' – and, likewise, the humanity of Christ. But this remained a secondary proof; the primary one depended on attending to and accepting the words of Christ 'in simple faith'. So he could say in his *Greater Catechism* (1529):

What then is the sacrament of the altar? Answer: It is the true body and blood of the Lord Christ, in and under the bread and wine through the word of Christ, of which we are commanded to eat and drink. . . . The word, I say, it is that makes and distinguishes this sacrament so that it is not and is not called simply bread and wine, but Christ's body and blood. For it is said, *Accedat verbum ad elementum et fit sacramentum*, 'When the word comes to the outward element, it becomes a sacrament.' . . . The word must make the element a sacrament, else it remains a mere element. Now it is not the word and command of a prince or emperor, but of the exalted majesty, so that all creatures should fall before his feet and assent that it is as he says, and receive it with all honour, reverence and humility. Out of the word can you strengthen your conscience and say: If a hundred thousand devils and all the *Schwärmer* urge, 'How can bread and wine be Christ's body and blood?' and so on, yet I know that all the spirits and the learned piled up together are not so clever as the divine majesty in his tiniest little finger. Now Christ's word stands here . . . we stand by it and will see what happens to those who set out to master him and to make it other than he has spoken. . . . For as Christ's mouth speaks and says, so it is, for he can neither lie nor deceive.

For Luther, genuine faith is shown in the willingness to take the words of institution literally; anything else is mere human would-be cleverness, travelling the same path as the 'Aristotelian quibblers'. Zwingli, by contrast, is convinced that these words must be interpreted within the general perspective of faith, and that their meaning cannot reduce to this insistence on the literal sense.

Coming as they did from opposite sides of the question, Luther and Zwingli were both equally right and equally wrong. Luther's vehemently rhetorical literalism betrays the characteristic inability of literalism to face the possibility that what it takes to be the 'simple meaning' is being read into the text rather than out of it. On the other hand, Zwingli's enlightened rejection of literalism diverts him from sufficiently pondering the full depths of the words of institution, and makes him too rapidly content with a reduction of their meaning to *mere* symbolism. Neither is a good guide to the sense of the matter: neither lingering scholasticism of Luther's brand nor progressive humanism of Zwingli's offers a reliable way forward, for neither offers an adequate understanding of the New Testament evidence itself.

In view of the inevitable opposition between these equally eccentric views, it is scarcely surprising that the one serious attempt made to reconcile them during the lifetime of the two main protagonists failed, albeit not with a bang, but a whimper. Towards the end of the 1520s, the preparations for the Diet of Augsburg made it seem more and more likely that the Emperor Charles V would at last embark on a sustained military campaign against the Reformation and against those rulers who supported it. At least partly for this reason, one of the most far-sighted German princes of the Reformation party, the Landgraf Philip of Hesse, persuaded both Luther and Zwingli to meet, together with their leading associates, for a colloquy in Marburg in the autumn of 1529. The chief participants were Luther, with Philip Melanchthon (his closest adviser), Justus Jonas of Wittenberg and later of Halle, Andreas Osiander of Nuremberg, Stephanus Agricola of Augsburg and Johannes Brenz of Schwäbisch Hall, who was later to play a leading part in consolidating the Reformation in Württemberg; and Zwingli from Zürich, Johannes Oecolampadius of Basle, and Martin Bucer and Caspar Hedio, both of Strasbourg (then a free imperial city, closely allied with the Swiss Reformation). The aim Philip of Hesse had in view was both a theological reconciliation and the laying of the foundations of a prospective military alliance that would give support to the Reformation within the Empire by the additional weight of the reformed Swiss cantons.

The Landgraf was, however, to be sadly disappointed, in spite of the considerable energy he devoted to pressing for an agreement. The colloquy lasted for several days, and we possess several fairly full reports of the proceedings from various angles.[2] They make lively and frequently entertaining reading! But while agreement was reached on a whole series of subsidiary points, the nub of the issue remained as unsettled as before. The final report of the colloquy was made up of fifteen articles. The first fourteen registered agreement; the last betrays in a subordinate clause that the Landgraf's project had failed:

> And although, however, we have not reached an accord at this
> time as to whether the true body and blood of Christ are
> physically in the bread and wine, yet each party should show
> Christian love to the other, so far as the conscience of each can
> bear it, and both industriously beg Almighty God to confirm to
> us the right understanding through his Holy Spirit. Amen.

The failure of the Marburg Colloquy can be seen in more than one light, as can its historical significance. On the one hand it set a first seal on the division between the German and Swiss Reformations, between what were to become known as the Lutheran and Reformed churches. Protestantism within the Empire, and in Scandinavia, became largely Lutheran, while the Reformed movement spread chiefly outside the boundaries of the Empire – from Switzerland through France and the Netherlands, and to England and Scotland. All this can be seen as stemming from the failure of the Marburg negotiations, and the resultant fact that at the Diet of Augsburg in 1530, where the *Confessio Augustana* ('Augsburg Confession'), the charter of Lutheran Protestant-ism, was laid before the Emperor, the Reformed churches and their theology were not represented. It was to be over a century until, with the Peace of Westphalia (1648) after the Thirty Years War, Reformed teaching achieved the same status in law within the Empire as the Lutheran enjoyed from the Peace of Augsburg in 1555.

On the other hand, Marburg nevertheless represented a step forward, in that it made some attempt to bring the two sides together after the years of polemical controversy. Those attempts were to continue in the succeeding years. In the process it became clearer that neither of the two positions maintained there was wholly adequate. Of the participants in the colloquy, Melanchthon on the Lutheran side and Bucer on the Reformed were the most willing to re-think and to urge their colleagues to do likewise. The gradual but significant shift in climate which began to result from this can be seen in two documents of 1536 – the (Swiss) *First Helvetic Confession* and the *Wittenberg Concord*. According to the first of these:[3]

> ... the Lord ... truly offers to his people his own body and blood, that is himself, to the end that he may live more and more in them, and they in him. Not that the body and blood are naturally united with the bread and wine, or locally included in them, or are made carnally present in any way; but the Lord himself, through the ministry of the church, makes the true communication of his body and blood to be exhibited not as perishable food for the body, but as the aliment of eternal life.

The second includes the explanation:

> And although we deny transubstantiation, and do not believe that there is any local inclusion in the bread, nor any combination enduring beyond the actual duration of the sacrament, nevertheless we grant that the bread is, by a sacramental union, the body of Christ, i.e. we believe that, with the offered bread, there is at the same time present and exhibited, the body of Christ.

The *Wittenberg Concord* was drawn up by Melanchthon as a basis for possible agreement with the Swiss, and it is interesting to contrast the language he uses there with what he had written in the *Augsburg Confession* (German version) six years before:

> X. Concerning the Lord's Supper it is therefore taught that the true body and blood of Christ are truly present in the Supper under the form of bread and wine, and are distributed and received there.

'True presence in the Supper *under the form* of bread and wine' has by 1536 become 'presence and exhibiting *with* the offered bread of the body of Christ'. A similar tone is struck in the revised *Augsburg Confession*, the *Confessio Augustana Variata*, which Melanchthon drew up in 1540, and which Calvin among others subscribed. Now the tenth article reads:

> Concerning the Lord's Supper it is therefore taught that the body and blood of Christ are truly presented and received with the bread and wine in the Supper.

Thus we have here on the Lutheran side a significantly modified expression of the presence of Christ's body and blood, on the Reformed a new and emphatic emphasis on genuine communication in and feeding upon Christ's body and blood as spiritual food. Convergence, and the desire for convergence, are apparent – and that precisely in the year 1536, when Calvin, who more than any other was to seek to reconcile the differences in a deeper consideration, began his work in Geneva.

3. Calvin's Eucharistic Theology

If Luther was a monk whose struggles with the question of faith and justification before God, and with the interpretation of Scripture, had led him to break with the prevailing teaching, and Zwingli a humanistically educated preacher whose work eventually took him in the same direction and led him to usher in the Reformation in Zurich, Calvin was a man of rather different background and intention. He had never been a priest of the pre-Reformation church; had never even formally studied theology, though his theological learning was eventually to surpass that of both Luther and Zwingli. He was a Reformer of the second generation, who became a Reformer without expecting or intending it. He had studied law, and thereafter set out at first to follow the career of a humanist and scholar in his native France. How and in what way he became a conscious and engaged advocate of reformation of the church remains to this day an unresolved puzzle; he himself later spoke of a 'sudden conversion', but no attempt to date that conversion precisely, or to uncover the circumstances surrounding it, has yet found a generally convincing answer. We know that in the autumn of 1533, when his friend Nicholas Cop, the rector of the university in Paris, was compelled to flee because of a Lutheran-tinged address he had held, Calvin also found it prudent to depart from Paris; that in 1534 he renounced certain ecclesiastical benefices which had earlier been acquired for him; and that in 1535 he settled in Basle and busied himself with the first edition of his *Institute of the Christian Religion*, which appeared early in 1536, and was an exceptionally powerful and closely argued presentation of a Protestant position. But when or how the decisive turn occurred remains a mystery. It seems at any rate that he made his own way through intensive study and reflection – and that he was not in any way the product simply of some already established direction or tradition or school, but one who from the start sought to engage freshly and directly with the message of the Bible and with the questions of the day.

His intention was, however, to engage with and to continue with this study and reflection and writing as a simple scholar, a free author, not a reconstructer of church organisation, a preacher or church leader – for which tasks he felt himself quite unsuited. But in the summer of 1536, after his last visit to France, when he was on his way to Strasbourg with the intention of settling either there or in Basle, he was forced by the military situation on the north-east frontier of France to make a detour by way of Geneva, where the Reformation had been ushered in a bare few weeks before through the preaching of William Farel. By this time Calvin was already known as the author of the *Institute*, and Farel, hearing of his presence in the city (in which he only intended to stay one night before travelling further) immediately sought him out. Farel's aim was quite simple: this gifted young man of twenty-seven years must remain in Geneva and join in the work of reformation of the church there. Calvin refused point-blank: this was not the work to which he felt himself called, and he had other plans for a quiet life of study, research and writing. Seeing that his arguments were of no avail, Farel took recourse to other means. Facing Calvin he uttered the hope that God would curse his studies if he did not stay and take up the burden of the hour. That made an impression on Calvin that he could not shake off: he heard, and stayed.

The first period of residence and work in Geneva did not last long – less than two years. Towards the end of April 1538 both Farel and Calvin were expelled because of disagreements with the city council, and Calvin moved to Strasbourg. Little more than three years later, however, he was recalled; and from 1541 until his death in 1564 he remained in Geneva and built up there the great centre of Reformed theology and churchmanship, from which impulses spread all over Europe. This period made him the Reformed theologian *par excellence* and, alongside Luther, the most influential single teacher of the entire Reformation. Both his training in law and the organisational powers he unsuspectingly possessed, together with his sharp eye for what was decisive in theological and practical issues, made him without (or even against) his will the framer alike of the greatest systematic theology of the Reformation and of the Reformed church order – to say nothing of his immense labours in biblical commentary, in lecturing and preaching week by week.[4]

These biographical and personal details are not without relevance for Calvin's treatment of the Eucharist, as of many other theological topics. Judicious scholarship accompanied by a lively sense for the heart of the matter set him free alike from the trap of simple literalism and from the temptations of a superficial rationalism, and gave him the freedom to tackle the questions afresh in their theological and practical bearing. The resulting independence can already be recognised in the 1536 *Institute* where, without naming names, Calvin nevertheless feels free to criticise and distance himself from positions taken up by Luther, Zwingli and others. Four years later he published his *Short Treatise on the Holy Supper*, and in the fifth and closing chapter came directly to address 'The Present Dispute'.[5]

He begins by stressing how regrettable the whole controversy is, and his hope that it can soon be forgotten. For this reason he does not want to rake over the whole history and argument yet again, but simply to give the necessary orientation to those of the faithful who have been unsettled and confused by the whole matter. So, to come to the debatable land itself:

> When Luther began to teach, he regarded the matter of the Supper in such a way, that, with respect to the corporal presence of Christ, he appeared ready to leave it as the world generally thought it. For while condemning transubstantiation, he said that the bread was the body of Christ, insofar as it was united with him. Further, he added some similes which were a little harsh and rude. But he did so as by constraint, because he could not otherwise explain his meaning. For it is difficult to give an explanation of so high a matter, without using some impropriety of speech.
>
> On the other hand, there arose Zwingli and Oecolampadius, who, considering the abuse and deceit which the devil had employed to establish such a carnal presence of Christ as had been taught and held for more than six hundred years, thought it wrong to dissimulate; since this view implied an execrable idolatry, in that Jesus Christ was adored as if enclosed under the bread. Now because it was very difficult to remove this opinion, rooted so long in the hearts of men, they applied all their mind to decry it, remonstrating that it was a gross error not to acknowledge what is so clearly testified in Scripture, concerning the ascension of Jesus Christ, that he was in his humanity received up into heaven, where he dwells until he descend to judge the world. While they were absorbed with this point, they forgot to define what is the presence of Christ in the Supper in which one ought to believe, and what communication of his body and blood

one there received. So Luther thought that they intended to leave nothing else but bare signs without any corresponding spiritual substance. Hence he began to resist and oppose them, even to the extent of denouncing them as heretics. . . .

Here we have the reason, then, why Luther failed on his side, and Oecolampadius and Zwingli on theirs. It was Luther's duty, in the first place, to make it clear that he did not intend to set up such a local presence as the papists imagine; second, he should have protested that he did not mean the sacrament to be adored instead of God; and third he should have abstained from the similes so harsh and difficult to conceive, or have used them with moderation, interpreting them so that they could not occasion offence. Once the debate was taken up, he went beyond measure . . . . For instead of explaining himself so that his opinion could be understood, with his accustomed violence in attacking those who contradicted him, he used exaggerated forms of speech, which were certainly hard to bear by those who otherwise were not very disposed to believe what he said.

The others offended also, by being so eager to decry the contrary opinion of the papists concerning the local presence of the body of Jesus Christ as superstitious and fantastic, and the adoration which followed from it as perverse, that they laboured more to destroy the evil than to build up the good. . . . I mean that in taking too great pains to maintain that the bread and wine are called the body and blood of Christ because they are signs, they took no care to make the reservation that they are such signs that the reality is joined to them; or to protest that they did not at all intend to obscure the true communion which our Lord gives us in his body and blood by the sacrament.

Calvin then concludes the chapter (and the *Treatise*) by looking to the future:

. . . it has pleased God at last, having humbled them thus, to bring to an end this unhappy disputation, or at least to calm it, in anticipation of it being quite resolved. I say this because there is not yet any published formula in which agreement has been framed, as would be expedient. But this will happen when God is pleased to bring into one place all those who are to draw it up. Meanwhile, it must content us that there is brotherliness and communion between the Churches, and that all agree in what is necessary for meeting together, according to the command of God.

We all confess, then, with one mouth that, in receiving the sacrament in faith, according to the ordinance of the Lord, we are

truly made partakers of the real substance of the body and blood
of Christ. How this is done, some may deduce better and explain
more clearly than others. But be this as it may, on the one hand
we must, to shut out all carnal fancies, raise our hearts on high to
heaven, not thinking that our Lord Jesus Christ is so abased as to
be enclosed under any corruptible elements. On the other hand,
not to diminish the efficacy of this sacred mystery, we must hold
that it is accomplished by the secret and miraculous virtue of God,
and that the Spirit of God is the bond of participation, for which
reason it is called spiritual.

It became a major part of Calvin's own programme over the
following years to try to bring about just such an agreement. Genuine
participation in the body and blood of Christ through the signs, which
are certainly to be *distinguished* but not *separated* from the reality joined
to them, constitutes the heart of the matter; and it is very apparent here
how far Calvin is from Zwingli. He also firmly and decisively rejects
Zwingli's earlier reduction of a sacrament to an expression of faith:[52]
this, as he had already stated in the 1536 *Institute*, is to make what is a
genuine but secondary element in a sacrament the only one, to overlook
that a sacrament is primarily God's sign of his promise, given precisely to
awaken and strengthen faith. Along the same line lies his insistence that
the Eucharist is a *mystery*, and his implicit subordination of *explanation* to
apprehension, recognition, acceptance of that mystery of communion with
Christ. There is also a special weight in his insistence that the Eucharist is
'spiritual' because it is *the Spirit of God* who brings about the union
between Christ and us. The unspoken implication is that the contrast
between flesh and spirit in John 6 should not be scaled down into an
antithesis between the physical/material on the one hand and the
'spirituality' of faith on the other. The real difference is between Creator
and creature.

In all of these respects excepting the last, which represents a
deepening of Zwingli's argument, Calvin is recognisably closer to
Luther than to Zwingli; but Luther's position cannot entirely satisfy
him. The essential question here is the nature of the humanity of Christ:
Luther is in danger, to put it no higher, of propagating a new
Marcionism, a form of gnosis which turns the human nature of Christ
into something of an utterly different nature from any human nature
otherwise known to us, of evaporating his individual particularity and
corporeality into a diffused ubiquity of a sort that would in effect
'spiritualise' him, turn him into something other than he is witnessed to
in the New Testament, the Word of God made flesh in the specific,
human individual Jesus Christ, incarnate, crucified, risen and ascended.
What happens to the overall message of the New Testament if, in the

interests of a particular interpretation of the words of institution, such a construction as the doctrine of ubiquity is spun out? Is this not precisely, Calvin asked, to distort the message in the interests of a theory? Is it not soteriologically vital to hold to the true, concrete and particular human nature, human body of Christ, and not to turn it into something else? To put it at its most pointed, where is our hope of resurrection, the resurrection of the body, if we do not firmly and properly hold to the risen corporeality of Jesus himself, and reject the temptation to transform it in this fashion? Luther could have argued, and certainly felt, that it was soteriologically vital to hold to the physical presence 'in' or 'with' or 'under' the bread to guarantee our own union with Christ; but Calvin detected here an undercutting of the real meaning of union with Christ through a misdirection of the question, through locating the problem in the wrong place, and asking too hurriedly about *the connexion between the body of Christ and the bread* instead of setting that issue in the wider and deeper horizon of *the whole relation between Christ and us*. The doctrine of ubiquity was only one of a whole string of false answers dreamt up for the wrong question. Attention must be directed again to the nature of the promise which the Eucharist holds out:

The sacrament does not make Christ the bread of life, but each time it calls to our remembrance that he has been made the bread by which we are constantly fed, it supplies us with the taste and savour of that bread. Again, it promises us that whatever Christ did and suffered, he did and suffered that we might be made alive. Finally, that this vivification is eternal, and by it we are nourished, sustained and preserved unendingly in life. For indeed, just as Christ would not have been the bread of life for us unless he had been born and had died for us, unless he had risen for us; so too he would not be that bread now, unless the effect and fruit of his birth, death and resurrection were an eternal and immortal reality.

If this force of the sacrament had been expressed and pondered as it deserved to be, there was plenty and more in it to satisfy us; nor would those appalling dissensions have been stirred up by which both in the past and within our own memory the church has been troubled, when busy-bodies wanted to define how the body of Christ is present in the bread. Some, in order to show their acuity, added to the simplicity of Scripture that he is present 'in reality and substance' (*realiter et substantialiter*); some went even further: present 'in the same dimensions with which he hung on the cross'; some thought up the monstrosity of transubstantiation; some, that the bread is the body itself; some, that it is under the bread; some, that only a sign and figure of the body is held forth.

... Yet those who thought in this way did not notice that the first thing to ask was how the body of Christ, as it was given for us, becomes ours, how the blood, as it was poured out for us, becomes ours. That is in truth to possess the whole crucified Christ and to be made participant in all his benefits. Now that matters of such moment have been left to the side, yes neglected and near buried, this one thorny question is fought over: how is his body eaten by us?[6]

This quotation from the 1536 *Institute*, written before Calvin himself became in any way personally involved in the debate, expresses the stance he adopted from the first, and maintained consistently thereafter. Neither the 'affixing' of the body to the bread nor the reduction of the bread to a 'mere sign' would do, for the first focuses attention too much on the bread, the second also focuses on the bread, but negatively, and so misses the point. Zwingli is right in what he denies concerning the bread, but wrong in his overall view of the Eucharist; Luther is nearer the mark in his overall view, but wrong in his attempt to identify the body with the bread, in which, whatever the differences in detail, he follows the line of his medieval predecessors.

In this perspective, two other elements in Calvin's position and argument fall into place. First, the insistence, in which he reflects but at the same time deepens Zwingli's position, that it is the Spirit of God who brings about the union between Christ and us. Against Luther's carrying-forward of the Western tradition, which focussed on the words, 'This is my body', and therefore sought in some fashion to 'bring the body of Christ into the Eucharist', Calvin took up again the insight of the Eastern tradition and the Greek fathers, pointing to the need for a proper place for the *epiclesis* of the Spirit in the eucharistic celebration. It is the Holy Spirit who is both the 'bond of union between the Father and the Son' (Augustine) and the 'bond of participation' in Christ in which we are joined with him. Calvin's eucharistic theology seeks to be properly trinitarian, whereas Luther's remains somewhat christomonistic, and ascribes to the human nature of Christ a characteristic that properly belongs to God as God. There is here a serious structural weakness in Luther's whole theology which Calvin more than any other Reformer diagnosed and corrected, not only in respect of the Eucharist, but in the whole broad theological framework. It would take us too far from our subject to develop this theme in the detail it requires, but a quotation from the final (1559) edition of the *Institute* may serve to show what is meant:

We must now see in what way we become possessed of the blessings which God has bestowed on his only begotten Son. . . . And the first thing to be attended to is, that so long as we are

without Christ and separated from him, nothing which he
suffered and did for the salvation of the human race is of the least
benefit to us. To communicate to us the blessings which he
received from the Father, he must become ours and dwell in us.
. . . the very nature of the case teaches us that we must ascend
higher and inquire into the secret efficacy of the Spirit, to which it
is owing that we enjoy Christ and all his blessings. . . . until our
minds are intent on the Spirit, Christ is in a manner unemployed,
because we view him coldly without us and at a distance from us
. . . it is by the Spirit alone that he unites himself to us. By the
same grace and energy of the Spirit we become his members, so
that he keeps us under him, and we in our turn possess him. (*Inst.*
III.i.1; 3)

Not an *extension of the humanity of Christ* but the *uniting and unifying
activity and energy of the Spirit of God* is what counts. It is neither necessary
nor appropriate to take Luther's path: he has fallen into the short-circuit
of a false objectivism, as Zwingli into an equally false subjectivism.
Neither gives the objective presence and reality, power and working of
the Holy Spirit its due place. Consequently Luther substitutes the
presence of Christ's physical body for union with him by the Spirit;
Zwingli dissolves the Spirit into the spirituality of faith; and Calvin
judges that neither does justice to the heart of the matter.

   The other aspect of Calvin's argument which now falls into place is
his criticism of medieval thinking (and indirectly, of Luther) on the
matter of a purported 'local' presence of Christ. This must at first sight
seem somewhat puzzling, as we have seen how both Aquinas and Luther
in their different ways avoided 'localising' the body of Christ. Calvin
was not so ignorant as to be unaware of that, though he was not
impressed by the cogency of either of the arguments advanced. But the
question still remains: why does he stress *local* presence as a grievous
error?[6a] The answer is not far to seek: he felt that the sophistication of the
arguments adduced, whether in respect of an incorporeal 'substance' or
an 'indefinite' 'true body' was inherently strained to the point of
absurdity and in any case far too rarified to be generally comprehensible.
In effect, all such theories served to reinforce a simple identification of
body with bread and bread with body – with the corollary that what
happens to the eucharistic elements also happen to the true body and
blood: they are eaten and drunk with the mouth of the communicants
(what was called the *manducatio oralis*), and, if one pursues the matter
consistently through to the end, even by those who receive the
sacrament without faith, in godlessness (the *manducatio impiorum*). Such a
conclusion seemed to him doubly unacceptable. First, by reducing
Christ in his body and blood to the victim of whatever happened to the

elements, it was both 'unworthy of his heavenly majesty' and a reduction to nonsense of the affirmation of his genuine humanness. Second, because Christ himself is the reality, the 'substance' and 'matter' of the sacrament, it is impossible for genuine participation in the sacramental reality to be other than salvific: he who eats and drinks unworthily can only receive in Calvin's view – here according with Augustine's – the *sign* of the divine promise, but not the *reality*, which can bring only salvation, but only to those who receive it in faith.

In view of these two critical reservations, the answers which became standard in Lutheranism must be mentioned. To take the second first: it eventually became the normative Lutheran view that all those who receive the eucharistic bread and wine do indeed receive the body and blood of Christ – but that only those who receive them in faith also receive what in medieval terms would be called the *res sacramenti* – not simply *the body and blood*, but *the forgiveness of sins*. In other words, the Lutheran doctrine does not offer such a solid assurance as might at first appear: one may indeed receive the true body and blood to one's own damnation. Against that, it was Calvin's conviction that he who truly receives the body and blood receives only salvation, not condemnation. To eat and drink the body and blood of Christ, who is himself the 'substance' or 'matter' of the sacrament, is to be savingly united with him, nothing else or less. Where and when this does not occur, the body and blood are not eaten or drunk. The Lutheran view gives the true body and blood to all who receive the sacrament, but this must then remain an ambivalent gift which does not guarantee a saving union with Christ: 'This is my body' can pave the way to hell as well as to heaven; which Calvin finds wholly unacceptable. In other words, there is no such clear 'advantage' to the Lutheran theory as its advocates have commonly imagined, for it offers no more 'objective' guarantee than does the sacramental 'sign' in Calvin's account. More seriously, the Lutheran theory drives back into the medieval distinction between the true body and blood of Christ and the authentic 'matter' of the sacrament, the forgiveness of sins, in a way which Calvin felt compelled to reject.

The other Lutheran counter has recently been formulated in a statement describing 'the Lutheran identity',[7] which in its initial thesis asserts a specifically Lutheran emphasis on the 'condescension' of God and the 'physicality' of the sacraments:

> God, the Creator of the world, comes to men and women for their salvation in his Son Jesus Christ. Disguised in weakness, he gives himself up to them and allows them to grasp him in the incarnation and humanity of Jesus, in his suffering and death on the cross for our sake. . . . For all times he creates faith by means of

the human character of the Word and the physical character of the sacraments through the Holy Spirit.

The appended commentary on the 'Historical and Present Context' adds:

By stressing God's stooping to us in Jesus Christ, the Lutheran Reformation aimed to counter, for example, the speculative currents within Catholic (sic) theology, false inwardness of the 'enthusiasts' and even specific aspects of Reformed theology: the focus was on the essence of the biblical message, the fact that in the saving encounter between God and human beings, God takes the entire initiative. God comes to us – we do not approach God through an effort of thought or mystical immersion. Thanks to the divine incarnation in Jesus of Nazareth, the meeting-point between God and men and women takes place in the finite, bodily sphere of this world. This fact determines the Lutheran view of God's Word as a word of human utterance, and of the sacraments as places of divine encounter precisely in their earthly elements.

Where precisely does the point of the implied critique of Reformed theology lie? The suggestion appears to be that the Reformed approach does not do justice to the scale and scope of the divine condescension that stoops to meet us in the very physicality of the sacramental elements, and consequently attempts to reach up to God through an 'effort of thought or mystical immersion' or, in Calvin's frequent language, by raising our hearts and minds to heaven where Christ is seated at the right hand of the Father, instead of recognising him where he meets us in humbleness, in, with and under bread and wine, in the 'finite, bodily sphere of this world'.

There is certainly a good deal that can be disputed in this (implied) characterisation of Reformed theology. To speak of the Holy Spirit as the bond of union with Christ is hardly the same as to urge 'an effort of thought' of 'mystical immersion'! Nor is it a proper interpretation of Calvin's urging that we 'lift up our hearts' to see it as an attempt to pull ourselves up to heaven by our own efforts; he can also, and equally rightly affirm that Christ 'descends to us, as well by the external symbol as by his Spirit' (*Inst.* IV.xvii.24), and it is clear that it is only on the basis of that movement of condescension that we can lift our eyes upwards. Nor, finally, is the Lutheran habit of drawing a direct line from the incarnation to the presence of the true body in the sacramental elements without its own problematic features, here resembling those of the similar Roman Catholic inclination to treat the church as an extension of the incarnation. But even if this analysis is too drastically simplified to be accepted as an adequate diagnosis, it can serve to draw attention to a certain legacy of lingering dualism which even Calvin did not entirely overcome, and which led him on occasion when speaking of the sacramental signs to distinguish so sharply between them and the reality that the connexion (on which he also insisted) could fall into the background. Then the signs could *appear* to be what he vigorously insisted they were not – 'naked and bare signs', rather than concrete vehicles of the promise which Jesus Christ himself is. Certainly, such an interpretation of him does not do justice to his intentions or indeed to his own statements. He, and the direction of thinking he represented and influenced, was no less insistent than contemporary Lutherans on the centrality of the incarnation, on genuine union with Christ, and on the setting of the Eucharist in that horizon – and so on the fact that the elements were *not* 'mere signs'. One witness speaking particularly vigorously here is the *Scots Confession* of 1560, in ch. 21:[7a]

> These sacraments . . . were instituted by God . . . to exercise the faith of his children and, by participation of these sacraments, to seal in their hearts the assurance of his promise, and of that most blessed conjunction, union and society, which the chosen have with their Head, Christ Jesus. And so we utterly condemn the vanity of those who affirm the sacraments to be nothing else than naked and bare signs. No, we assuredly believe . . . that in the Supper rightly used, Christ Jesus is so joined with us that he becomes the very nourishment and food of our souls. Not that we imagine any transubstantiation . . . but this union and conjunction which we have with the body and blood of Christ Jesus . . . is wrought by means of the Holy Ghost, who by true faith carries us above all things that are visible, carnal and earthly, and makes us feed upon the body and blood of Christ Jesus, once broken and shed for us but now in heaven, and appearing for us in the presence of his Father . . . Thus we confess and believe without doubt that the faithful, in the right use of the Lord's Table, do so eat the body and drink the blood of the Lord Jesus that he remains in them and they in him; they are so made flesh of his flesh and bone of his bone that as the eternal Godhood has given to the flesh of Christ Jesus, which by nature was corruptible and mortal, life and immortality, so the eating and drinking of the flesh and blood of Christ Jesus does the like for us . . . . Therefore, if anyone slanders us by saying that we affirm or believe the sacraments to be naked and bare signs, he is libellous and speaks against the plain facts.

At the same time there is a recognisable difference in emphasis between this and what appears to be the primary Lutheran concern. The latter moves, as it were, downwards: condescension, incarnation, leading to a stress on the physicality of the sacramental element; the other traces a movement downward *and* upward: condescension *and* elevation, incarnation *and* resurrection/ascension, and so stresses the distinction between the 'earthly' and the 'heavenly'. Here, if anywhere, lay the reason for the Lutheran mistrust, which, however, Calvin aimed and hoped to allay.

The attempt involved him in a campaign on two fronts, the Swiss as well as the German. It must soon have become clear to him that the going would be stiffer than he imagined when he wrote the *Short Treatise*, for 1541 brought a renewed and sharply acrimonious exchange between Luther and Heinrich Bullinger, Zwingli's successor in Zürich; and in 1544, two years before his death, Luther launched a final attack in his *Short Confession*. That, however, was only one side of the story. Calvin knew himself to be close to Melanchthon's view; and it is also reported that Luther himself was much impressed by the *Short Treatise* when he read it in 1545, remarking, 'Certainly a learned and pious man! I could have entrusted the whole matter of this debate to him. ... If Zwingli and Oecolampadius had expressed themselves thus at the beginning, we could have come to an agreement.'[8] That agreement remained Calvin's aim.

On the Swiss side he was finally able to reach his goal. The turning-point came in 1549 with the *Consensus Tigurinus*, the 'Zürich Consensus', hammered out between him and Bullinger. The *Consensus* consists of 26 articles.[9] The way in which they are ordered is significant: they fall into four groups, namely §§1–5; 6–9; 10–20; 21–26. §§1–5 lay the theological foundation for the whole by speaking, not right away about the Eucharist, or even about sacraments in general, but about Jesus Christ, in the conviction that a proper understanding of the sacraments must rest upon a due appreciation of who he is and how we are related to him (§2). He communicates himself to us, makes us one with himself as members of his body, and does so by the power of the Holy Spirit (§§3; 5).

§§6–9 then deal generally with the nature of the sacraments of Baptism and the Supper, stressing that they testify to 'the spiritual communication' by which Christ lives in us and gives all believers a share in the benefits subsisting in him (§6). Their primary purpose is *not* to be 'signs and badges of our profession' – though they are that as well – but lies in the fact that 'through them God himself testifies, represents and seals his grace to us' (§7). The Lord truly performs and guarantees what the sacraments 'figure' (§8), so that while 'sign' and 'reality' are to be distinguished, they are by no means to be separated (§9).

§§10–20 continue to deal with the nature of a sacrament, but are intended chiefly to draw necessary boundaries, to rule out any excessive or misplaced confidence in the power of sacraments by themselves to mediate salvation. What we are above all called to recognise in them is the divine promise that awakens faith and makes us sharers in Christ (§10), not the elements seen in themselves apart from him (§11); for the sacraments by themselves effect nothing – it is God alone who works through them (§12) and uses them as his instruments (§13). Strictly we must say that it is *Christ* who inwardly baptises, who makes us participant in himself, who fulfils what the sacraments represent, so that their whole power and working rests with his Spirit (§14). The effectiveness ascribed to the sacraments belongs to them only secondarily and derivatively; in the primary and proper sense it is of God's Spirit, and no portion of our salvation is to be transferred from its unique author to created elements (§15). It follows that not all who receive a sacrament receive the reality (§16); the sacraments do not automatically confer grace on all who do not actually put an obstacle in its way, as the medieval teaching asserted (§17); for the gifts of God are indeed *offered* to all, but *received* only through faith (§18). Finally, the faithful have communion in Christ before and apart from the use of the sacraments as well as in it (§19), and the benefits are not tied to the precise moment of reception, but may bear fruit later (§20).

All that is said, both in §§6-9 and §§10-20, is essentially in line with Luther's rejection of medieval sacramental theory and his reorientation of the matter around the theme of 'a sign given by God to confirm his promise and directed towards faith'. But it has a further latent force; for what is said here (consistently with Luther) about 'sacrament' and 'sign' *also* applies specifically to the eucharistic bread and wine. It is this that is then explicitly drawn out in the last five articles, which all deal with the Eucharist directly.

Every kind of 'local presence' is a fictitious fantasy which must be rejected (§21) for Christ in his human nature is finite and has his 'place' in heaven (§25). It is beyond all question that the words, 'This is my body', are to be taken figuratively (§22). The eating of Christ's flesh and drinking of his blood cannot mean or imply any 'mixture or transfusion of substance' from him to us, but rather that we draw our life from the body once sacrificed and the blood once poured out for our expiation (§23). Transubstantiation is to be rejected, and with it, all other absurdities inconsistent alike with Christ's heavenly glory and the reality of his human nature; in particular it is fully as ridiculous to locate him under the bread or bind him to it as it is to transubstantiate the bread into his body (§24). Finally, Christ is by no means to be worshipped in the bread; to venerate the sacrament with the intention of venerating him is to make it an idol (§26).

It was Calvin's hope that this agreement, somewhat laboriously negotiated with Bullinger, might supply the basis for a wider consensus among the Protestants generally. In the longer run, however, his success on the Swiss side was not to be matched by a similar agreement on the Lutheran, in spite of Melanchthon's sympathy for and closeness to Calvin's position. Other voices than Melanchthon's were to call the tune on the Lutheran side in the following decades. This was foreshadowed in the attacks launched on Calvin and the *Consensus Tigurinus* in the following years from somewhat extreme, not to say obscurantist Lutheran quarters. The first shots were fired by Joachim Westphal in his *Farrago of Confused and Mutually Contradictory Opinions concerning the Supper of the Lord, Culled from the Books of the Sacramentarians* (1552). This initiated a debate with Calvin which lasted until Calvin's *Last Warning to Joachim Westphal* (1557) – after which Calvin gave him up as a hopeless case. Westphal made no significant difference between Zwingli, Calvin and all the other Reformed theologians he cited, and took notice of divergences between them only as demonstrating the hopeless inconsistencies of their common position. They were all 'sacramentarians', that is, they all treated the eucharistic elements under the category of 'sacrament' or 'sign' instead of taking the words of institution in the only proper, i.e. literal sense. Against them, he intoned the old song of the *Ego Berengarius* recantations in the 11th century: the flesh and blood of Christ are so literally eaten and drunk that we must affirm that they are 'chewed with the teeth'; Christ's human nature is ubiquitous, though present *extra locum*, 'outside place'; whoever receives the sacrament, with or without faith, eats and drinks the true body and blood of Christ himself.

The exchange with Westphal is of significance only in two negative respects. First, it led Calvin in the final (1559) edition of the *Institute* to devote a great deal of space to rejecting such wild views (*Inst.* IV.xvii.17ff). Second, it helped to prepare the ground for the undiscriminating condemnation of the Reformed doctrine of the Eucharist in the Lutheran *Formula of Concord* of 1577. Calvin himself did not anticipate that matters would take such a sorry course, though yet a further controversial exchange was to show how the tide was beginning to run in Germany. This brings us to Tileman Heshusius and the Heidelberg Controversy of 1559 and its consequences.

Heshusius was Superintendent of the church in Heidelberg, but deposed by the Elector in 1559 because of his private feud with the Dean, Klebitz. Klebitz held to the presence of the body and blood of Christ 'with' the bread and wine, but not 'in' or 'under'. Heshusius was certainly less extreme than Westphal had been: he rejected the doctrine of ubiquity and the idea that Christ's body is 'chewed with the teeth'. He did, however, insist on the presence 'in, with and under' the elements, on the *oralis manducatio* and the *manducatio impiorum*. His deposition (along with Klebitz) was provoked less by their theological disagreement than by its manifestation when Heshusius sought to tear the chalice from Klebitz' hands during the celebration. The Elector then asked Melanchthon to give a judgment on the matter; part of Melanchthon's answer ran as follows:[10]

> The Son of God is present in the ministry of the gospel, and he is certainly effectively there in believers, and he is not present for the sake of the bread, but for the sake of man, as he says, 'Remain in me and I in you.' Again, 'I am in my Father, and you in me, and I in you.' And in these true consolations he makes us his members and testifies that he will give life to our bodies. Thus do the ancients expound the Lord's Supper.
>
> Yet some find this true and simple doctrine of the fruit too ethereal and demand to be told whether the body is in the bread or in the *species* of the bread. As if indeed the sacrament were instituted for the sake of the bread and that papistical veneration! Then they invent ways of enclosing it in the bread: some have thought up 'conversion', some 'transubstantiation', some 'ubiquity'. All these monstrosities were unknown to the ancient learning.

This shows how clearly Melanchthon had by now aligned himself with the position of Calvin. A further consequence of the Heidelberg Controversy was his recommendation that the young theologians Olevianus and Ursinus should be called there, both then played a major role in the formulation of the *Heidelberg Catechism*, which in §§75-82 gives a splendid statement of the Calvin/Melanchthon teaching on the Eucharist. The *Catechism* was then, however, bitterly opposed within Germany on the ground that its teaching was inconsistent with the *Confessio Augustana*; and this too served to harden the front of Lutheranism against the Reformed.

A further consequence of the controversy was the polemical tract of Heshusius, *On the Presence of the Body of Christ in the Lord's Supper against the Sacramentarians* to which Calvin replied, at Bullinger's request, in 1561 with his *Clear Explanation of Sound Doctrine .... to Dissipate the Mists of Tileman Heshusius*, a work which shows Calvin with all his rhetorical power and his capacity to reduce the opposed position to the object of devastating ridicule. This, too, certainly had a negative effect on future relations between the Lutheran and Reformed movements – though Calvin himself had no such aim, still believing it possible to distinguish between the individual views of an Heshusius and those of the broad Lutheran party. He appended to the *Clear Exposition* a statement of very different tone entitled *The Best Method of Obtaining Concord*, in which he summarised and explained his position, and once more expressed the conviction that an open and unprejudiced exploration of the matter could do away with all cause for contention.

By now, however, this was a lost and forlorn hope. Melanchthon was already dead, and his followers being driven to the wall in the internal Lutheran wranglings. By the time of the *Formula of Concord* in 1577, which sought to restore the unity of Lutheranism, their influence had dwindled to insignificance. The *Formula*, in the seventh chapter of the *Epitome* dealing with the Supper, asserted that the key question was:

> Whether in the Holy Supper the true body and blood of our Lord
> Jesus Christ is truly and substantially present, distributed with
> bread and wine and received with the mouth by all who make use
> of the sacrament, whether worthy or unworthy, pious or
> impious, believing or unbelieving – for the consolation and life of
> believers, for the judgment of unbelievers? The sacramentarians
> say No, we say Yes.

It went on to distinguish between 'gross sacramentarians' (such as Zwingli) and the Trojan Horse of the 'surreptitious sacramentarians, the most harmful of all' (which means such as Calvin and Melanchthon), 'who appear to speak with our words', yet really only believe in the presence of bread and wine. Then followed a lengthy and rather jumbled series of denunciations and affirmations demonstrating more than anything else how impossible it was on this basis to understand, let alone meet constructively with the concerns of Calvin and Reformed theology. So, thirteen years after his death, his attempt at mediation and reconciliation proved unsuccessful.

*   *   *   *   *

In the foregoing account we have already touched on the main aspects of Calvin's teaching on 'sacrament' and 'presence' (though not, so far, 'sacrifice'). But it may now be useful to summarise very briefly his handling of all three themes in the 1559 edition of the *Institute*, Book IV, chapters xiv and xvii–xviii. Ch. xiv deals with the nature of a sacrament; xvii with the nature of Christ's presence; xviii with the interpretation of the Mass as sacrifice; and so give us here his systematic treatment of the three main themes which we traced earlier in medieval theology and in Luther.

(a) *Sacrament*

Calvin begins by offering his own definition, which echoes but also develops Luther's:

> It seems to me . . . a simple and appropriate definition to say that it
> is an external sign by which the Lord seals on our consciences his
> promises of goodwill towards us in order to sustain the weakness

of our faith; and we in turn testify our piety towards him. . . . We
may also define more briefly by calling it a testimony of the
divine favour towards us, confirmed by an external sign, with a
corresponding attestation of our faith towards him. (xiv. 1)

A sacrament is thus located and defined within the Reformation horizon
of Word/promise/testimony and faith, and Calvin, like Luther, takes up
again Augustine's saying, *accedit verbum ad elementum et fit sacramentum*,
carefully noting at the same time that the word in question is not a
'magical incantation' which 'consecrates the element', but 'one which,
preached, makes us understand what the visible sign means' (xiv. 4). A
sacrament is thus 'a visible word because it represents the promises of the
God as in a picture, and places them in view in graphic, bodily form'
(xiv. 6).

Calvin marks this understanding off from two others. On his left, so
to speak, were those Protestants who, as Zwingli had done, treated
sacraments essentially as *expressions of our faith*; on his right the Roman
Catholics, who held them to be *effective causes of the grace they signified*.
Much of ch. xiv is taken up with these frontiers, §§5-13 being directed
chiefly against the left, §§14-17 against the right. He can agree neither
with those who 'impair the force and altogether overthrow the use of
the sacraments' nor with 'the others who ascribe to the sacraments a kind
of secret power which is nowhere said to have been implanted in them
by God' (xiv. 14). Rather it must be seen on the one hand that the
sacraments are given to strengthen faith, not merely to express it; on the
other, that the energy making them effective is that of God's Spirit, not
of the sacraments themselves:

. . . in assigning this office to the sacraments, it is not as if I thought
that there is a kind of secret efficacy perpetually inherent in them,
by which they can of themselves promote or strengthen faith;
but it is because our Lord has instituted them for the express
purpose of helping to establish and increase our faith. The
sacraments duly perform their office only when accompanied by
the Spirit, the internal master, whose energy alone penetrates the
heart, stirs up the affections, and procures access for the
sacraments into our souls. If he is lacking, the sacraments can avail
us no more than the sun shining on the eyeballs of the blind, or
sounds uttered in the ears of the deaf. Wherefore in distributing
between the Spirit and the sacraments, I ascribe the whole energy
to him and leave only a ministry to them . . . (xiv. 9)

This activity of God's Spirit is apprehended in the faith which the Spirit
enables, so that 'in order that you may not have the sign devoid of truth,
but the reality with the sign, the word which is included in it must be
apprehended by faith' (xiv. 15). So Calvin bluntly dismisses the

medieval theory of the effective working of the sacraments – the teaching that 'the sacraments of the new law . . . justify and confer grace, provided only that we do not interpose the obstacle of mortal sin' (xiv. 14).

> This sentiment . . . is plainly of the devil; for first, in promising a righteousness without faith, it drives souls headlong on destruction; second, in deriving a cause of righteousness from the sacraments, it entangles miserable minds, already of their own accord too much inclined to the earth, in a superstitious idea which makes them acquiesce in the spectacle of a corporeal object rather than in God himself. (xiv. 14)

Calvin goes on to reject the description of sacraments as 'causes of righteousness', the classic medieval distinction between the sacraments of the old law and the new in terms of 'signs' and 'effective causes', and the doctrine of the *opus operatum*;

> I say that Christ is the 'matter', or, if you rather choose, the substance of all the sacraments; for in him they have their whole solidity, and apart from him they promise nothing. Hence the less toleration is due to the error of Peter Lombard, who distinctly makes them causes of the righteousness and salvation of which they are parts. . . . the office of the sacraments differs not from that of the Word of God; and this is to hold forth and offer Christ to us, and in him the treasures of heavenly grace. (xiv. 16-17)

> The ancient sacraments had the same end in view as our own – viz. to direct and almost lead us by the hand to Christ. . . . There is only this difference, that while the former shadowed forth the promised Christ while he was still expected, the latter bear testimony to him as already come and manifested. . . . The scholastic dogma . . . by which . . . the difference is made so great that the former did nothing but shadow forth the grace of God while the latter actually confer it, must be altogether exploded. (xiv. 20; 23)

> . . . all the trifling talk of the sophists concerning the *opus operatum* is not only false but repugnant to the very nature of the sacraments, which God appointed in order that believers, who are void and in want of all good, might bring nothing of their own, but simply beg. Hence it follows that in receiving them they do nothing that deserves praise, and that in this action (which in respect of them is merely passive) no 'work' can be ascribed to them. (xiv. 26)

This last quotation shows how complex and many-layered were the conflicts between the medieval and Reformation perceptions. If the interpretation of the *opus operatum* quoted in our last chapter is correct, then it does not mean what Calvin here takes it to mean – the performance of a 'good work' by the celebrant or recipient of a sacrament. Rather it points to the objective activity of God – and Calvin, too, is concerned to preserve the objectivity and primacy of the divine action, and to set the sacraments in that light. Yet even with this qualification, the differences are not in the end removed. The objectivity of a sacrament is, for Calvin, as for Luther, twofold: the objectivity of the divine promise and the attached sign, and the objectivity of the working of the Holy Spirit evoking and nourishing faith through the sacrament. Only reception *in faith*, not reception *without faith*, is to be ascribed to the work of the Spirit; only there might one speak of an *opus operatum* in the sense actually intended by medieval thought, but not in the case of a mere 'valid' performance and reception of the sacrament *without* faith either then or following later. There, one must speak only of the holding forth of the authentic sign of the promise, not of its reception – and therefore not of a completed action, an *opus operatum* in the correct sense of medieval teaching. This shows clearly how the whole interpretative horizon had shifted, how the emphasis had moved from what is 'done' to what is 'received in faith'. The centre of the matter was not now sacramental grace, but Jesus Christ himself in his relation by his Spirit to those who believe in him.

Finally, as part of this same shift in perspective, Calvin is prepared only to admit Baptism and the Supper as sacraments in the strict sense. These, at any rate, are the 'ordinary sacraments', 'instituted for the use of the whole church. For the laying-on of hands by which the ministers of the church are initiated into their office, though I have no objection to its being called a sacrament, I do not number among ordinary sacraments' (xiv.20). The other medieval sacraments are dealt with in detail in *Inst.* IV.xix; Calvin's main ground for rejecting them *as sacraments* is the lack of proof of special divine institution and the suspicion that their 'sacramentality' is pure human invention. 'Man cannot institute a sacrament, because it is not in the power of man to make such divine mysteries lurk under things so abject' (xix.1). Only God can make a sign the pledge of his own promise. More is at stake here, however, than merely a point of constitutional legality, of whether or how far one can find a warrant for 'institution' in the New Testament, though that plays a considerable role in the argument. The reorientation of the very notion of 'sacrament' is also involved, and in particular the insistence that the divine promise to which the sacraments witness is nothing other than Jesus Christ himself. *That* is what now brings Baptism and the Eucharist to the fore in opposition to the medieval sense of a whole range and series of sacraments marking out all the key stages of the life of the individual and the church.

(b) *Presence*

Calvin's understanding of the presence of Christ is similar in structure to his conception of a sacrament; his treatment of the eucharistic elements is of a piece with his general understanding of sacramental 'signs' in their relation to the 'reality'. In this, he represents a consistent antithesis to medieval theology, where the teaching concerning the nature of a sacrament on the one hand, and the doctrine of transubstantiation on the other, reflect a parallel concern with objective presence 'in' the sacraments, 'in' the bread and wine. (Luther by contrast stands with Calvin on the general point of 'sacraments', but with the middle ages on the eucharistic 'presence'.) It is therefore natural that in respect of presence he should again mark off his position on two fronts:

> ... two faults are here to to be avoided. We must neither, by setting too little value on the signs, dissever them from their meanings, to which they are in some degree annexed, nor by immoderately extolling them, seem somewhat to obscure the mysteries themselves. (xvii.5)

The 'meaning' and 'mystery' is nothing other than the body and blood of Christ, given for us:

> We now then understand the end which this mystical benediction has in view – viz. to assure us that the body of Christ was once sacrificed for us, so that we may now eat it, and, eating, feel within ourselves the efficacy of that one sacrifice; that his blood was once shed for us so as to be our perpetual drink. (xvii.1)

> For these are words which can never lie or deceive: 'Take, eat, drink. This is my body which is broken for you; this is my blood which is shed for the remission of sins.' In bidding us take, he intimates that it is ours; in bidding us eat, he intimates that it becomes one substance with us; in affirming of his body that it was broken and of his blood that it was shed for us, he shows that both were not so much his own as ours, because he took and laid down both, not for his own advantage, but for our salvation. And we ought carefully to observe that the chief and almost the whole energy of the sacrament consists in these words, 'It is broken *for you*; it is shed *for you*.' (xvii. 3)

The bread and wine are indeed *signs* – but signs of a *reality* – that our life before God flows from the flesh and blood of Jesus Christ, that we are fed on his human nature in virtue of the 'wondrous exchange' by which, 'having become with us the Son of Man, he has made us with himself sons of God' (xvii.2). Calvin is adamant that this cannot be reduced simply to *believing* in him or sharing in his *Spirit*, for such reductions iron out the meaning of 'eating and drinking', 'flesh and blood', 'true communion' (xvii. 5; 7; 11). They do not do justice to

> a mystery which I feel, and therefore freely confess that I am
> unable to comprehend with my mind, so far am I from wishing
> anyone to measure its sublimity by my feeble capacity. No, I
> rather exhort my readers not to confine their apprehension within
> these too narrow limits, but to attempt to rise higher than I can
> guide them. For whenever this subject is considered, after I have
> done my utmost, I feel that I have spoken far beneath its dignity.
> And though the mind is more powerful in thought than the
> tongue in expression, it too is overcome and overwhelmed by the
> magnitude of its subject. All then that remains is to break forth in
> admiration of the mystery, which it is plain that the mind is
> inadequate to comprehend, or the tongue to express. (xvii.7)

Insofar as an explanation can be attempted at all, it must appeal to the power of the Holy Spirit truly to unite us with Christ:

> Therefore what our mind does not comprehend, let faith
> conceive – viz. that the Spirit truly unites things separated by
> space. That sacred communion of flesh and blood by which
> Christ transfuses his life into us, just as if it had penetrated our
> bones and marrow, he testifies and seals in the Supper, and that
> not by presenting a vain or empty sign, but by exerting an
> efficacy of the Spirit by which he performs what he promises.
> (xvii.10)

In all this, however, the true, concrete, physical humanity of Christ must not be lost to sight or transformed into something else in the interests of explaining this union and communion. Such theories are unnecessary, 'since the Lord by his Spirit bestows upon us the blessing of being one with him in soul, body and spirit. The bond of the connection, therefore, is the Spirit of Christ, who unites us to him, and is a kind of channel by which everything that Christ has and is is derived to us.' (xvii.12) As a general principle:

> The presence of Christ in the Supper we must hold to be such as
> neither affixes him to the element of bread, not encloses him in
> bread, nor circumscribes him in any way; for this would
> obviously detract from his heavenly glory. It must, moreover, be
> such as neither divests him of his just dimensions, nor dissevers
> him by differences of place, nor assigns to him a body of
> boundless dimensions, diffused through heaven and earth. All
> these things are clearly repugnant to his true human nature.
> (xviii.19)

The Roman and Lutheran theories must therefore be rejected as unworthy of the matter they seek to describe. 'I have no doubt that he

will truly give and I receive. Only I reject the absurdities which appear
to be unworthy of the heavenly majesty of Christ, and are inconsistent
with the reality of his human nature.' (xvii.) But, he adds:

> When these absurdities are discarded, I willingly admit anything
> which helps to express the true and substantial communication of
> the body and blood of the Lord, as exhibited to believers under
> the sacred symbols of the Supper, understanding that they are not
> received by the imagination or intellect alone, but are enjoyed in
> reality as the food of eternal life. (xvii.19)

There, rather than in the polemical negations developed at considerable
length in this chapter of the *Institute* lies the heart of Calvin's eucharistic
theology.

(c) *The Sacrifice of Praise*

In dealing with the sacrifice of the Mass in chapter xviii, Calvin nails
his colours firmly to the mast from the start, and in a way which echoes
both Luther and the generality of the Reformers before him:

> I am here combating that opinion with which the Roman Anti-
> christ and his prophets have imbued the whole world – viz. that
> the mass is a work by which the priest who offers Christ and the
> others who in the oblation receive him gain merit with God, or
> that it is an expiatory victim by which they regain the favour of
> God. And this is not merely the common opinion of the vulgar,
> but the very act has been so arranged as to be a kind of
> propitiation by which satisfaction is made to God for the living
> and the dead. . . . This mass, however glossed and splendid, offers
> the greatest insult to Christ, suppresses and buries his cross,
> consigns his death to oblivion, takes away the benefit which it
> was designed to convey, enervates and dissipates the sacraments
> by which the remembrance of his death was retained . . . (xviii.1)

Among his grounds, he stresses three in particular.

First, the only sacrifice which makes satisfaction to God for sins,
expiates them and makes him propitious to us, is that of Christ, offered
once and for all upon the cross. 'The Supper is the memento, or as it is
commonly expressed, the memorial, from which they may learn that
the expiatory victim by which God was to be appeased was to be offered
only once.' (xviii.6) Second – and this he calls 'the crowning point' – the
Supper is 'a gift of God which was to be received with thanksgiving, the
sacrifice of the mass pretends to give a price to God to be received as
satisfaction. As widely as giving differs from receiving does the sacrifice
differ from the sacrament of the Supper.' (xviii.7) 'The Lord therefore
has given us a table at which we may feast, not an altar on which a victim
may be offered; he has not consecrated priests to sacrifice, but ministers

to distribute a sacred feast.' (xviii.12) Third, this does not mean that there is no sense in which we 'offer' and 'sacrifice' to God, but a fundamental distinction is nevertheless to be drawn between two senses of the term 'sacrifice' itself. One kind may be called

> propitiatory or expiatory. A sacrifice of expiation is one whose object is to appease the wrath of God, to satisfy his justice, and thereby wipe and wash away sins, by which the sinner being cleansed and restored to purity may return to favour with God. (xviii.13)

> The other class, with the view of explaining, let us call *latreutikon* (worshipful) and *sebastikon* (reverential), as consisting of the veneration and worship which believers both owe and render to God; or if you prefer it, let us call it *eucharistikon*, since it is exhibited to God by none but those who, enriched with his boundless benefits, offer themselves and all their actions to him in return. (xviii.13)

The first of these is and can only be Christ's alone; the second which includes 'all prayers, praises, thanksgivings and every act of worship which we perform to God' (xviii.16), is ours. 'This is so necessary to the church that it cannot be dispensed with. It will endure for ever, so long as the people of God shall endure ... so far are we from doing away with *this* sacrifice.' (xviii.16) Further, 'This kind of sacrifice is indispensable in the Lord's Supper, in which, while we show forth his death and give him thanks, we offer nothing but praise.' (xviii.17)

In sum, we can only receive and give thanks for what Christ has done for us; there is an absolute qualitative difference between his one, atoning sacrifice and our sacrifice of thanks and praise. Here the Reformation sense of the uniqueness of the completed work of Christ finds its sharpest expression.

To complete the picture here, one more point must be stressed. Insofar as the category of sacrifice has its validity to describe Christian life and self-offering, it applies to *all* believers, not only, nor in any special sense, to ministers over against others. The concepts of 'sacrifice' and 'priesthood' apply primarily and uniquely *to Christ*, secondarily and in the sense just outlined *to all the members of his body*; they do *not* indicate a difference between 'clergy' and 'laity'. Calvin does indeed draw a sharper distinction than Luther between the calling of a minister as preacher and pastor and that of the baptized Christian; he stresses the divine institution of the office of the ministry, develops a clearly-outlined doctrine of ordination and lays great emphasis on the ordering of the ministry in the church. But the minister is not in any special or singular sense a 'priest', nor does he have the task of offering a distinctive 'sacrifice', but merely that of 'distributing a sacred feast' (xviii.12). One last quotation from his discussion of ecclesiastical orders in *Inst.* IV.xix may serve to make the point clear:

> Let us see how they wrest the ordinances of God to their own ends. We begin with the order of presbyter or priest. To these two names they give one meaning, understanding by them, those to whom, as they say, it pertains to offer the sacrifice of Christ's body and blood on the altar, to frame prayers, and bless the gifts of God. Hence, at ordination, they receive the patena with the host, as symbols of the power conferred upon them of offering sacrifices to appease God, and their hands are annointed, this symbol being intended to teach that they have received the power of consecrating. But of the ceremonies afterwards. Of the thing itself, I say that it is so far from having, as they pretend, one particle of support from the word of God, that they could not more wickedly corrupt the order which he has appointed. And first, it ought to be held ... that all are injurious to Christ who call themselves priests in the sense of offering expiatory victims. He was constituted and consecrated Priest by the Father, with an oath, after the order of Melchizedek, without end and without successor. He once offered a victim of eternal expiation and reconciliation, and now also having entered the sanctuary of heaven, he intercedes for us. In him we are all priests, but to offer praise and thanksgiving, in fine, ourselves, and all that is ours to God. It was peculiar to him alone to appease God and expiate sins by his oblation. When these men usurp it to themselves, what follows, but that they have an impious and sacrilegious priesthood? ... Christ odered dispensers of his gospel and his sacred mysteries to be ordained, not sacrificers to be inaugurated, and his command was to preach the gospel and feed the flock, not to immolate victims. (xix.28)

So Calvin, in common with the other Reformers, sharply rejected both 'the sacrifice of the Mass' and the conception of the ministry as a 'sacrificing priesthood'. This is at the same time connected with the dismissal of the doctrine of the *opus operatum* in the sense that it maintains that the objective action of God is bound up with the instrumental action of the priest, who alone is empowered to celebrate the sacrifice of the Mass and is in this sense a *necessary* instrument for the validity of the sacrament. So we end this chapter as we began it – with the question of 'priestly status' and 'priestly power' as an unavoidable issue in the whole confrontation between the medieval and Reformation views. While the question of ministry and/or priesthood has not been our primary concern, it cannot be left aside in consideration of the Eucharist then and now – as we shall see in the final chapter.

7

RECONSIDERATIONS

The accounts and interpretations of the Eucharist that we have tried to outline in the last two chapters are certainly very different. Not only that: they were forged and shaped in mutual conflict. The Reformed understanding crystallised in critical rejection of medieval teaching, while Trent, though reiterating that older tradition, framed its decrees and its anathemas in deliberate opposition to Protestant (Lutheran and Reformed) affirmations. The two views incorporate and rest upon contrasting convictions, not only concerning the Eucharist, but also and more profoundly concerning the relation between Christ and the Church.

In one, the church is seen in effect as an extension of the incarnation. The power and authority of Christ himself are transmitted and continue to operate in the ministry of the church; the eucharistic elements are transmuted into his very body and blood; in the eucharistic offering, priest and people are caught up into his once-for-all sacrifice. In the other, an absolutely fundamental distinction is recognised between Christ and the church: the church exists in total dependence upon the living power of his Word; his 'real presence' does not depend upon or require a 'substantial' transformation of bread and wine; there is a sheer qualitative difference between his one sacrifice of himself and the response of thanks and praise which we offer to the Father, and with it, ourselves. Further, each conception carries with it a radically different understanding of the nature of ministry in the church: the one sees the essential office of the ministry in the priestly work of the 'sacrifice of the altar', the other speaks rather of 'ministers of the Word and dispensers of the sacraments'.

When the position is stated as bluntly and sharply as that, it might appear that the oppositions are in every respect so absolute that no kind of reconciliation could be possible. That was certainly the general conviction on both sides in the sixteenth century, and through most of the generations since. It would indeed be wrong to underestimate the difficulties here, and by our order of treatment we have tried to bring them out as fully and clearly as possible within the available space. To say, however, that there are real and serious differences stemming from the Reformation is not to say that that is the end of the matter, or that these differences cannot be set in a new light. It is, rather, to pose the question what that new light might be; to ask whether, without trivialising the issues, we might yet be able to relativise the differences, wholly or in part, and so to recover a profounder understanding of our common ground.

A first step is to remind ourselves that it was *common* ground that the battles were fought over during the Reformation itself. The Reformation was a Christian family-quarrel, not a conflict between belief and unbelief, though it was often enough so regarded. That view of the matter has left its legacy. Dr Johnson is said once to have remarked that there were 'twenty thousand stout fellows in England who would fight to the death against popery, though they knew not whether popery be a man or a horse'. James Joyce captures the mirror-image of such sentiments when in *A Portrait of the Artist as a Young Man* Stephen Dedalus answers Cranly's, 'Then you do not intend to become a protestant?' with the riposte, 'I said that I had lost the faith, but not that I had lost selfrespect.' Whatever else may be said about such attitudes, they reflect such an identification of 'the faith' with one's own church or tradition as to deny the right of other forms of Christianity to exist. More clearly than in the sixteenth century can it be seen today that such a spirit is more likely to erode and deny the Gospel than witness effectively to it.

It would certainly be a grave injustice to the Reformers to accuse them of that spirit, but it is one that their successors today need to guard against – as do the heirs of the medieval church. What one can say of the men of the sixteenth century is that the pressures and challenges of the time could and did also conceal from them their own common ground. Two examples emerge very clearly from our last two chapters, and both have to do with central controversies concerning the Eucharist.

First, we have heard both Trent and Calvin affirming strongly that the presence of Christ in the Eucharist is a mystery that cannot be adequately explained or expressed in words.[1] Had each there heard the voice of the other, and sought to work out from that foundation, the entire debate about transubstantiation might have been put on a more promising basis by the relegation of *that* issue to its proper, secondary place. Where, however, transubstantiation was asserted on the one side as an article of faith, and attacked on the other as a pernicious blasphemy, the whole controversy moved at a level which did not allow the heart of the matter to be brought out and recognised as a common conviction.

Second, both affirmed equally strongly that the one complete and perfect sacrifice for the sins of the world was Christ's upon the cross, and that the Eucharist can neither add to nor detract from it.[2] Certainly the tone in which these affirmations were made was very different on each side: Calvin advanced his insistence on the uniqueness of Christ's sacrifice in criticising the medieval theory, Trent in defending it. But the point remains that the central conviction on which both implicitly agreed was not brought into the discussion as the primary theme; it arose only indirectly in the context of the argument about the sacrifice of the Mass, and was not directly faced. To that extent, the argument ran at least partially at cross-purposes.

All this is not to suggest that there were not at the same time real differences in both these areas; it is to suggest that the differences had to do with matters other than the most central, and that this was not at the time clearly seen. If that is indeed the case, it may be possible to obtain somewhat more leverage on the issues than our previous presentation might at first sight seem to imply.

To make this more precise, however, a little more thought must be given to the question of how and in what way differences of this kind can be overcome. The simplest method is simply to ignore them or to dismiss them with the argument that they were never really as important as they were taken to be, and at any rate need no longer be worried over today. This is *not* what we are proposing, and it may be as well to say so quite clearly – if only because there is at the present a certain wave of ecumenical thinking which is tempted to try to glide all too smoothly over genuine differences, and in the process to treat the Reformation largely as a piece of regrettable misunderstanding which can now be left out of sight and out of mind.[3] Against that, it needs to be said that there *were* profound issues at stake in the Reformation. The Reformers were right in their search for theological restatement which would more adequately place Christ in the centre, which would replace the doubtless well-intentioned but mechanical and objectifying categories of medieval sacramental theology with others more biblical, dynamic and personal, which would return with a new seriousness to the witness of Scripture and reverse the tendency of the previous centuries to write the existing church with its structure, tradition and practice into the Gospel itself. In this sense there can and should be no going back on the Reformation. It was and remains a moment of enormous weight and importance in the whole history of the church, and is in that sense a part of our common ecumenical heritage, whether we belong to a 'church of the Reformation' or not. It cannot simply be left behind.

The other side of this coin, however, is that we cannot simply anchor ourselves in the sixteenth century as if we were still living then, though we do well to learn from it. In the circumstances of the time, the attempts to reform the church led – perhaps inevitably – to its division; and we can see today what the Reformers could not foresee – what a process of fragmentation and separation spread from that beginning, and how ambiguous its consequences have been for the witness and work of the church in the world. (And our world today is no longer that of western European Christendom: it is a world in which Christians are in a minority, a world desperately needing to recover a new sense of the unity of mankind, a world in which the heartlands of the Reformation are particularly marked by the alienation of large sectors of the population from any and every church.) The challenge today is to search through the insights of the Reformers for the healing of our divisions and for a recovery of their vision of a revitalised church. In the process we must be willing to test the testimony of the Reformers afresh by the message of Scripture, just as much as that of Trent or the middle ages, and to keep in mind the possibility that the controversies of four centuries ago may at points have been set up on a false basis. Nor can we leave out of sight that eucharistic theology is no abstract theory, but related to the life and worship of the church. Changes in practice that have taken place and are taking place in different churches – not least in the Roman Catholic – may set many of the old issues in a new and more hopeful light.

With this we have hinted at three themes which should perhaps be developed a little more before we attempt to reconsider the three central topics of sacrament, presence and sacrifice: the new ecumenical climate of the twentieth century; fresh biblical and theological awareness; the transformation that has overtaken the Roman Catholic Church in the last generation. We can still only deal with them briefly, but they can help to introduce and set the scene for our final reflections.

Ecumenical conferences, meetings, dialogues, reports and organisations are so much a feature of the exchanges between the churches today that it is easy to forget what a recent development they represent, and what a change in atmosphere they reflect. The beginnings of the ecumenical movement lie in the nineteenth century, but it grew to maturity only in the twentieth, stimulated above all by the series of World Missionary Conferences which began in Edinburgh in 1910, by the Faith and Order and Life and Work movements, and by the establishing of the World Council of Churches shortly after the Second World War. The Roman Catholic Church is not a member of the WCC, but it too has become increasingly engaged in inter-church and inter-confessional conversations at all levels from the local to the international. This new kind of meeting, whose fruits are reflected in a veritable flood of joint studies and reports,[4] shows both a new willingness on many sides to reconsider the old divisive issues, and some degree of success in tackling them. Certainly by no means all problems have been resolved, and the search for solutions must still continue. Yet the very fact of the dialogue is itself of immense significance. It holds out hope that there may yet be further progress as Christians seek to rediscover what binds them together instead of focussing chiefly on what divides. Willingness to consider and look for possibilities of reconciliation, or at least of a better degree of mutual understanding, is itself a powerful new fact of our day.

In many of these conversations the Eucharist has figured prominently as a central theme. It is not possible here to survey all that has been said or suggested concerning it in the many different discussions,[5] but two ecumenical documents of the 1970s are particularly important in view of the approach we have followed here in outlining and contrasting the Roman and Reformation views. The first is the *Leuenberg Concord* of 1973, which aimed to offer the basis for intercommunion between Lutheran and Reformed churches, and has been very widely subscribed as such by churches of both confessions throughout the world. The second is *The Presence of Christ in Church and World*, the report of a dialogue between the World Alliance of Reformed Churches and the Vatican Secretariat for Promoting Christian Unity in the years 1970-1977. We shall draw on both of these later on.

Fresh biblical and theological awareness has also played its part in improving the climate. One sign of this is the fact that biblical and theological study have become ecumenical in a way that they were not only two or three generations ago, and that in a whole series of respects, ranging from co-operation in research, through the new interest shown by Roman Catholic scholars in the theology of the Reformers and the regular use of Roman Catholic writings in Protestant seminaries and faculties and vice-versa, to the springing up in the last decades of centres for ecumenical study. It is worth mentioning this, if only because it is otherwise too easy to forget how the landscape has changed within a relatively short period of time. But there are other aspects bearing even more directly on our subject. Most fundamental of all is the widespread recognition of what we have also here tried to underline by the order of our discussion – that priority must be given to the task of trying to enter into the meaning of the Eucharist as opened up for us in the New Testament; that neither the Tridentine nor the Reformation patterns of understanding and interpretation can be assumed from the start to be a simple republication of the truth of Scripture: that some at least of our problems stem from habits of thinking which have been imposed on the biblical evidence; that formulations developed in controversy become dangerous and misleading if absolutised and abstracted from their historical context. As *The Presence of Christ in Church and World* puts it:[5a]

> 67. Reflection on the celebration of the Eucharist must start from the biblical sources, i.e.:
> from the celebration of the Lord's Supper in the primitive church,

from the celebration of the Last Supper of Jesus,
from the Old Testament background, particularly the Jewish Passover.
70. If this background is taken seriously, new possibilities of mitigating the traditional confessional quarrels emerge ...
71. Reflection on the biblical sources along these lines can also help to relativise certain traditional alternatives (influenced by a dualistic anthropology and cosmology) which encumber the dialogue between the confessions (as for example, realism/symbolism, sacramentalism/inwardness, substance/form, subject/object. In relation to an objectification which tends to rigidity, the original biblical way of thinking helps us to a more profound understanding of the character of the Eucharist ....
89. ... In the course of history certain formulae have been taken up in dogmatic and liturgical usage, primarily as protective devices to safeguard the faith against misinterpretation. These formulae have usually been developed from a context of controversy, from which the passage of time has tended to detach them. Such formulations need to be re-examined in order to see whether they are still adequate as safeguards against misunderstanding, or have themselves become sources of misunderstanding, especially in the ecumenical situation.

There is therefore a pastoral responsibility on the churches to see that such formulae contribute to the genuine communication of the Gospel to the contemporary world.

What comes to expression here is a necessary sensitivity to the limitations of theological formulation. Both Trent and Calvin do show an awareness of these limitations; but we today must be even more acutely conscious of the extent to which the way in which we talk, think, describe and interpret – or, on occasion, seek to define – is conditioned by our own background, our own circumstances, the issues we are addressing. Our concepts and ideas, categories and terms are indeed forged – or should be – in the attempt to speak truthfully of the reality of God in his gracious relation to us through Jesus Christ; but they are always only imperfectly suited to the task, always in danger of distortion, misrepresentation or exaggeration. Our language and patterns of thought cannot be simply and neatly identified with the truth itself, albeit it is in and with them that we are helped to glimpse and grasp that truth. Theology is not and cannot be anything other than the work of pilgrims on the way; it is necessarily provisional and promissory, unfinished and imperfect; and can only become opaque or downright misleading if it forgets the fact and strives after absolute finality. In the very nature of the case, it speaks, when it speaks authentically, of more than it can adequately specify; it witnesses and points to more than it can contain in the web of its words. This is not to swallow everything up in the relativism that believes that there is no truth, that any formulation is as good as any other, that in the end we may say what we like, because it really does not matter what we affirm or deny. It is, rather, to recognise that the realities of which theology speaks, which theology attempts to bring to expression, transcend the power of the theologian or the theological school to formulate; that therefore theology must be tested and measured for its faithfulness as a pointer and sign to a reality surpassing the understanding of the theologian, for its functioning to deepen and strengthen the vision and the understanding and the hope which faith seeks and grasps after, and to communicate and convey the truth which is in Jesus Christ.

In this light, we dare not overlook the real risk of putting so much weight on particular positive or negative points of eucharistic theology – that it must be understood and taken *thus* and not *so* – as to make our understanding the be-all and end-all of the matter. The parallel histories of Protestant denunciation of the 'blasphemy of the Mass' and of Roman Catholic denial of the validity of eucharistic celebration in Protestant churches can indeed be understood in the light of the history we have traced; but they remain, to say the least, less than edifying. In each case the reality of the Christ who gives himself through bread and wine is simply and flatly denied on grounds that have more to do with the polemical stances built up in a controversial history than with the promises of the Gospel – or the evidence of the New Testament. Sound theological judgment would surely be at once more humble and more generous.

Yet a further point must be mentioned. In discussing the New Testament evidence we more than once emphasised the eschatological perspective which was rediscovered three generations ago through the work of Johannes Weiss and Albert Schweizer. In one sense, eschatology never disappeared from the theological scene. For long enough, however, it was reduced to a kind of appendix treating of 'the last things' – resurrection and final judgment – which, as coming after the history of this world, were thought of as correspondingly distant and remote. The sense, so present to St Paul, that in Jesus Christ the final, saving act of God had been realised, that, in him, the 'end' has already broken in, that our own existence is directed and drawn towards the conclusion and consummation realised in his death and resurrection, had largely faded from Christian awareness. Consequently the decisive, once-for-all character of Jesus Christ himself was chiefly seen as the once-for-allness of a *past* event, from which the onward march of time carried us ever further away, rather than of *the event* in the past in which the mystery of *our future* is *already* broken open. The Eucharist was then located and interpreted in a horizon defined and determined on the one side by the pastness of Jesus' own history and on the other by the present moment of eucharistic celebration. That made the question of Christ's presence take form as the question of the relation between this present and that past time.

If the question is posed in this way, then one of two alternatives is likely to force itself to the fore. Either one insists that what is done is done, that the past is complete, that all that follows must be distinguished radically from it and cannot add to or subtract from its finishedness; or one will find ways of speaking of that past as continually living on in the present. The first way was taken by the Reformers; the second is more characteristic of Roman Catholic thinking, as when *Caritatis Studium* affirms that Christ's once-for-all sacrifice is *continued* (not *repeated*) in the mass. These ways of thinking would seem to have left their mark on the debates about presence and sacrifice alike. Yet neither is wholly adequate. The danger along the first path is of failing to discern and express the connexion between the finished past and the continuing present; along the second of failing sufficiently to distinguish them.

By opening up the third dimension of the future which is already inaugurated in Christ himself, the eschatological perspective of the New Testament sets the matter in a wider room.[6] Our present time is related to a past which is not only past but future, in that Christ himself is the alpha and the omega, the first and the last. Our present stands in a twofold relation to him whose past is not merely past to us but also lies before us. He is not simply fixed in an ever-receding remoteness, for there he was, is and will be the creative and transforming and saving power of God in and as man for us. *There*, rather than in 'continuance', 're-presenting', 'remembering', or any other form merely of linear, temporal transmission, lies the secret of his presence now. His presence is not merely a continuation or extension of what he was two thousand years ago; it is his bearing upon our present to make it a form and means of *his* presence, opening it (and us) to his future. It is in the eschatological presence of the crucified and risen Christ that the main lines of the New Testament invite us to discern the significance of the Eucharist. What he was, suffered and did for us he makes ever and again contemporary in its completeness for us who are still *in via*. We have to do not only with past and present, but with past, present *and future* meeting in him, and making him the ground, accompaniment *and goal* of our journey. He stands *before* us, not merely behind or with us. This sets the issues in a different light from that in which they have very commonly been seen in western eucharistic theology, both Roman and Protestant. (It also sets them in a different light from the common suggestion that the problems can be overcome by a recovery of the sense of Christ's enduring intercession, his perpetual pleading of his sacrifice before the throne of the Father at the heavenly altar – a view which can easily remain anchored in a linear and temporal conception of eternity, and so fail to break out of the inadequacies of the underlying frame of reference.)

It may well be that this weakness is bound up with a common tendency to ignore or underplay the place and role of the Holy Spirit, and to reduce him to a merely historical influence or inward power flowing from Christ through the church and through history. It is the Spirit as the 'third moment' in the life of God who is supremely involved in the eschatological outworking of God's reconciling and redemptive act in Jesus Christ. Perhaps, too, it is no mere coincidence that the recovery of an eschatological perspective in recent times has run alongside a new desire to discern and respond to the activity of the Spirit, who both directs us back to Christ and forward to him, and so makes him present to us and us to him. Here, Calvin's stress upon the role of the Spirit in the Eucharist is of capital significance, though Calvin himself did not pursue it so far as we may need to do today.[7]

Finally, if only in a few words, we must at least mention the enormous changes that have overtaken the Roman Catholic Church in the last generation. These go far indeed to reversing trends in the late patristic and early medieval periods which gave cause for many of the Reformers' practical objections and complaints. The emphasis of the Second Vatican Council in the Dogmatic Constitution on the Church, *Lumen Gentium*, that the church is not simply a juridical or sacerdotal institution, but the 'pilgrim people of God', the rendering of the liturgy of the Mass into the vernacular, the revision of the liturgy itself along lines more closely resembling the ancient rather than the medieval and Tridentine pattern, the giving of the cup as well as the bread to the laity, the degree of active participation by the congregation in the service – all these give the celebration of the Mass today a life and vividness, a sense of festival as well as of devotion, which it must be admitted are often sadly lacking in much Protestant worship. It is also striking how the new ecumenical openness and attitude of brotherhood encouraged by the council has led not only to a considerable increase in co-operation, meeting and shared worship, but also to pressure for intercommunion and eucharistic hospitality resulting in numerous unofficial initiatives going far beyond what is officially and theoretically permitted. Certainly this is only one side of the story, and the *magisterium* has repeatedly in the last twenty years shown itself to be nervous and uneasy about the dangers of moving too far and too fast. Yet the changes that have taken place are a sign of hope, and should not be forgotten as we go on now to reconsider the three areas of traditional controversy.

1. *Christ the Sacrament*

In the last two chapters we have traced two rather different paradigmatic models of 'a sacrament'. One is controlled by the thought of *God acting through the action of the church*, the other by that of *God communicating by his Word to faith*. Yet each model has its strengths and its inherent dangers. The first is based on the sound recognition that a sacrament involves *action* and not merely *words*: 'Do this ...' is performative and not merely declaratory. The second builds on the equally fundamental awareness that God does not act upon us dumbly or impersonally, but in acting also communicates and evokes an answer. To this extent the two models may be seen as complementary and mutually corrective. Taken on its own, the first can lead to an uncritical identification of God's action and ours, and so to a magical view of sacramental efficacy, and the second to a reduction of 'sacrament' to a 'naked and bare sign', or to an activity of our own in which God is no longer believed to be involved directly. Yet the Word and the action of God cannot be sundered from each other; our own speech and action rest and depend on his; and both the activity of the church and the response of faith have their necessary place in the horizon. Each of the two models has something necessary and valuable to contribute – provided they are held together in proper complementarity rather than torn apart into stark opposition, in which each becomes opaque and absolute, with its more dubious aspects setting the tone.

This recognition, however, can only be a first step towards a profounder re-evaluation. The very concept of 'a sacrament' is not properly to be found in the New Testament at all. Both these conceptions of it rest largely on the theology of the early Latin fathers, and in particular on Augustine's explanations and interpretations of *sacramentum*. Behind that lies a wider tendency in the early church to focus attention on the rite, the sacred action, and to ask what was really happening in it. The danger there is that we can come to concentrate simply on the rite, or on a preferred definition of 'sacrament', and work out from there. Instead we do better to return to the central meaning of the whole matter and to remember that in the New Testament *mysterion* does not refer to ceremonies but to the secret of God's redemptive will, disclosed in Jesus Christ. Jesus Christ is *the* 'sacrament' in whom God and man are united, the Father's purpose for man declared, and man's true identity as the child of God affirmed. It is there that we must begin if we are to get our thought about 'sacraments' into sharper focus.

In this light, the established medieval and Reformation definitions of a sacrament, so far from being dispossessed, take on yet deeper meaning. If it is understood, along scholastic lines, as 'a form and cause of grace', that pattern can be applied, in the strictest propriety, to Jesus Christ himself. He is the actualisation of God's favour present for us in our world, and it is from and through him that that favour is extended to us. In similar style, the Reformed understanding of 'a sign given to confirm God's promise' also leads back into christology; for where is *the* sign and pledge of that promise but in Christ incarnate, crucified, risen and ascended? Obliquely though it may be, both definitions point back to him, and it is in their relation to him that the opposition between them can best be overcome.

In what sense, then, may we understand the claim that he is *the* sacrament? First, he himself, as God's Word made flesh, as true God and true man, is the place of meeting between God and man, the visible and the invisible, the natural and the supernatural. He is himself sign and pledge and reality of God's presence with and for us. Second, from and through him in his person, history and destiny, is given to us the life that is his and in which we share. Here certainly it is better to think less in terms of 'grace' than of the Holy Spirit; for the power and energy of that life is the power and energy of the Spirit that came upon him and was released and sent through his cross and resurrection/ascension. Third, in that Spirit we are gathered together, incorporated with Christ, and in him offered to the Father; and by this the whole creation is recalled to its promised future under the sign of the reign of God. The uniting of God with man, the coming of God to man, and the raising of man to God: these are the three moments which combine in him as the outworking of the *mysterion* which he himself is. It is by reference to this ground and criterion that all 'sacramentality' is established and measured.

This recognition has in recent times become almost a commonplace in much writing, both Roman and Reformed; but it can be followed through in more than one way. Either we may conclude, as Karl Barth does,[8] that there is *no* 'sacrament' apart from or other than Jesus Christ himself, and that the Reformers were mistaken in not rejecting the medieval notion of 'sacraments' altogether; or we may see in this christological foundation the basis for a reinterpretation of the 'sacraments', and indeed of the church itself as 'sacramental', as does the Roman Catholic theologian Eduard Schillebeeckx.[9] In part the issue is simply one of definition: whether or not we should retain the language of 'sacraments'; but there are profounder questions involved. Behind Schillebeeckx' position lies not only the tradition of medieval and later Roman Catholic thought, but also the development in the Roman Catholic Church in the last hundred years of a shift away from older, largely juridical conceptions of the church towards the *Mysterientheologie* of Dom Odo Casels and others and the Encyclical *Mystici Corporis* of Pius XII (1943). In this theology the sense of the church as the mystical

Body of Christ whose essence lies in the sacramentality supremely
manifested in the Eucharist gives new life and vigour to the description
of the church itself as inherently sacramental, and to the interpretation
of particular sacraments as acts in which that sacramentality is effectively realised. Behind Barth, by contrast, lies a somewhat zwinglian
rejection of 'sacramentalism', sharpened up by Barth's own insistence
that the so-called 'sacraments' of Baptism and the Eucharist are not
to be looked upon as vehicles of *God's* action, but of *ours*: they are our
witness and sign and response to the one sacrament which is Jesus Christ
himself.

Without pretending to explore all the possible ramifications and
implications of these alternatives – or of other, more differentiated
positions that might be taken up somewhere between them – we may
still notice that in effect they represent the ancient divergence in modern
dress, with the same old strengths and weaknesses on each side. Talk of
the church as the 'original and universal sacrament' alongside
descriptions of Jesus Christ as *the* 'sacrament', such as one commonly
meets in Roman Catholic writing, raises the question whether the
distinction between head and members of the body of Christ is being
quietly overlooked. Here Barth's critical distinction deserves to be
underlined. On the other hand, Barth himself seems to go much too far
in the opposite direction, so that though he can indeed speak of the
church as the 'earthly-historical form of Christ's presence' between his
past history and his future *parousia*, that presence undergoes a subtle
redefinition in terms of our response to him, our 'ethical act' of obedient
witness.

In view of this it is pertinent to ask whether the categories of
'sacrament' and 'sacramentality' whose roots lie in the early church
rather than in the New Testament do not after all have something of
value to contribute. Given that the central and fundamental *mysterion* or
sacramentum is Christ himself, may we not also recognise a strictly
secondary and dependent sacramentality in the forms and means of his
presence and action? In this sense the church may properly be called a
sacramental reality as his body. Its nature and meaning lie deeper than
the surface appearance; it is both visible and invisible, both an empirical
entity and a divinely grounded mystery. But it is not in and by itself a
sacrament apart from Christ, nor is it a sacrament of the same sort as he,
for only in him is its own identity grounded, disclosed and promised. It is
sacramental as a sacrament *of Christ, the sacrament*, as participant in him,
as imaging him, and as witnessing to him.

In this broad sense, every authentic expression of the being and life of
the church in the world has sacramental character, for it always rests on
and represents the mystery of Christ and his Spirit, of his life for us and

our life in him. This applies equally to the life of the believer: there too lies a hidden depth and a secret significance, for there too God in Christ is at work. It is in the divine call and promise in Jesus that our own identity is declared, and it is in response to that call and promise that our true life grows, grasped by the graciousness of the Father and made a testimony in the Spirit to his love in the incarnate Son. Each individual Christian life is essentially sacramental in its core, called and challenged and – however brokenly and fragmentarily – empowered to be a sign and channel of the everlasting mercy. This is not a recipe for unrealistic perfectionism or for pietistic escapism: rather it has to do with the essential orientation and direction of our human life in the world through which we are travelling. Precisely because it is sacramental, it involves from beginning to end the victory of grace over our failures, of forgiveness over our guilts, of liberation and promise over our enslavements and defeats. And unless the life of the Christian believer is indeed seized by grace, forgiveness, liberation and promise, how shall it be *Christian* at all?

Within this broad horizon, however, there are key moments in the life of the church and of the individual that do not merely express this given sacramental character but actually serve to constitute it. In them we not only *articulate* but *receive* our identity as Christians individually and in community; for the church is event as well as institution, called not merely to self-expression but to renewed realisation. These moments include all that most fundamentally belongs to the nature of the church and determines the shape of Christian life – worship and prayer, the speaking and hearing of the Gospel, confession and declaration of forgiveness, affirmation of faith, thanksgiving, offering and intercession, and – by no means least – the giving and receiving of God's blessing. (And all of these, while they naturally and properly receive liturgical expression, should by no means be narrowly conceived in exclusively liturgical terms, let alone regarded simply as matters of ritual ceremony.) But they also include in quite distinctive fashion Baptism and the Eucharist as the acts and declarations which centrally and decisively crystallise and focus our individual and corporate sharing in Jesus Christ. They are only real, effective and valid insofar as they are not simply *our* acts and declarations but *his* in the energy of his Spirit. As such they are and repeatedly become visible and tangible forms of the Word which he himself is. Baptism as initiation and Eucharist as regular participation are the signs and instruments by which the risen Christ unites us to himself, imparts himself to us, and engages us with him – these three moments corresponding to the three we traced above in speaking of his being the sacrament of union between God and man, of the coming of God to man, and the raising of man to God. In this secondary sacramentality his primary sacramentality is, as it were, projected on to the plane of his relation to us and ours to him.

If 'the sacramental' in general, and Baptism and Eucharist in particular, are set in this light, it is possible to move away from the tendency to think of them in the rather juridical terms that marked medieval theology, and also to some degree that of the Reformers. Where attention is focused more on a certain conception of 'validity', or of 'real presence' than on the *true* presence, or where a legalistic notion of 'what the Lord commanded' obscures the profound connexion of the Eucharist with the very person of the Word made flesh, then eucharistic theology can hardly fail to be diverted on to (doubtless well-intentioned) side-tracks. Both can find the needed corrective in a return to the centre of the matter, and in a measured working out from it.

2. *The Present Christ*

In the last chapter we saw how the question of the 'real presence' (in the sense of the presence of the true body and blood of Christ) became a controversial issue during the Reformation, not only between Protestants and Roman Catholics, but also between the Lutherans and the Reformed. Bound up with it in the Lutheran/Reformed debate were the christological divergences which developed in the course of the dispute. By the time of the *Formula of Concord* in 1577, yet a third point of conflict had joined them – the doctrine of 'double predestination' as it had been developed by Calvin and consolidated by Beza and others as a cornerstone of Reformed doctrine, but rejected and condemned in Lutheranism. All three issues were therefore unavoidably on the agenda in the Leuenberg conversations from 1971 to 1973, and the formula of agreement designed to restore fellowship and communion between the Lutheran and Reformed churches dealt with each in turn, and in each case along similar lines. Here, we must limit ourselves to the treatment of the Eucharist.

The *Concord*[10] falls into four sections. The first, 'The Road to Fellowship', deals with common aspects of the Reformation witness and then with changed elements in the contemporary situation in view of which the churches 'have learned to distinguish between the fundamental witness of the Reformation confessions of faith and their historically-conditioned thought forms' (p. 258). The second outlines 'The Common Understanding of the Gospel', stressing 'the message of justification as the message of the free grace of God' and 'the measure of all the Church's preaching' (pp. 258-259), and sums up the core of the significance of the Eucharist in a key formula, which appears again in the central third section:

In the Lord's Supper the risen Jesus Christ imparts himself in his

body and blood, given up for all, through his word of promise
with bread and wine. (pp. 259-260)
Section Three, 'Accord in Respect of the Doctrinal Condemnations of
the Reformation Era', then comments and declares:

The differences which from the time of the Reformation onwards
have made church fellowship between the Lutheran and
Reformed churches impossible, and have led them to pronounce
mutual condemnations, related to the doctrine of the Lord's
Supper, Christology and the doctrine of predestination. We take
the decisions of the Reformation fathers seriously, but are today
able to agree on the following statements in respect of these
condemnations:

1. *The Lord's Supper*

In the Lord's Supper the risen Jesus Christ imparts himself in his
body and blood, given up for all, through his word of promise
with bread and wine. He thus gives himself unreservedly to all
who receive the bread and wine: faith receives the Lord's Supper
for salvation, unfaith for judgment.

We cannot separate communion with Jesus Christ in his body
and blood from the act of eating and drinking. To be concerned
about the manner of Christ's presence in the Lord's Supper in
abstraction from this act is to run the risk of obscuring the
meaning of the Lord's Supper.

Where such a consensus exists between the churches, the
condemnations pronounced by the Reformation confessions are
inapplicable to the doctrinal position of these churches. (p. 260)
Similar brief statements on christology and predestination lead on to:

4. *Conclusions*

Wherever these statements are accepted, the condemnations of
the Reformation confessions in respect of the Lord's Supper,
Christology and predestination, are inapplicable to the doctrinal
position. This does not mean that the condemnations pronounced
by the Reformation fathers are irrelevant; but they are no longer
an obstacle to church fellowship. (p. 261)
Section Four, finally, deals with 'The Declaration and Realisation of
Church Fellowship' in the light of this agreement and recognition.

Detailed analysis of the central Leuenberg formulations on the
Eucharist would demand more space than we can give them here, but
one comment should be made. At almost every crucial point they betray
a measure of vagueness which would allow different emphases to be read
into or out of them equally well. For example, the phrase, 'communion

with Jesus Christ in his body and blood', *could* be interpreted in Luther's sense, but does not *demand* that interpretation. It could equally easily be taken in Calvin's. The agreement has indeed been criticised on just this ground. But there is another side to the matter. Arguably, it is precisely this 'ambiguity' that constitutes the strength of the *Concord* and has led to its being so widely accepted as a basis for mutual recognition between Lutheran and Reformed churches. The formulations chosen are designed to point to what is central as the decisive common ground, but at the same time to leave questions which are more properly regarded as secondary to the side, allowing the possibility of their being answered in more than one way, but not requiring or demanding a particular answer as the only possible or acceptable one. This may well seem unsatisfactory from the standpoint which requires every 'i' to be dotted and every 't' crossed; but it is in the longer run both more realistic and ecumenically more constructive. Leuenberg would certainly not be the first agreement which succeeded precisely because it left some room for manoeuvre or variation within the space it opened up, while at the same time pointing to what was needful and indicating limits that should not be transgressed in formulating what is needful. This involves at least an implicit recognition and admission that there can be significant truth in more than one of the alternative positions admitted, even if they cannot be brought neatly under a form which settles every detail without remainder of tensions or loose ends.

The classic instance of such a solution in the history of Christian theology is the *Symbol of Chalcedon* (451). This spoke of Jesus Christ as 'one person in two natures' 'without confusion, without change, without division, without separation', and so sought to integrate the divergent concerns of Alexandrian and Antiochene christology, while at the same time ruling out the extremer forms of each. It can hardly be overlooked that the divergent Lutheran and Reformed emphases in christology display recognisable Alexandrian/monophysite and Antiochene/nestorian traits. If, in christology, room can and must be made for both, with the limitation that neither can be pushed too far, must not the same apply to the eucharistic presence of Christ? The connexion between the two issues and the modes of tackling them so briefly formulated at Leuenberg becomes more apparent in the *Arnoldshain Theses* of 1957, the product of an earlier Lutheran/Reformed dialogue in Germany which directly paved the way for Leuenberg.[11] The fifth thesis states the boundaries of an acceptable understanding of the eucharistic presence in a fashion directly reminiscent of the chalcedonian negative procedure:

> It is therefore not appropriate to interpret what happens in the communion in any of the following ways:

(a) to teach that, through the words pronounced by our Lord when he instituted the Last Supper, the bread and wine are transformed into a supernatural substance, and cease to be bread and wine;

(b) to teach that a repetition of the act of salvation takes place in the communion.

(c) to teach that in the communion a natural or supernatural material is presented;

(d) to teach that two parallel but separate processes take place, one a physical and the other a spiritual form of eating.

(e) to teach that physical participation in the communion ensures salvation, or that participation in the body and blood of Christ is a purely spiritual procedure.

Here, the classical Lutheran and Reformed concerns are taken up negatively as demarcating limits which must not be passed. Certainly the *Arnoldshain Theses* do more than that. The fourth thesis, for instance, is a direct source for the key positive formulation used at Leuenberg:

He, the crucified and risen Lord, permits us to participate through his word of promise with bread and wine in his body, given up to death for all, and his blood, poured out for all . . .

What is decisive, however, is that a space, a room for manoeuvre and variation is left between the positive statement and the negatively-defined boundaries. The *Theses* do not attempt to fill up that space completely by comprehensive theological definitions or decisions on every possible question. Therein lies the resemblance to the procedure of Chalcedon – and the model Arnoldshain and Leuenberg offer for further ecumenical reflection.

The same tone can be overheard in the Roman Catholic/Reformed report, *The Presence of Christ in Church and World*, from which we have already quoted. §70, which speaks of the possibility of overcoming traditional conflicts by renewed concentration on the New Testament accounts of the institution, gives these examples:

In the words of institution the emphasis is on the fact of the personal presence of the living Lord in the event of the memorial and fellowship meal, not on the question as to how this real presence (the word 'is') comes about and is to be explained. The eating and drinking, and the memorial character of the passover meal, . . . proclaim the beginning of the new covenant.

When Christ give the apostles the commission, 'Do this in remembrance of me!' the word 'remembrance' means more than merely an act of recalling.

The term 'body' means the whole person of Jesus, the saving presence of which is experienced in the meal.

The section, 'The Presence of Christ in the Lord's Supper', includes the affirmations:

82. As often as we come together in the Church to obey our Lord's command to 'do this in *anamnesis* of me', he is in our midst. This is the presence of the Son of God, who for us men and for our salvation became man and was made flesh. Through the offering of his body we have been sanctified and are made partakers of God. This is the great mystery (*sacramentum*) of Christ, in which he has incorporated himself into our humanity, and in partaking of which the Church is built up as the body of Christ. ... The realization of this presence of Christ to us and of our union and incorporation with him is the proper work of the Holy Spirit. ...

83. It is in this light that we may understand something of the specific presence of Jesus Christ in the Eucharist, which is at once sacramental and personal. He comes to us clothed in his Gospel and saving passion, so that our partaking of him is communion in his body and blood (John 6, 47-56; I Cor. 10, 17). This presence is sacramental in that it is the concrete form which the mystery of Christ takes in the eucharistic communion of his body and blood. It is also personal presence because Jesus Christ in his own person is immediately present, giving himself in his reality both as true God and true man. In the Eucharist he communicates himself to us in the whole reality of his divinity and humanity – body, mind and will – and at the same time he remains the Son who is in the Father as the Father is in him.

Unlike the *Arnoldshain Theses*, this report does not spell out explicitly what conceptions of the matter must be ruled out; but there are clear enough hints in and between the lines just quoted. Neither a diversion of attention from the present Christ to the 'how?' of his presence, nor a doctrine concerned more to insist on what might be called 'a bare remembering of the really absent body and blood' than on communion with the whole Christ, can meet the case. Positively, the meaning of the Eucharist reflects the meaning of the Gospel: to Christ's taking and sharing of our humanity in his incarnation, life, death and resurrection corresponds and answers our incorporation and participation in him.

The report is also in another significant respect different in aim from the *Leuenberg Concord*. It does not seek to lay out the basis for a full agreement leading to the restoration of broken communion between Roman Catholic and Reformed churches, but has a much more provisional character, as an early step in a dialogue which will continue into the future. The question has not yet been settled whether Roman

Catholic and Reformed teaching can in fact be reconciled along the lines it suggests. One key issue in that future discussion will doubtless be the doctrine of transubstantiation, which the report does not directly tackle. It had, however, been the subject of considerable debate within the Roman Catholic Church a few years before.

The excitement and rethinking surrounding the Second Vatican Council provoked much reflection on eucharistic theology among Roman Catholic theologians.[12] In particular, renewed attention began to be paid to the idea of 'sign' or 'symbol' as an avenue for fresh exploration of the nature of the sacramental elements. New terms – in particular 'trans-signification' and 'trans-finalisation' began to be advanced virtually as alternatives to 'transubstantiation'. The first labels a change of *meaning*, the second a change in *end* or *purpose*.

The common element in such suggestions was the aim to by-pass the difficulties associated with the Aristotelian notion of 'substance', and to employ categories more obviously viable and comprehensible in present-day ways of thinking. By and large we do not habitually locate the identity of a thing in a 'substance' perceived by the mind, but relate that identity to its significance and use. A coin, for instance, takes on a new identity when it is struck from a piece of metal; but that is a matter of the fact that it has been officially shaped and stamped, possesses an officially authenticated 'value' and can be used as a means of exchange. It has a new form and a new significance and a new use, and that is what differentiates it from what it was as a mere piece of metal. But it has not lost its metallic character, nor do we generally feel a need to bring in the category of 'substance' to explain what has been done with it.

Suggestions of this kind come very close indeed to what Calvin, for instance, also held. Speaking of the term 'conversion' applied to the elements, he attacks the theory of transubstantiation – but not any and every notion of 'change':

> I admit, indeed, that some of the ancients occasionally used the
> term *conversion*, not that they meant to do away with the
> substance in the external signs, but to teach that the bread devoted
> to the sacrament was widely different from ordinary bread, and
> was now something else. . . . This we deny not. But, say our
> opponents, if there is conversion, one thing must become another.
> If they mean that something becomes different from what it was
> before, I assent. (*Inst.* IV.xvii.14)

If suggestions of this kind were to become acceptable to official Roman Catholic teaching, the debate about the 'changing of the elements' could become a matter of past history.

So far, however, this has not happened: rather the reverse. Particularly important here is Pope Paul's 1965 encyclical, *Mysterium*

Fidei,[13] which dealt with 'the doctrine and worship of the Holy Eucharist' and set out deliberately to correct all such views. The Pope singled out for special defence three related matters: private celebrations of the Mass, the dogma of transubstantiation, and the proper devotion to the Eucharist and the reserved sacrament, the first and third of which are of course closely bound up with the second. The Pope's anxiety is clearly expressed in §11.

> It is not right to exalt the 'community' Mass, so-called, to the detriment of Masses which are celebrated privately. Nor is it right to be so preoccupied with considering the nature of the sacramental sign that the impression is created that the symbolism – and no-one denies its existence in the most holy Eucharist – expresses and exhausts the whole meaning of Christ's presence in this sacrament. Nor is it right to treat of the mystery of transubstantiation without mentioning the marvellous change of the whole of the bread's substance into Christ's body and the whole of the wine's substance into his blood, of which the Council of Trent speaks, and thereby to make these changes consist of nothing but a 'trans-signification' or a 'trans-finalisation', to use these terms. Nor, finally, is it right to put forward and to give expression in practice to the view which maintains that Christ the Lord is no longer present in the consecrated hosts which are left when the sacrifice of the Mass is over.

In paragraph 14 he remarks:

> We do not deny the praiseworthy zeal of those who disseminate these remarkable views. Their desire has been to investigate this great mystery, and to elucidate its riches, which are not yet exhausted, and to unfold its meaning to the men of our day. On the contrary, we recognize their zeal and approve it. We are unable, however, to approve the opinions they are putting forward. We are commanded to warn you of the serious risk to right belief which they entail.

The crucial positive statement then comes in paragraph 46:

> If no-one is to misunderstand this mode of presence, which oversteps the laws of nature and constitutes the greatest miracle of all in its kind, our minds must be docile and we must follow the voice of the Church through her teaching and prayer. This voice continually re-echoes the voice of Christ. It informs us that Christ becomes present in this sacrament precisely by a change of the bread's whole substance into his body and the wine's whole substance into his blood. This is clearly a remarkable, a singular change and the Catholic Church gives it the suitable and accurate

name of transubstantiation. When transubstantiation has taken place, there is no doubt that the appearance of the bread and the appearance of the wine take on a new expressiveness and a new purpose since they are no longer common bread and common drink, but rather the sign of something sacred and the sign of spiritual food. But they take on a new expressiveness and a new purpose for the very reason that they contain a new 'reality' which we are right to call *ontological*. For beneath these appearances there is no longer what was there before but something quite different. This is so in very fact and not only because of the valuation put on them by the Church's belief, since on the conversion of the bread and wine's substance, or nature, into the body and blood of Christ, nothing is left of the bread and the wine but the appearances alone. Beneath these appearances Christ is present whole and entire, bodily present too, in his physical 'reality', although not in the manner in which bodies are present in place.

Thus the position of Trent is restated, with repeated echoes of the Tridentine statements themselves. The Roman Catholic Church is right to speak of 'transubstantiation', for it points as other terms do not to the objective change in virtue of which a new 'ontological reality' is present 'beneath the appearances' of bread and wine. As at Trent, however, a closer definition of the precise nature of transubstantiation is not offered: it is less a theoretical explanation of *how* the alteration occurs than the fitting received formula by which the *fact* is affirmed. This is a mystery of faith to be believed rather than explained, and docile reverence before the voice of Christ re-echoed in the teaching and tradition of the church is demanded rather than the 'poisonous rationalism' that leads men to adhere to human arguments rather than divine revelation (paragraphs 15-16).

It is hard to detect here any real shift from the stance of Trent over against the Reformers, or any critical assimilation of their genuine concerns, of their questioning of the equation of venerable tradition with primal revelation, of their challenge not simply to the dogma of transubstantiation, but to the habits of thinking which called it forth and fed upon it. Certainly the Pope's implicit recognition that that dogma is to be understood more as authoritative *witness* than as *explanation* of the real presence still holds out the point of departure for ecumenical dialogue. At the same time the imprecision that enters the whole subject at this point leaves crucial questions without an answer. What is it in fact that the dogma is to be taken as affirming? Not apparently every detail of, say, Aquinas' doctrine. Yet that doctrine had the singular advantage of being precisely stateable, so that one could know to what one was being asked to say yea or nay. In *Mysterium Fidei*, as in Trent, that degree of precision is lacking – yet it would appear that a good deal of the scholastic metaphysics still lurks behind the 'new "reality" which we are right to call *ontological*' and to which 'the Catholic Church gives . . . the suitable and accurate name of transubstantiation'. One need not be a poisonous rationalist to ask *why* the name is suitable and accurate, and Reformed theology must certainly feel that there remains here a continuing unclarity in the official Roman Catholic position.

Nevertheless, the fact that this has been a topic of such lively debate in the Roman Catholic Church in recent times is itself a positive sign, while the liturgical changes in the same period have gone a very long way towards removing an excessive concern with and veneration for the sacramental elements and the unbalanced emphasis on the role of the priest apart from the community. Nor must it be forgotten that the doctrine of transubstantiation never did mean the crude magic that a good deal of popular imagination has taken it to entail. Reformed theology does better to recognise gladly what, with all its problematic aspects, it is attempting to affirm – that in the Eucharist Christ makes himself present to us, and gathers us with him into the presence of the Father, and that this is indeed 'the mystery of faith' which, as Calvin put it, is better *felt* than *explained*.

3. *His Sacrifice and Ours*

Now, at the end of our reflections, we come to what has been since the Reformation the most deeply divisive issue of all in eucharistic theology. We have seen how the question of the nature of the 'eucharistic sacrifice' gradually came to the fore in the middle ages; how Aquinas distinguished the devotion with which the Mass is offered from the objective value of Christ's sacrifice in itself, and saw it as possessing further propitiatory power in proportion to that devotion and offering; how Trent eventually affirmed that it is Christ who offers himself in the Eucharist through the ministry of the priest, and that because the fruits of his unique sacrifice on the cross are thereby received, each celebration has its own specific sacrificial value and may be offered for the living or those in purgatory. The Reformers on the other hand – and this applies pretty well across the whole Reformation spectrum – drew a radical contrast between the unique sacrifice of Christ, which he and he alone once-for-all offered to the Father, and the church's offering of *thanks* rather than *propitiation*; and at the same time rejected the equation of the Christian ministry of Word and sacraments with a 'sacrificing priesthood'. We have to do here with not merely one but two deeply controverted themes – on the one hand the meaning of sacrifice and the connexion and distinction between Christ's sacrifice and ours, on the other the nature of Christian ministry with specific reference to the eucharistic celebration and to conceptions of 'priestly power' to perform the 'objective work' of the sacramental celebration. It is betraying no secret to say in advance that the second of these is still today the thornier, and likely to remain so into the future, at last at the official level of ecumenical exchange. But in respect of the first we may find a little more room for manoeuvre than our forefathers suspected to be available. Let us therefore begin with it.

Wherein does the classical antithesis lie? Medieval thought generally tended to operate with a fairly broad conception of 'sacrifice' and 'offering', seeing all kinds of worship, devotion and good works as 'sacrifices' with which God is pleased. The supreme, unique and universal sacrifice was Christ's; but it reached out, so to speak, to enable and empower its own re-echoing in the life and worship of the church, which thus became a kind of 'meritorious co-operation' with divine grace, enabling and leading to its yet richer outpouring. The Reformers, by contrast, emphasised the absolute difference in kind and the objective, finished character of the one sacrifice of Golgotha over against any and every other 'sacrifice' that could be brought or offered. Hence the very different answers proposed to the question, 'What sacrifice do we bring and offer in the Eucharist?'

Behind both answers, however, there seems to lurk something of that radical disjunction between Christ and ourselves that came more and more to the fore after the Arian controversy. So Trent, while striving to hold together his sacrifice and the eucharistic celebration, nevertheless felt compelled to describe the Mass as *a different form* of his sacrifice with its own *distinct* measure of power to please God and make him favourable. It is not 'another' sacrifice, yet something 'more' appears to be achieved by it in each repetition. When one asks what that 'more' is, however, the answer amounts in the end to saying that it is the *same* sacrifice, for there is no other. That is certainly correct, but the position remains less coherent than it might be. The 'something more' is always in danger of detaching itself and becoming 'something additional', 'something other', 'something *we* do'. And it was against that that the Reformers so vehemently reacted.

Yet the Reformers' radicalisation of the disjunction between Christ and us does not *solve* the problem, but rather seems to *intensify* it. If our sacrifice is only that of thanks and praise for what Christ has objectively done, that can only mean that at the very heart and core of Christian worship, *anamnesis* and offering, he stands over against us, apart from us, rather than with us – and that our offering of ourselves is something *we* bring in response to his offering of himself for us. Once that is seen, Reformed and Protestant theology generally needs to ask itself whether the vital centre of the matter is not obscured and endangered. In making us sharers in himself – as Calvin, for example, repeatedly insists is the real meaning of the Eucharist – does not Christ give us part in all that he is and has done for us in its abiding freshness and newness? Is it not only on that ground, only in and with him by the power of his Spirit, that we can offer anything at all – even thanks and praise? To put it at its sharpest, is there not a valid sense in which it is always and only *the sacrifice of Christ himself* that we set forth and hold out to the Father, because he has so identified himself with us that we are united with him? This union lies at the heart of Calvin's theology, but when it comes to the controversial matter of the sacrifice of the Mass he is so anxious to avoid any idea of repeating or adding to Christ's sacrifice that he also seems to rule out our *participation* in his self-offering. Our offering becomes simply a response – response *to* him rather than sharing *with* him in his offering, not only *of himself for us*, but *of us with himself*.

In putting the matter like this, we have already shifted the question from the secondary – What sacrifice do we bring and offer in the Eucharist? – to the primary – What is the sacrifice of Christ, and what has it to do with us and we with it? In answering that question, a simple disjunction and contrast between his sacrifice of expiation and propitiation and our sacrifice of praise – the categories in which Calvin more or less exclusively handles the matter in his controversial writing on the Mass – is something of a short-circuit. It narrows down the meaning of Christ's sacrifice and self-offering too much to reduce it to the single point of expiation or propitiation, though that moment cannot properly be removed. But if it is once so narrowed down, then *only* the absolute contrast between his sacrifice and ours can possibly remain. It can then only be seen as vicarious, not as inclusive, as substitutionary, not as incorporating. That means that only one side of the matter is expressed, and the link between Christ and us, which is grounded and forged in his own person through his assumption of our humanity, falls into the background.

Let us try to open the matter out a little further. In offering himself for us, Christ stands uniquely apart from us. He and he alone offers and is the sacrifice by which our reconciliation is achieved. Yet his self-offering is not *only* a sacrifice of expiation and propitiation; it is at the same time the sanctifying and offering of our sinful human nature to God. In both respects he stands first of all alone, apart from us; yet he does so on our behalf, precisely so that we may be included with him; and it is to that inclusion that the Eucharist witnesses. His sacrifice was made for us; he himself is our offering to the Father; we have no other to bring, but he is the sacrifice who puts himself into our otherwise empty hands. To offer Christ is to present him as our sacrifice because he has made himself so;

and in the power of that offering to offer ourselves 'a living sacrifice'. It is not to add to what he is and has done, nor is it to repeat it. It is to accept, affirm and share in it – or, better, in him – so that our life, our worship, our Eucharist is our participation in and our setting forth before God and man of Christ crucified and risen, the Lamb of God who takes away the sin of the world and offers that world anew to the Father.

In this light, the Eucharist is both a *receiving* of Christ as the Father's gift to us and a *sharing* in his offering to the Father of our nature, indeed of *us*. Each moment is empowered and enlivened by the Holy Spirit, who bears him to us and unites us to him; each requires and complements the other. Neither can stand on its own without distortion of the whole. The theology of Aquinas and Trent sought to give expression to both sides, but in a manner which – in spite of its intentions – too easily toppled over into treating the sacrifice of the Mass in practice as an *additional* sacrifice. Calvin sought to eliminate that danger, but at the cost of tearing the two moments apart.

Considerations of this kind seem to underly some of the statements in *The Presence of Christ in Church and World*:

80. . . . Christ the mediator . . . is himself personally the mediation. In him and through him God's self-offering to us as human beings is accomplished; in him and through him humanity's surrender to God.

The sacrifice brought by Jesus Christ is his obedient life and death (cf. Hebr. 10, 5-10; Phil. 2, 8). His once-for-all self-offering under Pontius Pilate is continued by him for ever in the presence of the Father in virtue of his resurrection. In this way he is our sole advocate in heaven . . . He sends us his Spirit so that we weak human beings, too, may call upon the Father and can also make intercession for the world . . .

81. In its joyful prayer of thanksgiving, 'in the Eucharist', when the Church of Christ remembers his reconciling death for our sins and for the sins of the whole world, Christ himself is present, who 'gave himself up on our behalf as an offering and sacrifice whose fragrance is pleasing to God' (Eph. 5, 2). Sanctified by his Spirit, the Church, through, with and in God's Son, Jesus Christ, offers itself to the Father. It thereby becomes a living sacrifice of thanksgiving . . .

85. . . . He is both Apostle from God and our High Priest (cf. Hebr. 10, 19-20) who has consecrated us together with him into one, so that in his self-offering to the Father through the eternal Spirit (cf. Hebr. 9, 14), he offers us also in himself and so through our union with him we share in that self-offering made on our behalf. It is the same Spirit who cries, 'Abba, Father' (cf. Mk. 14,

36) in him who cries, 'Abba, Father', in us, as we in the Eucharist take the Lord's Prayer into our own mouth (Rom. 8, 15f., 26).

With the exception of the use of the doubtful word 'continued' in §80 – where the idea of a temporally-conceived 'heavenly altar' seems to have slipped in surreptitiously – these paragraphs show how, consistently with the profoundest insights of Reformed theology, the theme of eucharistic sacrifice could and indeed should once again be taken up to revitalise our sense and awareness of the meaning of Christian worship. Understandable and in its way justified as the reaction of the Reformers was, it ran the risk of snapping an essential connexion to which Roman Catholic theology rightly sought to witness, albeit in ways that were more dangerous than helpful. At any rate, this is a field where more needs to be said than was said in the sixteenth century, and where we would do well not to rest content with the polemical negations of our forefathers.[14]

That does not mean, however, that there are no more questions to be raised, no more issues to be explored in the ecumenical dialogue in the future. As we have already remarked, *The Presence of Christ* is a provisional statement, a step along the way, not a final agreement. If, from the Reformed side, we can see the need to revise some of our traditional stances, we still have to see whether that is enough to overcome all the old conflicts, and how the matter is currently regarded in official Roman Catholic treatments. This will also confront us with the second major issue – the question of ministry as 'sacrificing priest-hood'.

How, then, are they handled in contemporary Roman Catholic teaching? Again, it is to *Mysterium Fidei* that we should look. Behind Pope Paul's words lies the restatement of the Tridentine doctrine by his predecessor Pius XII in *Mediator Dei* (1947):

> The sacrifice of the altar is not the mere and simple
> commemoration of the crucifixion and death of Jesus Christ, but
> the true and proper sacrifice, in which indeed the High Priest
> through a bloodless immolation does that which he once
> performed on the cross, offering himself to the eternal Father as
> the most acceptable victim . . . (DS 3847)

Pius went on, again following the lines of established doctrine, to locate the distinctive role and office of the priest in the sacrifice of the Mass in his 'bearing the *persona* of Christ' (DS 3850), whereas the people do not. As members of the Body of Christ, however, they do share in a more general way in his priesthood, and while they do not '*perform* the bloodless immolation' through the words of consecration, they share in its *offering*, and with it, offer themselves (DS 3850-3852). The same distinction is drawn by Vatican II:

The ministerial priest, by the sacred power that he has, forms and rules the priestly people; in the person of Christ he effects the eucharistic sacrifice and offers it to God in the name of all the people. The faithful indeed, by virtue of their royal priesthood, participate in the offering of the Eucharist . . . Taking part in the eucharistic sacrifice, the source and summit of the Christian life, they offer the divine victim to God and themselves along with it.
(*Lumen Gentium* II 10-11)

Against this background let us now set the main points made by *Mysterium Fidei* about the sacrifice of the Mass, described in the brief formula of paragraph 34 as 'The Lord's immolation in the sacrifice of the Mass without bloodshed, his symbolic presentation of the sacrifice of the cross and his application of its saving virtue'.

27. The first point which it is useful to recall is, as it were, the summary and summit of this doctrine. It is that, by means of the eucharistic mystery, the sacrifice of the cross, achieved once on Calvary, is marvellously symbolised, continually recalled to the memory, and its saving virtue is applied to the remission of the sins which are daily committed by us.

31. There is another point which may well be added, for it is most helpful in throwing light on the mystery of the Church. When the Church, together with Christ, performs the function of priest and victim, it is the whole Church that offers the sacrifice of the Mass and the whole of the Church is offered in it. This is the wonderful doctrine which the Fathers of the Church once taught and was expounded a few years ago by Our Predecessor Pius XII. The Second Vatican Council recently gave it clear expression in the Constitution 'De Ecclesia' in the section on the People of God . . .

32. Mention ought to be made, further, of the conclusion derived from this doctrine on 'the public, social nature of every Mass.' For any Mass, even if celebrated by a priest in private, is not private; it is the act of Christ and the Church. The Church, indeed, in the sacrifice which she offers, is learning to offer herself as a universal sacrifice; she is applying to the whole world, for its salvation, the redemptive virtue of the sacrifice of the cross, which is unique and infinite. Every single Mass that is celebrated is offered not just for a certain number but for the salvation of the whole world as well. The consequence is two-fold: a numerous and active participation is most suitable for the celebration, as if demanded by its nature. Nevertheless no criticism may be made, on the contrary approval should be given, in the case of a Mass which, for adequate reasons, is celebrated privately according to the rules and lawful traditions

of holy Church, even if there is only one assistant at the celebration serving and making the responses. For this Mass gives rise to no insignificant supply of graces, but an abundance of them for the salvation of the priest himself, the faithful people and the whole Church, and for the world at large. These graces are not obtained in the same abundance from Communion alone.

33. It is Our paternal and earnest recommendation to priests, Our particular joy and crown, that they should keep in mind the power which they received at the hands of the consecrating bishop. This is the power of offering the sacrifice to God and of celebrating Masses for the living as for the dead in the Lord's name. They should celebrate Mass worthily and devoutly each day if they and the rest of the faithful are to have the benefit of the application of the abundant flow of fruits from the sacrifice of the cross. In this way they can make the very greatest contribution to the salvation of the human race.

If our criticisms above of weaknesses in some Reformed theology are justified, then it can surely both welcome and learn from the recognition in these statements on the one hand of the primary agency of Christ in the eucharistic celebration and on the other of the sharing of his whole people in his self-offering to the Father. These, we would argue, are profoundly consonant with the deepest impulses of Reformed doctrine, however obscured that may have been by dispute and polemic. But what of the essential middle term – essential, that is, in the horizon of Roman teaching? What of the way in which here the celebration of the Mass and the role of the priest are presented? Just here it is necessary to take along with the statements of *Mysterium Fidei* the traditional understanding stated in *Mediator Dei* of the priest's acting *in persona Christi*, for it is on that that those statements ultimately depend. The action of the priest in 'performing' or 'effecting' the bloodless immolation in virtue of which Christ in the Mass offers his one unique and universal sacrifice to the Father is what makes the Mass more than mere sign and memorial of Calvary and constitutes *every* Mass an offering for the celebrant, the church and the world, through which the fruits of Christ's sacrifice are richly and broadly bestowed *because the Mass is celebrated*. By the same token, it is on this that the participation of the faithful in the offering also depends. It is a *mediated* participation, mediated through the agency of the one empowered to act as the representative of Christ, so that Christ acts through him. And all this turns on the moment of consecration which only the ordained priest can bring about: 'The Lord's immolation in the sacrifice of the Mass without bloodshed, his symbolic presentation of the sacrifice of the cross and his application of its saving virtue, all these take place at the moment when, by the words of consecration, he begins to be present sacramentally, as the spiritual food of the faithful, under the appearances of bread and wine.' (*Mysterium Fidei* 34)

It would be easy at this point for Reformed theology simply to respond with an outright rejection of the whole pattern of thinking that it here confronts. Yet it is better to attempt a more differentiated critique, however briefly. There is, surely, a proper sense in which each celebrant at the Eucharist should be aware of speaking and acting *in persona Christi*, in which each celebration is a participation in the totality of the mystery of Christ which reaches out to embrace not only those present but the church and the world entire, in which the sharing in the Eucharist, however few the number there, has cosmic and universal import, in which the Eucharist itself is the central channel of the church's life. In that Roman teaching affirms all this, it is not wrong, and Reformed theology should beware of criticism so sweeping as to evacuate the Eucharist of its full range and depth of meaning. The difficulty, from a Reformed standpoint, lies rather in the way in which these lines are drawn together in the Roman *theology of priesthood*, meeting and gathering there into a solid body of doctrine which, with all its qualifications, projects the action of the church, focussed in that of the priest, into the centre of attention so that Christ's unique and infinite sacrifice is threatened with displacement behind the priestly work of mediation which completes upon the altar the bloodless form of that self-offering and makes its benefits available afresh. The issue the Reformers addressed remains living still, at this point where the Roman Catholic conception of priesthood intersects with eucharistic theology in the doctrine of the sacrifice of the Mass. And its importance for future ecumenical dialogue can hardly be ignored, for it is around this centre that the related problems of intercommunion and recognition of ministries also gather, problems to which little real prospect of a solution has yet appeared.[15]

Are we then saying after all, in spite of our earlier, more hopeful comments, that nothing has really changed? Not at all. The fact that official Roman doctrine still holds to the position of Trent on priesthood and sacrifice certainly cannot be ignored or dismissed as unimportant. But it is an open question whether or how long Rome will be able *plausibly* to maintain that position, given the way in which the celebration of the Mass itself has altered in the last two decades. Talk of the Mass as sacrifice cannot remain unaffected by this; even if it is retained, it is likely to shift in sense and colouring, in the meanings it evokes and the associations it carries. Reformed theology today would probably do best not simply to reject it as 'false doctrine', as the Reformers did, but to look upon it as reflecting a scheme of interpretation which draws on authentic insights, but casts them in a form too narrow, rigid, and consequently opaque. The understanding of the Christian minister as 'a sacrificing priest' cannot properly be read out of the New Testament, but developed from the second century onwards. While in some respects it may be illuminating, it needs to be firmly controlled and supplemented by other, more fundamental aspects of ministry. A clear-eyed awareness of this is necessary if Reformed theology is to make its proper contribution to ecumenical discussion as it proceeds into the future. But that discussion must also proceed, both to clarify genuine differences and to discover where even under unfamiliar forms and strange or even suspicious expressions the common faith is nevertheless held, the hope of deeper understanding leads us on, and the gift of charity is held out and received.

EPILOGUE

Our survey is ended. What can it bring, if not to our extra-terrestrial observer, then to us? What have we covered and offered in it? Something, I hope, to encourage reflection on the meaning of the Eucharist disclosed in the New Testament. Over and above that it has, in the second part, traced some perspectives on the understanding of the Eucharist through the centuries, on the traditional conflicts between Roman Catholic and Reformed approaches, and, in a fashion that is certainly tentative and to some degree inconclusive, on the present situation respecting these controversies.

In the process, for all the material that has been included, a very great deal has been left out. Even within the controversial areas there is much more that could have been usefully drawn in. For instance, we have barely referred to, let alone explored, the kind of understanding of the Eucharist which does not merely assert but *turns upon* the 'bloodless immolation upon the altar', and which led in the middle ages to a form of piety and spirituality which centred and fed upon the enactment of Golgotha at the hand of the priest. That sort of piety evoked the Reformers' shuddering revulsion; but it is not perhaps in the end of the day so very far removed from what is heard in those Protestant hymns which avow that I 'thy Pilate and thy Judas' was, or that 'I was there when they nailed him to the tree'. Nor, on the other hand, have we taken up the indisputable fact that wide tracts of Protestantism today follow more in the footsteps of Zwingli than of Calvin, and take for granted that the only possible approach to the matter is along the lines of 'our remembrance of what Christ once did for us'. The sheer simplicity of a 'zwinglian' form of eucharistic celebration, conducted without any elaborate liturgical form and focussed by reflective meditation on the mighty act of God which secured our salvation, can nevertheless be powerfully moving and sometimes better adapted to concentrate attention and stimulate response than a liturgy more 'correct' in form and 'profound' in intention and expression. Yet in our presentation we have treated both these ways of seeing the matter as one-sided and inadequate, and sought to point a different path. Have we then run the risk of speaking past rather than addressing the motives and concerns on either side?

A similar question can be put from a rather different angle. Would it be more useful, instead of what we have attempted here with our eye on classical Roman Catholic and Reformed positions, to sketch a range of ways of seeing and interpreting the Eucharist, all of which have their own value? From all the rich resources of Christian reflection and meditation on which we have here selectively drawn, it would be possible to hew out a series of overall views of the Eucharist and to develop and present each as having its own contribution to make. From the early fathers we could catch the vision of a world illumined and transformed by the Incarnation, of matter sanctified and ennobled by the presence of the divine Spirit, of bread and wine, eating and drinking, as symbols of that grand transfiguration by which the children of men become the children of God. From the thought of the middle ages we could take the powerful sense of the presence of Christ, of the perennial contemporaneity and cosmic outreach of his one sacrifice, of the institution of the church as his body in which that sacrifice is ever and again realised, represented and entered into through the eucharistic action. From the Reformers we could learn afresh of the message of the divine promise evoking and heard in lively faith, of our participation in Christ by his life-giving Spirit, of communion, remembrance and commitment. From our ecumenical reflections we could follow the leading thought that all of these patterns of understanding may have their own truth and validity as echoing and responding to the ground-tone of the Gospel, that each may have its voice in the polyphonous symphony of Christian faith and worship, that even where they differ, they should be seen as *completing*, not as *competing with* each other. The very same material we have presented here under the scheme of development, divergence and possible convergence could have been shaped rather by a pattern of complementarity, unblurred by insisting on the points of historical or present disagreement. Would that not have been more constructive, more ecumenical, than what we have actually done?

This thought may be reinforced by a further admission. In all that we have discussed, we have focussed very largely on *theological interpretation* of the Eucharist – certainly, at any rate, in the last three chapters. But is that perhaps a too selective approach, doomed in advance to by-pass the heart of the matter? What of the experience of eucharistic worship itself; what of the rich diversity of hymns and prayers, which may open up and hold together complementary vistas more richly and rewardingly than the rather abstract and theoretical approach we have generally taken? For example, the hymn book most widely used today in the British Presbyterian Churches, the *Church Hymnary* (3rd edn) includes among the hymns for Holy Communion such as Aquinas' 'Now, my tongue, the mystery telling Of the glorious body sing', the Presbyterian Horatius Bonar's 'Here, O my Lord, I see thee face to face; Here would I touch and handle things unseen', and the Anglican William Bright's rendering of the medieval *Unde et memores*:

> And now, O Father, mindful of the love
>> That bought us, once for all, on Calvary's Tree,
> And having with us him that pleads above,
>> We here present, we here spread forth to thee
> That only offering perfect in thine eyes,
> The one true, pure, immortal sacrifice.

When all these can be sung in Reformed worship, have the real problems not already been in principle resolved? And is not perhaps such an exchange of liturgical resources a better and surer way to mutual understanding and recognition than the comparatively historical and cerebral procedure we have followed?

In this connexion, there is also a whole range of immediately practical issues, some of which have been referred to here or there in passing, but not thematically treated. What is the appropriate frequency of the celebration? Calvin wanted it to be weekly, but was never able to get the city council in Geneva to agree; and for a variety of reasons most Reformed churches have through the centuries celebrated the sacrament very much less frequently: only in very recent times has this begun to change. Again, what elements deserve and demand to be generally recognised as belonging to the proper constitution of the Eucharist, and so as criteria for mutual recognition of its dispensing in different communions? Or how far should the shared, ecumenical Eucharist be seen (as usually in the Reformed view) as a means of growing together towards unity, how far (as is the Roman Catholic position) as a sign of unity already achieved, and therefore not normally to be permitted between Roman Catholics and Protestants? What, finally, of the current lively debate in more than one Reformed church on the admission of children to communion at a much younger age than has been customary, and on the basis of their Baptism, not of instruction, confirmation and admission to 'communicant membership'? The list could go on, but these not unimportant examples may serve to show how much has *not* been discussed that is of relevance for practical, ecumenical exchange today.

All these qualifications are valid and important. But if they show how limited has been the exercise we have undertaken, they do not make it redundant or demonstrate it to be valueless. Rather, they can throw into relief what it *has* and what it has *not* tried to do. It has sought to explore the sensitive areas of classical controversy, the issues which are still widely felt, both officially and unofficially, to be divisive; and has done so with the aim of seeing how far they can or could be resolved at the level of theological reflection (which has its own part to play in shaping both liturgy and practice, even if it does not exist in total independence of them) – and also of finding how far we have got along that road in the present ecumenical situation. The aim has not been to stress the divisive in any sectarian sense, but to face it openly and squarely in the conviction that the Lord of the church does not will the sacrament of his body and blood, of himself, to be a cause of disunity. In the words of yet another hymn inspired by his high priestly prayer in John 17:

> O Thou, who at thy Eucharist didst pray
>   That all thy Church might be for ever one,
> Grant us at every Eucharist to say,
>   With longing heart and soul, 'Thy will be done.'
> O may we all one bread, one body be,
> One through this sacrament of unity.

NOTES

PROLOGUE

1. Justin Martyr, *First Apology*, 66.
2. *Didache* ix.5. The *Didache* (Teaching) is of uncertain date, but may derive from the early second century – in which case it would be one of the oldest extra-canonical witnesses we possess to the understanding of the sacrament in the early church.
3. *Inst.* IV.xviii.16-17. References to the *Institute*, unless otherwise indicated, are to the edition of 1559. In quoting, I have followed the translation of H. Beveridge, Edinburgh: T. & T. Clark, 1863, rather than the McNeill-Battles version in the *S.C.M. Library of Christian Classics*, vols. 20-21. London, 1960.

CHAPTER ONE

1. See e.g. J. Jeremias, *The Eucharistic Words of Jesus*. 3rd edn. London: S.C.M., 1966, pp. 139-159; A. J. B. Higgins, *The Lord's Supper in the New Testament. Studies in Biblical Theology*, No. 6. London: S.C.M., 1952, pp. 37-43. Jeremias opts for the long text, Higgins for the view that Luke has combined two distinct sources.
2. H. Lietzmann, *Messe und Herrenmahl*. Eine Studie zur Geschichte der Liturgie. Bonn: A. Marcus & E. Webers Verlag, 1926.
3. R. Bultmann, *Theology of the New Testament*, vol. 1. London: S.C.M. Press, 1952, pp. 144-152.
4. Jeremias, *The Eucharistic Words of Jesus*.
5. See e.g. A. C. Cochrane, *Eating and Drinking with Jesus*. An Ethical and Biblical Enquiry. Philadelphia: Westminster, 1974, pp. 60-64 and note 2 ad loc.
6. J. Austin Baker, 'The "Institution" Narratives and the Christian Eucharist', in *Thinking about the Eucharist*. Essays by members of the Archbishops' Commission on Christian Doctrine. London: S.C.M., 1972, pp. 38-58.
7. J. Betz, *Die Eucharistie in der Zeit der griechischen Väter*, Bd I/1: *Die Aktualpräsenz der Person und des Heilswerkes Jesu im Abendmahl nach der vorephisinischen griechischen Patristik*. Freiburg: Herder, 1955; Bd II/1: *Die Realpräsenz des Leibes und Blutes Christi im Abendmahl nach dem Neuen Testament*. Freiburg: Herder, 1961. A useful English study which reports and builds on Betz' interpretation is E. J. Kilmartin, *The Eucharist in the Primitive Church*. Prentice-Hall, 1965.

CHAPTER TWO

1. *The Eucharistic Words of Jesus*, pp. 15-88.
2. *A Passover Haggadah*. The New Union Haggadah, revised edn, 1975, prepared by the Central Conference of American Rabbis. Edited by Herbert Bronstein. Harmondsworth: Penguin, 1978.
3. P. Tillich, *Systematic Theology*, vol. 1. London: S.C.M., 1978, p. 239.
4. E.g. A. R. Peacocke, *Creation and the World of Science*. Oxford: Clarendon, 1979, p. 290. His argument, however, tilts towards an account of an immanental

'sacramental universe', in which the whole cosmos is seen as 'incarnation', whereas *the* Incarnation in Jesus Christ is 'myth' (cf. p. 289). This is too back-to-front to be theologically helpful; we would rather follow T. F. Torrance's incisive remarks on science, sacrament and the 'sacramental universe' (*Theological Science*. London: O.U.P., 1969, pp. 18; 57; 66-67).

5. See e.g. M. Thurian, *The Eucharistic Memorial*, Parts One and Two (*The Old Testament* and *The New Testament*). *Ecumenical Studies in Worship*, Nos 7 & 8. London: Lutterworth, 1960; 1961.

6. J. B. Torrance, 'Covenant or Contract?' *Scottish Journal of Theology* 23 (1970), pp. 51-76; 'The Covenant Concept in Scottish Theology and Politics and its Legacy'. *Scottish Journal of Theology* 34 (1981), pp. 225-243.

CHAPTER THREE

1. Two examples from many must suffice: N. Hook, *The Eucharist in the New Testament*. London: Epworth, 1964; and A. C. Cochrane, *Eating and Drinking with Jesus*. Philadelphia: Westminster, 1974. Hook's determination that the meaning of the Eucharist must be found only in 'personal communion' with Jesus leads him to an account which does not seem to square with what Paul actually says (pp. 79-83). Cochrane is more extreme, for his whole thesis is that eating and drinking can only be *with* Jesus, not *of* him and that any 'sacramental' understanding of the Eucharist must be rejected (pp. 119-148) – and this involves him in extraordinary contortions in his exegesis of I Cor. 10-11. Both writers, it may be added, have even greater difficulty with John 6 (Hook, pp. 88-103; Cochrane, pp. 139-148) – not perhaps astonishingly!

2. E.g. Betz, op. cit vol. I/1, pp. 38-64; vol. II/1, pp. 35-59; 95-97 and Kilmartin, *The Eucharist in the Primitive Church*, pp. 74-92 both tend too rapidly to read in later sacramental theology to Paul's words – or at least, to express their interpretation of Paul in language drawn from that source without sufficient differentiation. The fact that the parallel Paul draws with pagan sacrifice actually *undermines* later theories of transubstantiation and eucharistic sacrifice is well made by F.-J. Leenhardt, *Le Sacrement de la Sainte-Cène*. Neuchatel: Delacheux & Nestlé, 1948, pp. 81-85.

3. On the Agape in general: Cochrane, *Eating and Drinking with Jesus*, pp. 78-100 and note 6 on p. 78.

4. Kilmartin, *The Eucharist in the Primitive Church*, pp. 93-140.

5. *Smyrnaeans* vi.2.

CHAPTER FOUR

1. R. C. D. Jasper & G. J. Cuming (ed.), *Prayers of the Eucharist: Early and Reformed*. London: Collins, 1975, pp. 18-19.

2. *Smyrnaeans* viii.

3. *Prayers of the Eucharist*, pp. 22-23.

4. We follow, with minor alterations, the translation of F. L. Cross, *St Cyril of Jerusalem. Lectures on the Christian Sacraments*. London: S.P.C.K., 1951.

5. *De Prod. Jud.* I.6; *Hom. 82 in Matt.*

6. *De Mysteriis* 52-54.

7. *Address on Religious Instruction* (The Great Catechism) 37.

8. *Paedagogus* I.vi.42-43.

9. *Stromateis* V.x.67.
10. *Enarr. in Ps.* 98.9.
11. *In Ev. Joh. Tract.* xxvi.11.
12. In Ev. Joh. Tract. xxv.12.
13. *De Doctr. Christi* iii.24.
14. *In Ev. Joh.* Tract. xxvi.15
15. *Adv. Haer.* IV.xviii.6.
16. *De Exhort. Castitatis* xi.
17. *De Corona* iii.
18. *Hom. in Lev.* IX.1.
19. *Hom. 82 in Matt.*

CHAPTER FIVE

1. T. F. Torrance, 'The Mind of Christ in Worship. The Problem of Apollinarianism in the Liturgy', in his *Theology in Reconciliation*. London: Geoffrey Chapman, 1975, pp. 139-214; J. B. Torrance, 'The Vicarious Humanity of Christ', in T. F. Torrance (ed.), *The Incarnation*. Edinburgh: Handsel, 1981, pp. 127-147. Both these essays take up from the centre of Reformed theology the dialogue with the new Roman Catholic liturgical thinking represented particularly by J. A. Jungmann, *The Place of Christ in Liturgical Prayer*. London: Geoffrey Chapman, 1965.
2. *Hom. in Eph.* iii.4.
3. *De Sacr.* V.25.
4. DS = Denzinger-Schönmetzer, *Enchiridion Symbolorum* . . ., 34th edn. Herder, 1967.
5. DS 860.
6. The different forms and operations of grace are discussed in considerable detail by Aquinas, *Summa Theologica* II/1, *quaestiones* 109-114.
7. On this distinction as grasped in Aquinas' 'christological interpretation of sacramental *ex-opere-operato* causality', see E. Schillebeeckx, *Christ the Sacrament of Encounter with God*. London: Sheed & Ward, 1963, pp. 100-109.
8. Aquinas, *Summa Theologica* III, *qu.* 79, *art.* 5; 7.
9. Aquinas, *Summa Theologica* III, *qu.* 83, *art.* 1.
10. *Scots Confession* xxii. The relevant passage runs, in the modern translation by James Bulloch published in *The Scots Confession of 1560*. Edinburgh: St Andrew Press, 1960, pp. 57-80: '. . . in the Roman Church . . . the whole action of the Lord Jesus is adulterated in form, purpose and meaning. What Christ Jesus did and commanded to be done is evident from the Gospels and from St Paul; what the priest does at the altar we do not need to tell. . . . But let the words of the mass, and their own doctors and teachings witness, what is the purpose and meaning of the mass; it is that, as mediators between Christ and his Kirk, they should offer to God the Father a sacrifice in propitiation for the sins of the living and the dead. This doctrine is blasphemous to Jesus Christ and would deprive his unique sacrifice, once offered on the cross for the cleansing of all who are to be sanctified, of its sufficiency; so we detest and renounce it.' (p. 77)

CHAPTER SIX

1. Our quotations follow the translation in Bertram Lee Wolf, *Reformation Writings of Martin Luther*, vol. 1. London: Lutterworth, 1952.

2. E.g. H. J. Hillerbrand, *The Reformation in its Own Words*. London: S.C.M., 1964, pp. 155-162.
3. Both quotations from A. Barclay, *The Protestant Doctrine of the Lord's Supper*. Glasgow: Jackson, Wylie & Co., 1927, pp. 109-110.
4. See especially T. H. L. Parker, *John Calvin: A Biography*. London: J. M. Dent & Sons, 1975.
5. We quote from the translation in J. K. S. Reid (ed.), *Calvin: Theological Treatises*. *S.C.M. Library of Christian Classics*, vol. 22. London, 1954. Ch. 5 is on pp. 163-166.
5a. It should be added that Zwingli too towards the very end of his life had moved back to the conception of a sacrament as a sign of *God's* faithfulness rather than the Christian's faith; but this played no role in his exchanges with Luther. He fell in 1531 at the battle of Kappel; Oecolampadius died in the same year.
6. *Institutio* (1536), ch. iv, trans. from P. Barth (ed.), *J. Calvini Opera Selecta*, vol. 1. Munich, 1926, pp. 138-139.
6a. We cannot here explore the further philosophical and scientific problems involved in the concepts of space underlying the controversy. See T. F. Torrance, 'The Paschal Mystery of Christ and the Eucharist', in his *Theology in Reconciliation*. London: Geoffrey Chapman, 1975, pp. 106-138 (esp. pp. 124ff.).
7. *Lutheran Identity*. Lutheran World Federation Institute for Ecumenical Research, Strasbourg, 1977, pp. 14-15. Cf. also the nuanced account, which comes very close to Calvin on the nature of the 'real presence', but stresses more strongly than Calvin the connexion between creation and redemption and the place of the created elements in the sacraments, given by the distinguished Lutheran theologian Regin Prenter, 'The Doctrine of the Real Presence', in his *Theologie und Gottesdienst*. Gesammelte Aufsätze. Århus: Forlaget Aros and Göttingen: Vandenhoek & Ruprecht, 1977, pp. 166-174.
7a. *The Scots Confession of 1560*, pp. 74-76.
8. Barclay, op. cit., p. 149.
9. Text in P. Barth & W. Niesel (ed.), *Johannis Calvini Opera Selecta*, vol. 2. Munich, 1952, pp. 247-253.
10. Trans. from R. Stupperich (ed.), *Melanchthons Werke in Auswahl*, Bd 6. Gütersloh: Bertelsmann, 1955, p. 485.

CHAPTER SEVEN

1. Trent, *Decree on the Eucharist*, ch. 1; Calvin, *Inst.* IV.xvii.7.
2. Trent, *The Doctrine of the Most Holy Sacrifice*; Calvin, *Inst.* IV.xviii.6.
3. This seems to be the main attitude in the two major ecumenical reports of 1982 – less surprisingly in *The Final Report* of the Anglican-Roman Catholic International Commission. London: S.P.C.K. and C.T.S.; more surprisingly in the Lima report of the W.C.C. Commission for Faith and Order, *Baptism, Eucharist and Ministry*. Geneva: W.C.C. The positive intention of such reports is to be warmly welcomed, but the failure to take the Reformation sufficiently seriously is both tactically unsound and theologically indefensible.
4. See e.g. N. Ehrenstrom and G. Gassmann (ed.), *Confessions in Dialogue*. 3rd edition. Geneva: W.C.C., 1975; *Modern Eucharistic Agreement*. London: S.P.C.K., 1973; and the more recent reports mentioned in n. 3 and below.
5. See *Confessions in Dialogue*, pp. 165-179.
5a. Our quotations follow the original xeroxed report and its paragraph numbering.

The section of the report dealing with the Eucharist was published (without the paragraph numbering) in *The Reformed World* 35.3, Sept. 1978, pp. 106-113.

6. Eschatology has figured prominently in discussion of the Eucharist in the last thirty or forty years. A particularly fine presentation is by G. Wainwright, *Eucharist and Eschatology*. London, 1971. But see also Cochrane, *Eating and Drinking with Jesus*, pp. 100-117 and note 18 ad loc.

7. T. F. Torrance, 'The Paschal Mystery of Christ and the Eucharist', in his *Theology in Reconciliation*. London: Geoffrey Chapman, 1975, pp. 106-138; also chs. 11-14 of his *Theology in Reconstruction*, repr. Grand Rapids: Eerdmans, 1975.

8. *Church Dogmatics* IV/2, pp. 54-55.

9. *Christ the Sacrament of Encounter with God*, esp. ch. 3 on 'the ecclesial character of sacramental action'.

10. We follow the translation of the *Leuenberg Concord* in *The Reformed World* 32.6, June 1973, pp. 256-264.

11. A translation of the *Arnoldshain Theses* with commentary by T. F. Torrance and I. A. Muirhead may be found in the *Scottish Journal of Theology* 15 (1962), pp. 1-21 under the title, 'Doctrinal Consensus on Holy Communion'.

12. A useful contemporary discussion of the debate is J. Powers, *Eucharistic Theology*. New York: Seabury, 1967.

13. London: Catholic Truth Society, 1965.

14. R. Prenter, 'Eucharistic Theology according to the Lutheran Tradition', in his *Theologie und Gottesdienst*, pp. 286-295, quotes both Luther and the Anglican Lambeth Conference of 1958 in support of this way of seeing the matter. One of the Luther quotations (from the 1520 *Sermon on the New Testament*) runs: 'Faith I call the true priestly office which makes all of us priests and priestesses. Through faith we place ourselves, our misery, our prayer, praise and thanksgiving in Christ's hands, and through Christ offer it all to God in the sacrament. Thus we offer Christ to God, that is, we give him occasion and move him to offer himself for us and us with himself.' (Prenter, p. 196)

15. *The Presence of Christ in Church and World* also discusses the ministry, but throws up more questions than answers (§§108-110, published in *The Reformed World* 35.4, Dec. 1978, pp. 152-158). The 1982 *Lima Report* seems to find the designation of the Christian minister as a 'priest' in some third sense between the priesthood of Christ and of the whole people quite unproblematic – and consequently gives the issue much too little attention to convince those not already so minded. See the chapter on Ministry, §17.

BIBLIOGRAPHICAL NOTE

For the reasons indicated in the foreword, I have not attempted in the notes to refer to more than a tiny handful of books or articles. Nor do I intend to go back on that general principle here. However, for readers who wish to read further in the literature, I would first mention two recent and far-ranging German surveys which give a great wealth of bibliographical reference, including much (if not all) of the important English material. The first of these is

H. Feld, *Das Verständnis des Abendmahls. Erträge der Forschung* 50. Darmstadt: Wissenschaftliche Buchgesellschaft, 1976.

The second is the lengthy series of distinct articles (each with bibliography) to be found under the titles 'Abendmahl' and 'Abendmahlsfeier' in

Theologische Realenzyklopädie, Bd 1. Berlin/New York: De Gruyter, 1977, pp. 43-328.

To these may be added the following select list of books in English which are *not* mentioned in the Notes.

J.-J. von Allmen, *The Lord's Supper*. London: Lutterworth, 1969.

G. Aulén (ed.), *Eucharist and Sacrifice*. Edinburgh: Oliver & Boyd, 1958.

L. Bouyer, *Eucharist. Theology and Spirituality of the Eucharistic Prayer*. Notre Dame, Indiana, 1968.

Y. Brilioth, *Eucharistic Faith and Practice*. London, 1930.

G. B. Burnet, *The Holy Communion in the Reformed Church of Scotland, 1560-1960*. Edinburgh: Oliver & Boyd, 1960.

F. Clark, *Eucharistic Sacrifice and the Reformation*. London: Darton, Longman & Todd, 1960.

R. E. Clements and others, *Eucharistic Theology Then and Now*. London: S.P.C.K., 1968.

G. Dix, *The Shape of the Liturgy*. Westminster: Dacre Press, 1943.

W. B. Frankland, *The Early Eucharist (A.D. 30-180)*. London: C.U.P., 1902.

F. C. N. Hicks, *The Fullness of Sacrifice. An Essay in Reconciliation*. London: Macmillan, 1930.

B. J. Kidd, *The Later Medieval Doctrine of the Eucharistic Sacrifice*. First published 1898; repr. London: S.P.C.K., 1958.

I. H. Marshall, *Last Supper and Lord's Supper*. Exeter: Paternoster, 1980.

G. Martelet, *The Risen Christ and the Eucharistic World*. London: Collins, 1976.

K. McDonnell, *John Calvin, the Church and the Eucharist*. Princeton: Princeton University Press, 1967.

J. I. Packer (ed.), *Eucharistic Sacrifice*. London: Church Book Room Press, 1962.

P. F. Palmer, *Sacraments and Worship*. London: Longmans, Green & Co., 1957.

R. S. Paul, *The Atonement and the Sacraments*. London: Hodder & Stoughton, 1961.

K. Rahner, *The Church and the Sacraments*. New York: Herder, 1963.

E. Schillebeeckx, *The Eucharist*. London: Sheed & Ward, 1968.

D. Stone, *A History of the Doctrine of the Holy Eucharist*, vols. 1 & 2. London: Longmans, Green & Co., 1909.

R. S. Wallace, *Calvin's Doctrine of the Word and Sacrament*. Edinburgh: Oliver & Boyd, 1953.

J. Wilkinson, *The Supper and the Eucharist*. London: Macmillan, 1965.

F. Young, *The Use of Sacrificial Ideas in Greek Christian Writers from the New Testament to John Chrysostom*. Cambridge, Mass.: Philadelphia Patristic Foundation, 1979.

INDEX OF BIBLICAL REFERENCES

INDEX OF NAMES

SELECT INDEX OF SUBJECTS*

* For such central topics as 'Presence' and 'Sacrifice' see the Table of Contents.